Toward Legacy

Toward Legacy

Design Workshop's pursuit of ideals in landscape architecture, planning and urban design.

Toward Legacy

Published by

Grayson Publishing

James G. Trulove, Publisher

1250 28th St., NW

Washington, DC 20007

ISBN: 0-9749632-6-7

Researched, written and edited by Val Moses

Graphic Design by Lisa McGuire

Photography by D.A. Horchner (except as otherwise noted)

Image Research by Julia Timmer

Project Management by Eliot Hoyt

Digital Prepress by Thomas Brunet

Final Document Production by Nino Pero

Printed in Canada

on recycled paper with 10% post-consumer waste

Contents

PREFACE   006

INTRODUCTION   008

FORMATIVE
PROJECT   022

1
NATURE

Nature is critical to human well-being and the continuation of life on Earth. This bond is nurtured by protecting natural areas or rejuvenating damaged ones.

028

2
PLACES

Place-making summons beauty into daily life and offers a platform for people to create meaning in their lives and in the built landscapes of their surroundings.

076

3
COMMUNITY

The design of neighborhoods, villages and towns succeeds when it values and honors both the natural world and the human need for community.

130

4
CONNECTION

Configuring the way people come together and engage with nature in urban settings must draw on existing galaxies of information and pattern.

174

5
LEADING CHANGE

Change begins in people's hearts and minds. Helping people create a vision for the future gives them the means for making major transitions.

228

AFTERWORD	272
THE PARTNERS	274
STAFF OVER THE YEARS	276
BIBLIOGRAPHY	280
ACKNOWLEDGMENTS	281
INDEX	282
AWARDS	284
PHOTOGRAPHY CREDITS	288

Preface

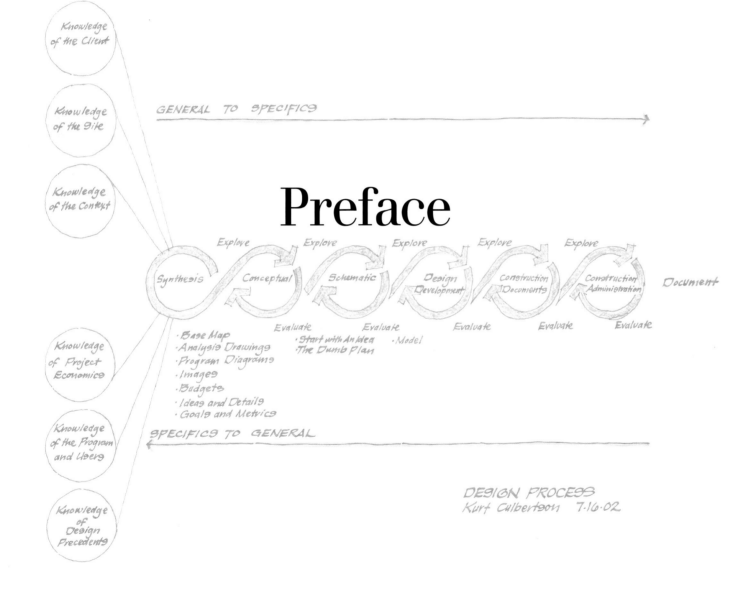

Knowledge of the Client

Knowledge of the Site

Knowledge of the Context

GENERAL TO SPECIFICS

Explore   Explore   Explore   Explore   Explore

Synthesis   Conceptual   Schematic   Design Development   Construction Documents   Construction Administration   Document

Evaluate   Evaluate   Evaluate   Evaluate   Evaluate

· Base Map
· Analysis Drawings
· Program Diagrams
· Images
· Budgets
· Ideas and Details
· Goals and Metrics

· Start with An Idea
· The Dumb Plan

· Model

Knowledge of Project Economics

Knowledge of the Program and Users

SPECIFICS TO GENERAL

Knowledge of Design Precedents

DESIGN PROCESS
Kurt Culbertson   7·16·02

What's in this book,
why we wrote it
and how to read it

When we set out to write a book about our work, we decided to do something deeper than a traditional review of projects over the past 35 years. We wanted to share what it's like to run a business based on ideas, how our experience and thinking have refined each other over time and what challenges we face and triumphs we've enjoyed. Two years ago, we chose our best projects and began to mine them for ideas, methods, outcomes and documentation. We focused on the main thrust of each one and found that these could be grouped under five tasks: preserving the natural environment, making places, fostering community, creating connection and leading change. Many projects might fit multiple categories but we found they would speak most eloquently in only one. Each chapter begins with our thoughts on its message, followed by projects that illustrate that thinking, including an in-depth discussion of projects that have come as close as possible to what we call Legacy Design. These projects offered complex challenges and had from their beginnings more potential to become legacies for future generations.

In this book, you will find examples of affordability as well as the kind of creative expression that only great wealth can support. You will find both conservation and examples where development saved the environment. Some projects seemed intractable — unsolvable over many years, a lightning rod for dissension and so clearly impossible from the beginning that the planners and designers could only keep faith with the firm's ideals and lead the client and the community in fathoming a single step at a time. We have also included projects that have achieved only limited success and a few projects that were simply learning experiences. We offer them here in the hope of educating and inspiring others and awakening people to possibilities for the future.

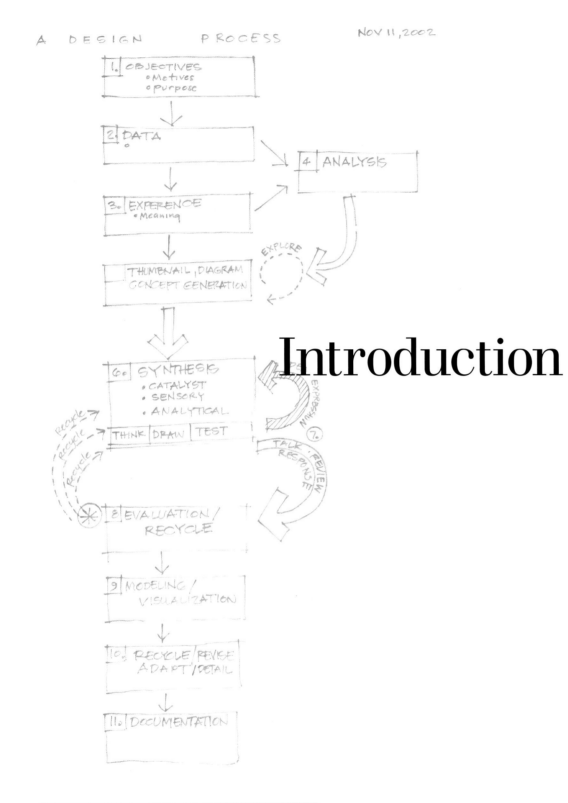

Introduction

Design Workshop is an ideologically based firm that originated in academia

I t has evolved as a learning organization, seeking out complex and challenging projects wherever intellectual interests lead. From the beginning, the members of the firm have sought to be generalists, willing to tackle any project concerning the land. Their guiding tenet has been that the work must take the most comprehensive perspective and use a collaborative approach to resolve issues. The goal is to do work that matters, work that makes a difference, work that contributes to the well-being of the planet — in other words, to do well by doing good.

The firm is driven by two values: transparency and holism.

Transparency embraces openness at all levels. It is manifest in the firm's name, which was chosen to describe the collaborative process the founders wished to foster, a process that values and invites every opinion and that keeps the decision-making process out in the open. Input is sought from a wide array of people. This doesn't mean design by committee and it doesn't mean senior designers relinquish leadership roles. It does mean input from everyone is valued, down to front-desk personnel, the marketing team and finance staff, all of whom frequently take part in open-studio design reviews.

Holism refers to the comprehensive approach that has been practiced at Design Workshop since its founding in 1969. From the beginning, the emphasis has been on using a comprehensive and holistic approach to design and planning that takes into account a spectrum of elements, including those outside the purview of a particular project. It does so at a multitude of scales in order to understand the broader context of an individual project and allow various levels of interest and authority to cross boundaries that usually separate them or to integrate technical disciplines that ordinarily operate in relative isolation from each other.

Both of these values promote the gathering of as much information as possible in order to make the best possible decisions, ones that serve the widest possible constituencies, including the client, the community and the end users of a project. "We knew intuitively from the beginning," says Don Ensign, one of the firm's founders, "that this work needed to be comprehensive. And that idea became embedded in the company genes."

Legacy Design

As the firm grew, it became necessary to define the comprehensive approach and to make it more tangible and teachable. In a board retreat in the 1990s, the partners came together over questions of how they could structure the concept. "Comprehensive" certainly meant considering the widest possible context but it also meant getting under the surface of a project. The partners wanted to give designers the tools that would allow them to "go deep." By this, they meant that while a project's "surface" conditions would identify the critical question of any given project, "going deep" would define the core of that question and lead to investigations into deeper meaning, which could yield synthesis of all aspects and more profound results from the planning and design effort.

In formalizing this idea, the board grappled with the emerging idea of sustainability, which was focused narrowly on the environment. What their approach brought to the equation was a broader consciousness of who we are, a broader accountability than what we used to see. Board members agreed that this formal version of the comprehensive approach would encompass the traditional elements of landscape architecture (art and environment), but also include community and economics — significant aspects of the profession of landscape architecture that are often not acknowledged.

These four elements bear similarity to those of triple bottom-line accounting, which began to emerge at about the same time (see *Cannibals with Forks* by John Elkington). But it broadens the idea by insisting that beauty is essential to human meaning. To represent this element, the word "art" was chosen as a more tangible term than "aesthetics," which can be understood as perceptual study or philosophical exploration. These four elements are understood as values:

ENVIRONMENT: Human existence depends on recognizing the value of natural systems and organizing its own activities to protect them. Design should fit purpose to the conditions of the land in ways that support future generations, driving value long-term.

COMMUNITY: Connection among people supports the culture of family, groups, towns, cities and nations and is the foundation on which they prosper. Design should organize community to nurture relationships and mutual acceptance.

ECONOMICS: The flow of capital that is required to develop a project and the capital generated over its life defines economic viability. Projects need long-term economic mechanisms to promote and protect the integrity of a place.

ART: Beauty is a timeless quality. It helps create real destinations that bring us meaning and act as a restorative on the human spirit. It boosts economic value, supports viability and attracts capital, helping to ensure a project's longevity.

To get at the essence of the idea, board members distilled it down to a single paragraph, using simple, accessible language:

We believe that when environment, art, community and economics are combined in harmony with the dictates of the land and needs of society, magical places result, places that lift the spirit, sustainable places of beauty, significance and quality. We are dedicated to designing extraordinary landscapes that leave a legacy for future generations, creating such places for our clients, for society and for the well-being of our planet.

The name of the approach was drawn from this description, using the word "legacy" to acknowledge the temporal character of design, the idea that such work should endure and sustain itself over a long period of time. The idea is symbolized by four overlapping circles, one for each element. The center of these rings, where the four are in balance, is the ideal profile for a project. If the work begins with a heavy emphasis on one element, the process seeks to move it as close to the center as possible. In order to anchor this rigorous intellectual process in the day-to-day process of the practice, a fifth circle was added, representing design and management. The outer circle represents synthesis: It speaks to both the design process and the stewardship of a project's resources, which reconcile conflicting choices and help optimize the outcome.

"What the Legacy rings diagram and dialog really created was a target," says partner Rebecca Zimmermann. "It was a way to focus energy and effort. As we're working on projects that have an environmental emphasis or an economic emphasis, we keep our consciousness in bringing those projects closer to the middle and integrating the other elements into the project. This helps us take projects that at first lie outside some of the rings and moving them more towards the center. Will they be Legacy? Maybe, maybe not. Have we made them better because we were thinking about it? Absolutely."

Legacy Design grew out of the idealism of Design Workshop's academic origins. One of its goals was to bridge the rifts that divide the profession into various factions, which begin with the education process. "The fragmentation of design values and skills begins in the Academy," says partner Todd Johnson, the firm's chief design officer. "At Harvard, there were those professors who were oriented to form and composition and those who were oriented to problem-solving. These biases created polemic schisms among impressionable students. Form givers dressed in black, read certain magazines and talked a common language. Problem solvers were less predictably attired and focused more on science and rational thought processes. Students, being impressionable, get caught up in the rightness of certain values at the expense of comprehensive problem-solving connected to highly resolved formal solutions. The trap is always to enslave one set of skills and values to the other. Legacy Design acknowledges the difficulty of holistic solutions yet strives to make the connection between high purpose and form."

The idea is grounded in personal values and beliefs. In some measure, it is an act of faith. It recognizes that the few designs that have stood the test of time did so by bringing together elements of environmental sensi-

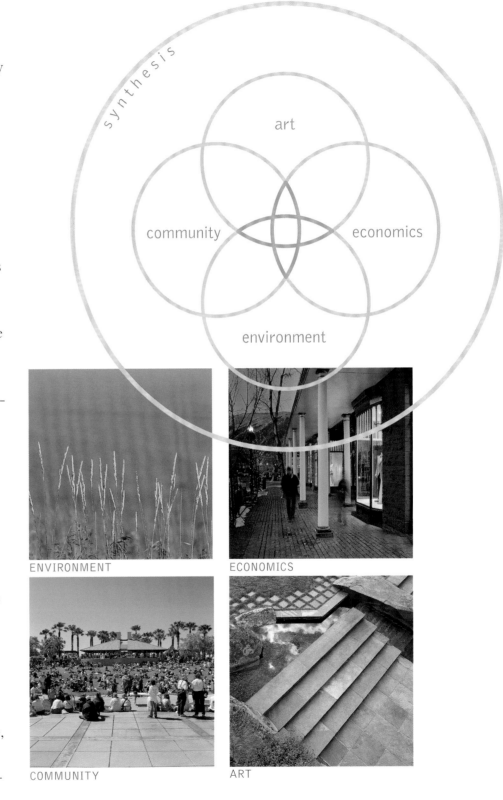

ENVIRONMENT

ECONOMICS

COMMUNITY

ART

tivity, economic viability and community values in a manner that raised the executed work to the level of art. Such places represent the noblest strivings of our profession; their very existence forms part of the legacy upon which modern civilization is built. While many emphasize one Legacy element or another, they go a long way toward fulfilling all aspects. Prominent examples would include New York's Central Park designed by Frederick Law Olmsted, the intensively "green" island of Ærø in Denmark, Spiral Jetty by Robert Smithson on the Great Salt Lake of Utah and the new communities of Columbia (Maryland), The Woodlands (Texas), Seaside (Florida) and Verrado (Arizona). In our own work, we have come closest to achieving the Legacy Design ideal in the projects that are presented with an in-depth discussion at the end of each chapter of this book.

At the inception of this idea, board members recognized that Legacy Design is essentially a theory. It asserts that creating a dialog among these four elements during the analysis process leads to synthesis and integration of all aspects and produces the most viable response. At the same time, although efforts to achieve these ideals can be measured, it is not possible to fully prove that balancing art, economics, environment and community will leave legacies for future generations. The firm persists in applying this approach because the results so far are encouraging and the process itself has yielded a great store of knowledge. In the view of the firm's practitioners, Legacy Design is the future.

Challenges and Benefits

"I think we were a little naïve about what it takes to really walk that talk," says Joe Porter, a co-founder of the firm. Much of the journey has been a process of growing and learning, expanding the understanding and then using it to influence how development is done. Sometimes the lessons were straightforward; sometimes they were only understood in the aftermath of a project.

"Many clients have not taken a broader view of all the components," says partner Richard Shaw. "The result may not be the optimal outcome." Legacy Design can often be a concept that needs to be promoted with an educational approach, in order to show the client the array of benefits of taking a comprehensive, collaborative approach.

Partner Kurt Culbertson recounts just such a situation. "We had an interview [recently] and put up a slide of the Legacy rings and I got stopped in mid-sentence by the president of the company. He says, 'You know that's a really interesting diagram but our owners are only concerned with that circle on the left, which is economics.' And I said, 'I appreciate that but there's greater economic value in projects that are successful for the community, at an environmental level and at the level of art. So if your owners really are interested in economics, they need to be interested in the whole puzzle.' And when they thought about it a little bit further, they said, 'Well, you know, we really hadn't thought about it in those terms but we would like to feel like when we're done with this that we had made something nice out of an old steel mill.' It really goes beyond a do-no-harm philosophy to a more activist position."

Partner Greg Ochis, president of the firm, has also seen this effect. "One of the most interesting aspects of Legacy," he says, "is how powerful it becomes in application both for the project team and the client. It is enormously useful to get people to think in non-traditional ways if they are used to concentrating in only one of the four areas. It's got the accountants thinking about what really creates value and maybe the people who are interested in community understand what community has to do with form and environment. I am usually surprised by how quickly it pushes a project to a higher level."

Porter sees at least a partial realization of the firm's mission in this process. "The concept of doing projects that set in motion change, that really do make a difference over a long period of time, has always been important to us," Porter says. "We've spent a lot of our professional lives working outside our comfort zone to move this Legacy agenda forward. After 35 years, we can honestly look people in the eye and say we're making progress. We seem to have more clients who are buying into the idea and working to figure out how to make it work."

The process also supports designers because the concept helps structure the work. "I think the Legacy definition of design is really helpful for young project managers," says Ensign, "when they get overly focused on managing budgets, schedules and processes and they stop thinking comprehensively. The Legacy idea brings them back to focus on the quality of projects in order to reap the substantial intrinsic rewards."

The firm has developed several structural supports in recent years to support Legacy Design, from the abstract to the concrete. These are incorporated into the firm's electronic systems, which allow design teams to track progress and evolve the thinking behind the work. Using analysis to understand context, designers develop a dilemma and then a thesis that responds to it. From these emerge the narrative principles that will guide the project. These are used to craft Legacy Design goals that deal with issues such as form and the use of materials. The projects then undergo a series of design reviews and rapid-cycling iterations to promote more profound synthesis and a more layered outcome.

The Value of the Workshop

The workshop is one of the most important means for moving a project toward the ideals of Legacy Design. Rather than bowing to the cult of personality and perpetuating the myth of the lone genius, the firm's founders chose a name and a way of operating that would foster an open working environment where clients and designers could embrace design and problem-solving together. Certain conditions are required to make this work: encouragement of diverse opinions, willingness to search for knowledge, a sense of equality among the team and an attitude of discovery.

Workshop is an ideal notion, a state of the working environment where discovery and communication are an open process. It is a delicate state. Rapport is required for it to be creative and effective. It is established by design leadership and upheld by all those who participate. Just as the quality of democracy is related to the quality of the polis, the studio's character requires a certain tenor in the workshop. In the workshop, while teams of professionals are led by those with more experience, the central guiding tenet is that everyone participates. Behaviors essential for the performance of the workshop include communication between experience levels, decisions based upon project-guiding principles and keeping

the decision-making process out in the open. The workshop is literally a territory of discovery, trust, discernment, refinement and resolution, not once but again and again, to make projects responsible to the highest measures.

Planning and design require combining information from varied sources, bringing these facts to bear on alternative solutions, which are set out as models and evaluated by designers, clients and others in order to be improved and refined. This process sounds simple, but doing it well with unique circumstances and different teams of people is always challenging. The organization of the workshop has evolved within the company to promote the open communication of problem-solving and design processes. Central to this process is the need to balance creativity with critique. The design review process includes a collaboration and re-visioning of the work in which the power of the workshop is most readily evident, the power to move toward Legacy ideals. "It builds an atmosphere within our studio of common objectives and an understanding of how our projects move forward," says Johnson. It also rejects any practice of imposing designs on clients. As Culbertson says, "Legacy implies that in the work, you have to be optimistic but you have to be humble, that you have to engage in listening."

Toward Legacy Design

The firm is not alone in this interest in a new way of doing things, a new way of living. The pursuit of Legacy Design is moving in parallel with a broader social movement, in synchronicity with a growing call from many quarters for a society that sustains the environment, nurtures humanity and incorporates spirituality into our daily lives. Fellow travelers include:

- General Electric, the largest firm in America, which announced in 2005 its intent to become a "green" company
- Wal-Mart, whose CEO made a surprise announcement last November committing the company to sustainability goals and backing it up with an investment of $500 million
- the coming together of MacArthur Prize-winning Harvard professor Howard Gardner, Mihaly Csikszentmihalyi and William Damon to form

Goodwork, an organization committed to work that is technically excellent and that seeks outcomes that are ethical, moral and responsible
- Al Gore's exploration of global warming in the movie *An Inconvenient Truth* and the affiliated website that helps people reduce their energy use and carbon footprint http://www.climatecrisis.org/

Such moves raise hopes that commitments to sustainability will be contagious and emulated throughout the business world. These ideas are becoming more engrained in the culture. The market is catching up with the movement toward more responsible living. But there's more. People are learning that it's important to combine the idealistic with the practical and they are searching for ways to live out their ideals or work out of them. And they are looking to those in the forefront for leadership. This has been a significant lesson for Design Workshop, which has created several mechanisms that support its intention of designing to ideals, including an annual gathering of staff from all offices to delve more deeply into both the theoretical and implementation aspects of Legacy Design. These efforts and investments have aligned that infrastructure with the firm's values.

This book is about Design Workshop's journey along the path of Legacy Design. Creating the book has been a trek of its own, as firm members marshaled and refined their thoughts and scavenged through years of projects to find the right work to illustrate their thinking and approach to design. We recognize that the process is a journey, not a destination. In the space of a single lifetime, the firm has accomplished much and learned how much farther there is to go. Operating from principles is a challenge — at the corporate level, in individual offices and discrete teams, and for each individual. This cannot be achieved by simply "adding on" goals and activities; it requires a fundamental transformation of the mental models under which a design firm typically operates. The firm has committed the resources to create a structure to push every project as far toward Legacy Design as possible, but the challenge is ongoing. The goal remains elusive, the means for reaching it not entirely clear, but 35 years of practice have shown there is power in collaboration when it is guided by ideals.

Has Design Workshop always sought to balance economics, environment, community, and art in its work? No. Have all the firm's projects achieved the Legacy ideal? No. Is there a constant drive for improvement? Yes. Is the theory being tested and refined? Are results measured and accountability held? Does each project build upon the lessons of the past? If not, Legacy would simply be a marketing slogan seeking to deceive others and, worse, ourselves.

To ensure against such self-delusion, one must test, measure efforts and ask the right questions. In the arena of economics, can one look beyond profit margin and return on investment to questions of a project's fiscal impact on a community? Environmentally, how close can a design come to creating a continually restorative landscape? Can one predict the effect of a landscape intervention on social factors like crime rates, employment and public health in the surrounding area? And finally, does the built work delight the eye, touch the soul and respect both sacred geometries and the narratives of the cultural landscape in a way that is timeless, not merely provocative or sensational?

The decision to formalize the Legacy Design theory was a decision by Design Workshop to work toward becoming a sustainable organization that also champions the human need for beauty. This is a critical point. A society that meets the needs of the environment and people is healthy. One that meets the demands of the environment and economy is efficient. To bridge the economy and society is to seek justice. But we must strive to create a civilization that also uses artful design to hearten the spirit. At the intersection of all four of these values, in the dialog among them, design can begin to build and sustain more than built work. It can give meaning to existence.

Homes are reflected in the windows of the visitors' center of Utah's Daybreak community, a highly successful project that mandated significant environmental measures and that offers intense engagement with natural beauty.

The Beginning

The founders were teachers and professors who had in common a desire to change the world for the better.

Design Workshop was formed in 1969 at North Carolina State University as an effort to give real-world experience to landscape architecture students. The founders were teachers and professors who had in common a desire to change the world for the better. After a few years, they realized that they saw this mission in different terms: Two of the founding partners, Dick Wilkinson and Vince Foote, thought of the workshop's value as purely educational, while the other two wanted to effect change from within the powerful development industry. There was an amicable parting of the ways and Joe Porter and Don Ensign created Design Workshop, Inc., naming it for the process of collaboration they wished to foster.

One of the firm's earliest efforts was work with The Rouse Company at Columbia, Maryland, where the partners learned not only about the planning and design of new communities but about managing the complexity of such undertakings. That work increased their capacity for managing more and more intricate projects and nurtured their sense of mission. With a 1972 residential development plan for the Pine Island Gun Club in North Carolina, the partners got a rigorous introduction to public policy, the complexity of integrating different scales of planning and the design challenges of reconciling the environment with economics. In applying their values to this very sensitive environment, the partners made the island's ecosystem the framework for preserving the decades-old hunting club, a plan that has succeeded in keeping 6,000 acres of Pine Island preserved and protected as a sanctuary by the Audubon Society.

That ecology-based project led the partners in an unexpected direction, bringing them to the attention of visionary developer George Mitchell, who was building the thriving new community of The Woodlands in Texas. Recognizing the correlation between two sensitive environments, Mitchell hired Design Workshop in 1974 to design the ski area and base village of Owl Creek near Aspen, Colorado. Highly influenced by Ian McHarg's book *Design with Nature*, the developer hired McHarg's office to assess the site's ecology and used this information to support the firm's design of an auto-free village on a very small portion of the site between Aspen and Snowmass. The environment and wildlife corridors were preserved and the design introduced ideas that were innovative for the time, including a transit system and a central parking garage. The project was defeated for political reasons but the plan's careful balance of growth and environment became a model for future development in Pitkin County, significantly influencing the land-use regulations later adopted in and around Aspen. Ski resort work that followed benefited from the growing firm's continuing emphasis on holistic thinking, including projects in Europe and the original planning in Canada for Blackcomb, which has become one of the world's most popular and most sustainable ski resorts.

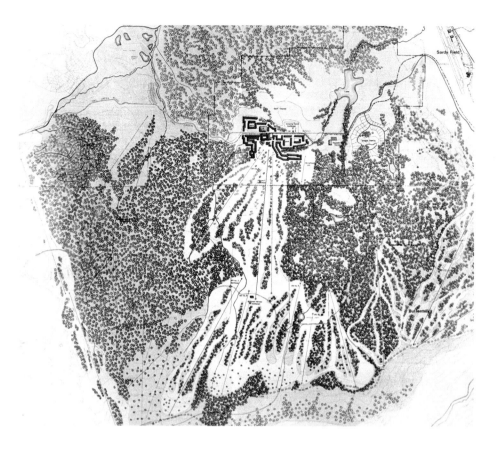

The firm earned an impressive reputation for its ski-area projects but the lessons from that period went far beyond developing in a sustainable manner in the mountains. The partners saw that the same principles that worked in resorts also worked in new community development. Although higher expectations and greater resources in resort communities allowed work to move at a more intense pace than typical community development, the heart of the projects was the same. The firm's staff also began to see that, in order to carry their values through a project, they would need to go beyond ideas, plans and designs, building the skills to take the work through implementation. In 1978, they got their chance with a project where everything they had learned came together, where thinking and practice merged seamlessly, in the Kananaskis Valley of the Canadian Rockies (see page 022). Creation of this resort village in the largely undeveloped valley was a 10-year-long landmark project for

Kananaskis Village lies gently on the land, melding the natural and built environments at the head of the largely undeveloped valley.

Design Workshop, where it became clear that the firm's ideals would work at a large scale on a complex project if the process were carefully managed through design development, public process and construction.

Kananaskis laid the foundation for many of the firm's most successful projects to come, including a series of new communities during the 1980s. These began at The Meadows in Castle Rock, Colorado, south of Denver along Interstate 25 (incidentally, an area that McHarg had identified as a major growth corridor). Plans and designs for that development included village clusters and innovative infrastructure, including riparian drainage spines. The same developer hired the firm to work on Estrella, a project near Phoenix, which led to creating the original master plan and community design for the 20,000-acre development of Summerlin along the western edge of Las Vegas.

Many powerful forces were arrayed against creating a holistic, integrated plan for Summerlin. The region was growing at breakneck speed and development was occurring at an extremely fast pace and in high volume. Las Vegas is a relatively young frontier city in a harsh desert environment and lacks the traditional neighborhoods, public institutions, parks and integrating boulevards and parkways that the City Beautiful movement brought to other American cities. Its population is more concerned with security than community, a trend that has spawned walled and gated neighborhoods.

The firm found, in a decade-long engagement at Summerlin, that it is almost always possible to move projects closer to the ideal, although the designers had both successes and disappointments. Balancing opportunities against constraints, they proposed village clusters, which survived the process and became part of the design guidelines for the entire development, as well as large portions of walkways linking neighborhoods, which were eliminated from the plan.

The firm's greatest success at Summerlin came with the creation of Hills Park in the very first village. There was only grudging acceptance for the proposed park, because parks in Las Vegas had a history as havens for motorcycle gangs and drug deals. The firm's idea of fronting homes on it went down to defeat when project engineers insisted that it be made into a separate recreational area. But ultimately, the ideas behind the park would be vindicated, both by opening-day response when families from all over Las Vegas came to picnic and the park's popularity since that time as a major venue for special events, performances and celebrations. By demonstrating the importance of parks, the success of Hills Park also affected planning in the area, moving both the City of Las Vegas and Clark County planners to pass ordinances requiring parks in new developments.

The projects in this book, which built upon the foundation of these early projects, flesh out the firm's history. The firm has kept education as a cornerstone of the practice, establishing a corporate university, Design U, which encourages a culture of ongoing learning. Designers are expected to return to graduate school at some point in their careers, and the firm continues to explore ways to participate in and engage the academy both through teaching and through joint research. Design Workshop's concept of Legacy Design emerged from the idealism of academia and is supported on both the theoretical and pragmatic levels as a major initiative that guides the firm's efforts going forward. Over many years, Design Workshop has cultivated a solid, diverse practice aspiring to sustainability in community planning, transit-oriented development, urban design, brownfield redevelopment and tourism planning and design. Its leaders and staff look forward to a future of creating legacies for generations to come.

Hills Park at Summerlin, shown during a concert early on in the park's existence, has proven to be a highly successful gathering space in Las Vegas.

The first project where all aspects of the firm's practice came together was Kananaskis, a 10-year project that created a resort village in an undeveloped valley in the Canadian Rockies. This project was a culmination of thinking and practice and it fulfilled many of the conditions of Legacy Design. It is presented here in retrospective analysis to show its formative influence on the evolution of the firm.

DILEMMA: As foreign visitors began to overwhelm Alberta's national parks in the 1970s, provincial officials turned to an undeveloped area to create recreational venues for local citizens. Analysis of the site revealed serious environmental and economic hazards, which were complicated by political pressures when Calgary won the bid to host the 1988 Winter Olympics.

LEGACY GOALS:

Community
Develop a resort aimed primarily at Canadians that would give easy access to both summer and winter recreation; configure accommodations as a village that will encourage social interaction; create a central hub where people come together to meet.

Environment
Analyze all ecological aspects of the entire valley to choose the most appropriate site; design the resort and recreation offerings so that they lie lightly on the land; decrease pollution by making the village auto-free and walkable.

Economics
Let analysis guide the sizing and number of villages and recreation stops; site these in a way that minimizes infrastructure costs; combine accommodations, retail and restaurants in a village layout that encourages foot traffic.

Art
Tuck the village into the landscape in a way that keeps the focus on the spectacular mountain environs; build a trail system that leads people through the valley and gives them a direct experience of nature.

THESIS: A deep understanding of the land and the economics of the situation will help people make appropriate choices in creating a resort village in the Kananaskis Valley. The process will work best through active collaboration among citizens, officials, special interest groups and developers. It will become a legacy for future generations if the design and construction process are guided at all scales by the firm's holistic approach.

KANANASKIS VILLAGE

Alberta, Canada

Planning for a wilderness village helps secure an Olympic bid

Overview

In the mid-1970s in an effort to increase recreational options for provincial residents, Alberta officials used oil severance tax revenues to begin planning skiing, golf and accommodations in the Kananaskis Valley. Canadian cabinet ministers had a vision of scattering European-style alpine resort towns up and down the valley, but Design Workshop, in collaboration with LandPlan Associates of Calgary, demonstrated instead the wisdom of thoroughly vetting the almost completely undeveloped 100,000-acre valley and creating a regional plan to guide development decisions.

History/Context

The planning and design team began in 1978 with the goal of structuring a logical, reasonable, sensitive and just decision-making process to direct development of recreational resources in the valley while preserving its waters, wildlife and scenic views, using comprehensive land analysis. One of its first discoveries was that the sites being considered for resorts were completely impractical, for reasons ranging from prohibitive utility costs to ground that was too steep, areas that would disrupt wildlife migration routes and places with too little sun, too much wind or a complete lack of views. The designers also found that the initial plan of scattering three small alpine villages across the valley ignored land conditions, lack of infrastructure, access and support issues. They focused on determining the suitability of the land for limited, sensitive development.

This high-altitude inland region was so remote that its analysis required a satellite survey. Located at 52 degrees north latitude, the valley is completely shadowed by mountains in certain areas. In winter, sunlight is at a low angle. Most of the valley is bedrock, not soil, which is difficult, expensive and environmentally detrimental to build on and does not readily lend itself to re-vegetation. But the ancient glacier that carved out the valley had created depressions called kettle holes, where giant blocks of ice had been left behind and melted. These were 10 to 12 feet deep and as wide as 300 to 400 feet and sheltered lush landscapes in which soils had had a chance to build up. Other factors included natural hazards such as wildfire and the harsh, warm, unpredictable Chinook winds, which had had a strong effect on the building of soils, on microclimates and on plants and animals.

Process

The team completed a wide array of studies of everything from habitat and scenic vistas to infrastructure costs and recreational preferences and created predictive models that interwove this information. In thinking that was advanced for the pre-computer era, the team devised innovative methods for interweaving land data, creating more than 40 hand-drawn analyses of such things

as aspect, slope, views and wind, and weighting these according to officials' expressed values and objectives. This identified the site most favorable for human comfort year-round, at the lowest construction cost, with the most attractive features, least natural hazards and lowest impact to the site's ecology and views. They presented this information to a broad spectrum of interest groups, including public and private natural resource officials, environmentalists, forest service and other agency representatives, and political officials ranging from the provincial level to the Canadian prime minister. The in-depth research and analysis created a powerful logic and a defensible regional plan that guided 10 years of development decisions in the valley and later stood in stark contrast to the self-interest efforts of those who wanted to profit from creation of venues for the 1988 Calgary Olympics.

Plan/Design

The focus of the plan was to create accommodations in a single village plan on a site on Ribbon Creek not far from the mouth of the valley and about 20 miles east of Banff. Here, a village could lie lightly on the land but still be a place of comfort and such surpassing beauty that it would have a natural and authentic appeal. Provincial officials

committed first to the extension of roads and utilities and then to construction of a 27-hole golf course and finally to creation of the Kananaskis Village, which featured nearly three times the original number of overnight accommodations. In 1980, Calgary was chosen as host for the 1988 Winter Olympics, a decision that would have a galvanizing effect on the creation of Kananaskis Village. Canadian officials hired Design Workshop to help site and configure skiing event venues in the valley. Later, the province would commit to facilities for fishing, water-based recreation and a handicapped recreational outdoor program to complement Kananaskis Village.

The design allows the village to look like it has been dropped gently onto the landscape. The team gave it the feel of a destination by keeping it auto-free and configuring a village of four hotels around a central gathering area that preserves major features of the landscape. They also created trails that lead out from it into the wilderness and persuaded individual restaurant and retail venues to locate around this hub, to enliven the space.

Wrangling and jockeying delayed major decisions for five years, leaving only 30 months to construct the village in time for the Olympics. The team managed the construction process in adherence to the original design, work-

ing with four developers and architects of four different hotels, preserving the auto-free zone and core village concept, with its sheltering of central spaces, architectural unity, focused plaza, the perimeter of dining and commercial uses and scenic views.

Outcome

This 10-year effort was a landmark project that deepened the firm's expertise in organizing the elements of recreational resort villages to create a successful whole. Kananaskis advanced the firm's thinking in regard to the elements that are critical to a holistic approach and made clear the necessity of managing construction so that the built work remains consonant with the design intent. The designers worked at all levels, from regional planning to the tiniest details of landscape architecture, and also solved the problems of economic and market viability and established governance of the village, ski area and golf course. Kananaskis Village continues to enjoy success over and above its original purpose of serving local residents. In addition to helping host the Olympics, the village has been the site of several prominent events, including the G-8 conference of the world's leaders in 2003.

Rock quarried from the site was used to establish a large pond and a stream and to build an imposing stone-slab plateau from which a waterfall cascades. A network of bicycle and walking trails encourages visitors to experience the landscape at different scales and speeds. The village is tucked into the landscape in a way that complements the valley's majestic beauty.

Nature

ESSAY

Partner Richard Shaw, who joined the firm in 1976, opens this
chapter with thoughts on the restorative power of nature, exploring our
culture's ambivalence toward it and the need for a reconciliation of
development and preservation. Following are descriptions of five projects,
which are intended to illustrate how working with nature deepens the
meaning of the places we create.

PROJECT DISCUSSIONS

Aguas Claras: A master plan gives a mining pit a second chance at
life, transforming it into a mixed-use community.

Walnut Creek National Wildlife Refuge: Farmland is turned back
into a tall-grass prairie oasis and is embraced by the surrounding towns
and cities.

Interstate-25 Conservation Corridor: Ten years of challenging
negotiations preserve a scenic corridor between two urban areas.

Glacier Club: A spectacular setting, unusual environmental practices
and strategic golf design create a memorable experience.

IN-DEPTH ACCOUNT

Clark County Wetlands Park: A piece of damaged, derelict ground
finds a new identity as a nature preserve for the city of Las Vegas.

We need to recognize as a society that nature can be a restorative force for the community.

AN ESSAY BY RICHARD SHAW

Human beings can single-handedly render the Earth uninhabitable, not just through apocalyptic weaponry but also through our everyday lives. The world is now supporting billions of people, technology produces byproducts beyond what other societies have ever had to reckon with and our reliance on nonrenewable resources is threatening our very existence. The consequences of some of our actions are now irreversible because of the scale at which we live and the immense power we wield. What we do counts in ways we are only just beginning to understand, and sometimes our actions come back to haunt us. Nature damaged at this scale cannot sustain civilization.

As our numbers grow, nature shrinks. Once, we had a wealth of wilderness to draw upon. Now, we must be more careful; we must learn nature's limits, its resilience, how we can support it and how it fits with the rest of our lives.

Our relationship with nature over the millennia has been ambivalent and changeable. It has been both boon and threat. We have subsisted on it, feared it, controlled it and exploited it, but we have also found within it aesthetic experiences that restore us. And we have edited, shaped and crafted nature in myriad ways in order to re-create these experiences for ourselves. The garden is a microcosm of this and has taken many forms. In traditional Japanese gardens, personal restoration comes from the cherishing gesture of emulating the landscape, where boulders are mountain ranges and ponds are oceans. In classic French gardens, a haven emerges from strict order imposed on profligate nature, managing it with the controlling formality of the straight line and the precision of perfection in a tightly dominated composition. The English garden constructs picturesque ideals, framing the existing landscape with composed natural elements. These purposeful efforts to create and subsequently control nature are single, dimensional, human imprints imposed on nature as a way to engage with it, to craft it, dream it or idealize it, according to the values of the culture.

We have all experienced at the personal level the power of nature to revive us: When we need to get away, we go to a sandy beach, a mountain retreat, an urban park or our own backyard. What we have not

Human beings have imposed structure and design on nature in many ways, including this hedge maze at the Château de Villandry in the Loire Valley in France.

recognized as a society is that the aesthetics of nature can be a restorative force for the community. Our current challenge as a species mandates that we take this understanding of and engagement with nature to a higher and broader level and cultivate this same nurturing relationship with the land at all scales.

Nature in America

Americans have had a unique tie to nature with a highly compressed history. Urban America discovered its own appreciation for natural landscapes following the nation's intense 18th-century urbanization, when social reformers created urban open spaces to bring light and air to people and restore the health and social welfare of the newly formed communities. But beyond the urban edge, the frontier beckoned and Americans largely saw nature as something to be conquered, an impediment to the manifest destiny of the future. They set upon these wild, unmanaged and seemingly limitless lands, prospecting them for unimaginable wealth. And they found, on those excursions, magical places — places they would ultimately work to preserve against exploitation.

Another culture might have designated such places as sacred; in a capitalistic culture devoted to equality and freedom of religion, people simply recognized their intangible value and the fairness of sharing them. Those who had visited Yellowstone embraced the previously unheard-of concept that private economic interests should be denied in favor of the preservation of land in perpetuity. In 1872, it was made our first national park. By the early 1900s, the U.S. had created an entire system of national parks, so that now 3 percent of the continental United States is entitled to all Americans. By the mid-20th century, this would evolve to include the preservation of wilderness areas, those vast regions of pristine and unmanaged land that lie beyond the urban edge. Americans chose to protect them in perpetuity for no other reason than, in the words of Wallace Stegner, "to drive to the edge and peer in; to know that it is, gives us sanity." These tracts would not be logged or mined or grazed, only appreciated. And this act made us see ourselves as stewards of the land.

Nature is resilient and thrives despite human interference, often against great odds. (**above**) Early California settlers enjoy a ride through a tunnel bored in a giant sequoia tree.

(**opposite**) Mule deer thrive at the former Rocky Mountain Arsenal, seen here against the Denver skyline. Although the highly toxic center of the Arsenal is a Superfund site that is slowly being remediated, the surrounding areas have long harbored hundreds of wildlife species, including nesting bald eagles. Design Workshop led the process to create a 15-year comprehensive management plan for transforming the 27-square-mile site into a national wildlife refuge.

In the end, our society will be defined not by what we create, but by what we refuse to destroy. — John C. Sawhill, past president, The Nature Conservancy

This inheritance is ambiguous and has inherent conflicts. Our national parks and wilderness suffer from lack of support and are threatened with resource extraction; the areas surrounding them are often not supported well enough to bear the weight of hordes of visitors. It also isn't clear whether we are preserving these lands in a pristine state or if people should be allowed to enjoy them, or whether we are preserving them for future generations to enjoy. But they remain a gift we have given to ourselves and an acknowledgment of the power of nature to heal us.

We see the need for this kind of healing every day in our towns and cities. In stark contrast to these pristine and scenic regions are the lands damaged by human habitation and industry, from the vast urban industrial swaths of our great cities to outlying lands impacted by new settlement. Often we did the best we could at the time. Often we didn't realize the effect we were having on ourselves and the land. Economic or other necessity drove our efforts and created practices and patterns that didn't look beyond tomorrow or beyond the borders of the community. What we know now is that just as nature can heal us, it can heal itself, if given enough support. These lands can recover from this bleakness. We can pay the price of such practices and find in even the darkest scenarios new possibilities and new hope.

Understanding natural systems within the larger landscape has a comparatively short history. Early research and applied analysis was tightly focused and was only finally broadened when Ian McHarg and others introduced the concept that the environment can and should directly influence land use. McHarg's method, articulated in his book *Design with Nature*, uses overlays and so-called filter mapping to get at spatial and locational land-use solutions. His approach, which has become the foundation for current planning and environmental design strategies, was based on the idea that landscape and environment are the principles by which design and development decisions must be made in order for humans not to destroy their own environment.

McHarg's transforming methodology was expanded by the work of Carl Steinitz of Harvard in research sponsored by the National Science Foundation in the 1970s. Through extensive predictive modeling, Steinitz was able to combine information about water quality, habitat loss, social change, visual qualities and myriad other environmental constraints to create methodical and, more importantly, comprehensible plans that resolved the conflict between natural resources and urbanization. Suddenly, land-use strategies informed by intelligence, forethought and analysis tools could effectively shape the future of communities, cities and landscapes.

The Reconciliation of Nature and Economics

Landscape restoration and preservation are inextricably linked as we approach a future that augurs unforgiving pressure on the use of our most precious resource: the environment. The conflict between development and preservation starts with those innate combinations of natural features and ecological systems — water, fertile soils and flat land — that are the very geographical resources most suitable for human settlement, development, growth and migration. For the most part, this is an ideological battle, fought by two sides that acknowledge the need for both to exist. The plans with the most appeal and power are also the most enlightened, wherein development preserves such things as rare and critical habitat or offers a kind of open space that fosters social equity.

Over the course of recent decades, there's been a paradigm shift toward valuing "green," but the relationship between nature and economics is still largely adversarial. Only by balancing these two factors with community and aesthetic values, can we help them achieve their natural symbiosis. Integrated and holistic thinking about the landscape recognizes that human civilization is a fundamental part of the natural world; if the human community is to sustain itself, then nature must be preserved, restored and perpetuated. The 20th century ushered in the concept of sustainability. While the term remains undefined in its application, its effect on our relationship with nature is multifaceted. In essence, *sustainability* refers to our ability as citizens to make thoughtful decisions, being ever-mindful that our every action has a result that is defining and consequential to the future. We are linked to our environment, the land we live on and the earthly resource we all share. Without this essential understanding, nature will cease to exist. And so will we.

Owners of this iron-ore mine in Brazil saw mining as a temporary use of the land and began planning in the early 1990s to reuse the excavated pit once mineral resources are depleted. The master plan transforms the massive open pit and waste areas into a satellite village for a metropolitan region.

PROJECT DISCUSSION:
AGUAS CLARAS

Belo Horizonte, Brazil

An iron-ore mine is configured as a community in its next life

In recent decades, leading mining companies have begun at the start of mining operations to design end-use plans as part of their mining plans. Company officials realize it is more cost-effective to mine with a plan for reuse and that the future of the industry depends on its ability to look beyond compliance and come to grips with issues of economics, environment, community and the aesthetics of what they leave. The Aguas Claras mine demonstrates an approach to planning the reuse of more destructive mines from an older era.

Brazil's second-largest iron-ore mining company, Mineração Brasileiras Reunidas (MBR), has mined the rich iron-ore quadrangle southeast of the city of Belo Horizonte in southern Brazil since the 1940s, including the Aguas Claras mine, which was opened in 1965. Officials calculated in the early 1990s that they would be closing the mine in the next decade. The company was dedicated to efficient and profitable mining, which is critical to the country's economy, but officials also acknowledged that the land should have a life after mining, one that restored and protected the environment and contributed to the area economy. Design Workshop prepared a master plan for MBR to rehabilitate and reuse the land at a later time.

Land analysis revealed that the mine presented no issues of toxicity that would prohibit human use. Aguas Claras is an ideal location for a village since the mine is on the rear slope of mountains that form the southern boundary of the burgeoning city of Belo Horizonte, which at more than three million people is Brazil's third largest city.

The design team and operations managers collaborated to prepare a

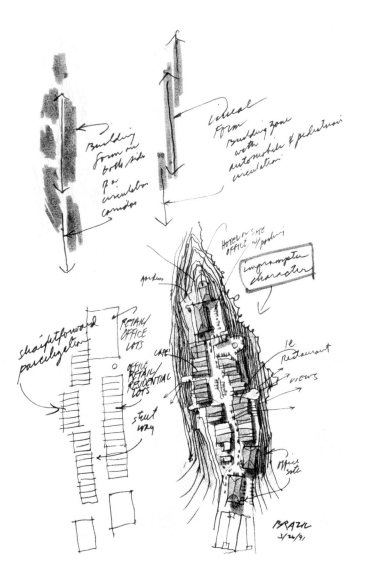

An early sketch fitted the Aguas Claras Village center to the mine-processing area, with neighborhood platforms surrounding the lake created out of the pit.

redevelopment plan that would ultimately transform the site into a new mixed-use village as a model for how walkable satellite villages can accommodate growth demands in the region with minimal disturbance to the environment. The plan places a nucleus of community life at its center, including a church, a school, shops, restaurants, a recreation club and conference and office centers, to provide an economic base for the village and to place jobs and services within walking distance of homes. The village plan also minimizes the need for cars and gives middle-class residents an alternative to automobile-oriented suburban living, which is beginning to choke the region with traffic.

The plan utilizes principles of adaptive reuse to apply elements of the mine and mining process to urbanization. The design creates a beautiful and functional garden setting for the village, using design standards for future development projects, site design and architectural standards for the community and revegetation strategies to add biodiversity to the massive site. The central feature of the village design is a lake created out of the mine pit, which is to be slowly filled with groundwater and surface runoff. Water-treatment facilities, once used to purify runoff from the mine, were incorporated into the plan as a means of

protecting Aguas Claras Creek from village construction and urban runoff. The plan also called for contouring the tops of waste areas during the last phases of mining to better accommodate village development. MBR began implementation of the plan with construction of its own office building in a planned office park on the site.

MBR originally anticipated it would close the mine in 1997, but mining operations continued until December 2003. The company was acquired in 2001 by CVRD, another Brazilian iron-ore producer, and Japanese trading company Mitsui. Company and government officials are continuing to explore options and detail plans for reuse of the site. The Aguas Claras master plan was featured as an example of sustainable mining in the Brazil exhibit at the Earth Summit in Rio de Janeiro in 1992.

PROJECT CREDITS

PLANNING/DESIGN: Design Workshop, Inc.
PIC: Joe Porter, Sergio Santana
Designer: Sergio Santana
Project Advisor: Kurt Culbertson

CLIENT: Mineraçãos Brasileiras Reunidas (MBR), a division of Caemi Mineração e Metalurgia SA

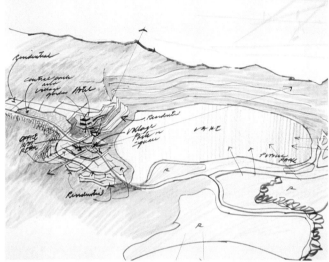

(above left) A comparison of existing conditions and a vision for the site shows the pit in the distance becoming a lake, Aguas Claras Village on its shore and transformation of ore-stocking areas in the foreground into offices and an employment district.

(above right) Prototype sketches apply hillside building patterns of the region to platforms, or terraces, that were created during mining operations.

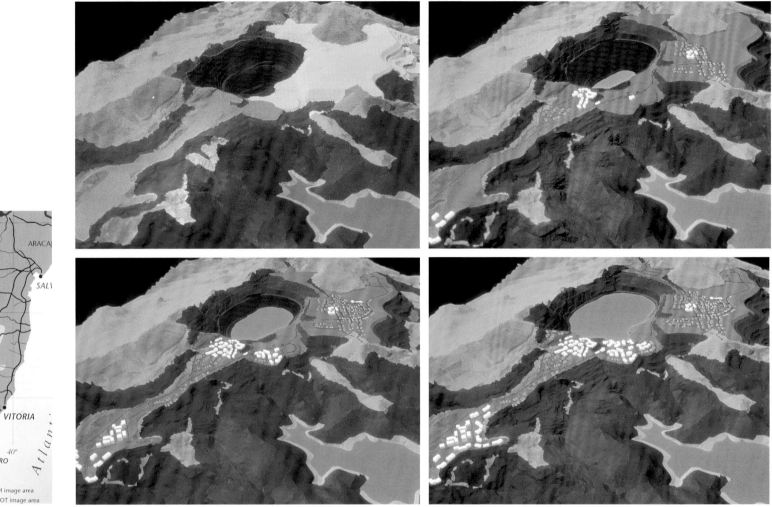

(above left) A GIS map shows the rich iron-ore quadrangle southeast of the city of Belo Horizonte in southern Brazil, which has been mined since the 1940s. The plan for transforming the Aguas Claras mine into a satellite village for Belo Horizonte was featured at the Earth Summit in Rio de Janeiro in 1992.

(above right) A series of computer simulations shows the proposed transformation of the site through a series of evolutions, from modifications at the later stages of mining to settlement of the area. The mine pit, or cava, is slowly filled to create a lake, around which are built the village core and neighborhoods and an employment center.

(right) Sustainable mining is reinvestment of mine revenues to create a perpetual income stream. This diagram, created by World Bank economist Salah El Serafy, illustrates the same principle applied to reinvestment at Aguas Claras to create a self-sustaining environment and community.

Sustainability Model
(Dr. El Serafy)

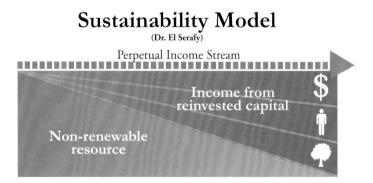

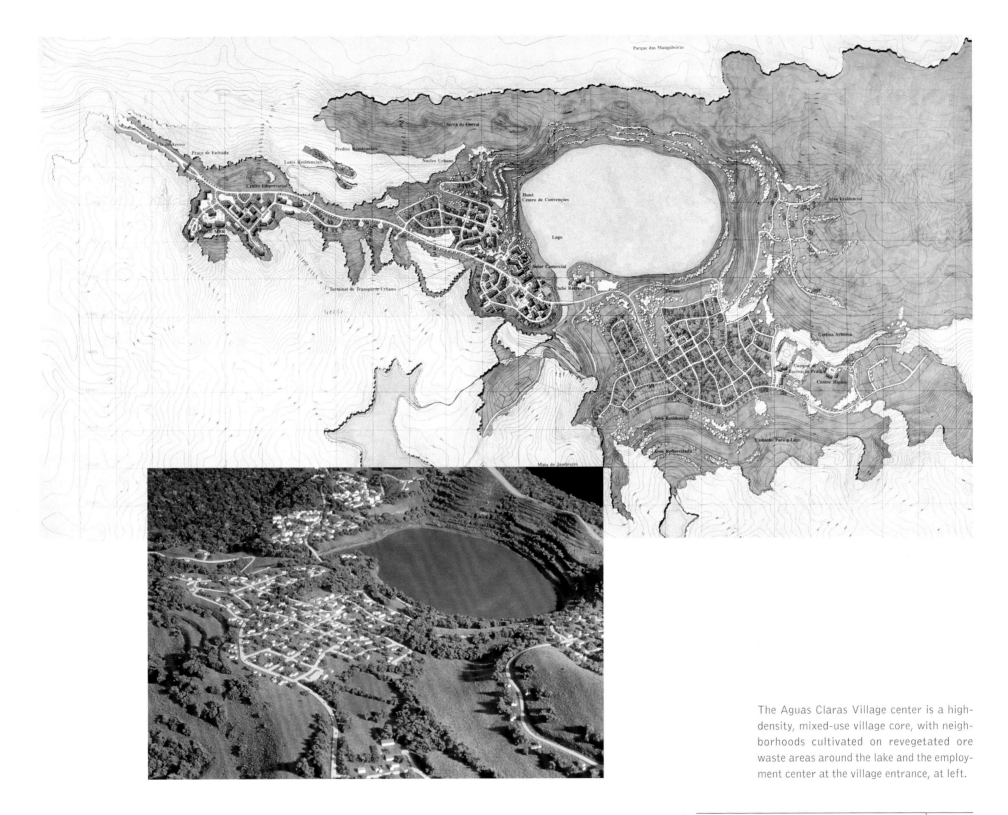

The Aguas Claras Village center is a high-density, mixed-use village core, with neighborhoods cultivated on revegetated ore waste areas around the lake and the employment center at the village entrance, at left.

When plans for a proposed power plant fizzled, a parcel of farmland became public land that could serve nearby communities. A design collaboration returned the land to its original state, creating a prairie learning center where visitors of all ages can rediscover the natural history of the area.

PROJECT DISCUSSION:
WALNUT CREEK NATIONAL WILDLIFE REFUGE

Jasper County, Iowa

Restored prairie engages the community with the land

During the 1980s, an Iowa power company assembled 8,000 acres of farmland as a site for a nuclear power plant. Changes in the industry led company officials to decide against building the plant and they began to explore options for divesting themselves of the land. Congressman Neal Smith suggested the federal government should acquire the land as a site for a national wildlife refuge that would study, restore and celebrate the tall-grass prairie ecosystem that formed the original landscape of Iowa and much of the Midwestern United States. Congress approved purchase of the land by the U.S. Fish and Wildlife Service in 1990 and land acquisition began the following year. At that time, the prevailing site condition was modern crop agriculture.

Design Workshop was part of a multidisciplinary team chosen through an extensive interview process to design the refuge. The Fish and Wildlife Service had historically made wildlife refuges focused on the preservation and creation of wildlife habitat, places that had no public access and that did not require education facilities or marketing efforts. But at that time, Department of Interior funds were being directed increasingly to projects that served the general public. In an effort to secure greater funding, the agency shifted its approach and proposed to give ordinary citizens access to the Walnut Creek site.

This new orientation brought challenges and benefits. The refuge's design would have to encompass education, interpretation and explanation of the complex natural and cultural forces at work on the site over time. But this focus could also foster community partnerships and bring in volunteers who

(above) By locating the visitor center 2 miles into the site, the refuge gives people a chance to first experience the tranquility of the prairie before reaching the educational exhibits and trails around the visitor center.

(opposite) The visitor center, constructed from local materials and designed to resonate with the horizontal feel of the prairie, almost disappears in the landscape.

would support refuge staff, as well as funding initiatives that could supplement federal revenues.

The landscape architects, architects and interpretive designers focused on the idea of creating an environmental conservation and restoration project that would create new and meaningful ways for people to understand and experience a unique North American landscape. Their design approach was an unusual combination of the pragmatic and the sensitive. The team first completed a market study to determine whether the refuge could be viable as a publicly visited facility. An intensive period of research followed, supported by Fish and Wildlife. Agency officials accompanied the design team on a tour of several prairie environments, bringing them together with botanists, biologists and educators who specialize in the prairie ecosystem and even rousting them out of bed one morning to watch the sun come up over the prairie landscape.

The team spent weeks on the site devising methods for immersing visitors in the landscape, both by preserving and containing views and by creating places that would give a sense of what the tall-grass prairie environment was originally like. Instead of locating the visitor center near the refuge boundary, the design gives people a 2-mile drive into the site

that allows them to leave the normal world behind and to start to become curious about this new place.

The design team collaborated in a series of charrettes, or workshops, to generate physical forms for the project's manmade structures, exploring the materials and patterns developed by Native Americans and early European settlers. Historic park architecture and the work of early Prairie School designers such as Jens Jensen and Frank Lloyd Wright became the primary inspiration for the project. This resulted in a design that allowed the project's four buildings — the 40,000-square-foot visitor center and three outdoor classrooms — to grow organically from the site but still visually and physically connect to it.

The design forms resonate with the broad, horizontal character of the landscape, and the project employs building materials such as stucco, concrete and wood, which are drawn from elements native to the region. The project also uses natural processes to support its presence on the land: Constructed wetlands are used to filter waste, while solar orientation and earth-berm design naturally help to heat and cool the visitor center.

To restore this now-rare ecosystem, the team located areas of relic and remnant prairie on the site, most of which were degraded, and managed them with

the goal was not only to resurrect the prairie
but also to engage people with it

(left) Visitors watch a herd of bison grazing high on a hillside of restored prairie vegetation.

(above) As restoration progresses, the landscape continues to evolve from former farmland to true tall-grass prairie.

(opposite) Volunteers support the refuge by gathering seed and replanting farmland with indigenous prairie plants, a project that will take many years to complete.

annual burning to eliminate exotic species and revive native plants. Eroded stream banks and other features were regraded and restored to a more natural condition in preparation for replanting, which was done with native seed collected by hand from original prairie plants — an ongoing process that volunteers continue to support.

The 200 species of indigenous plants now established on the site include cottonwood trees, Indian grass, bluestem grass, Canada wild rye, prairie blazing star, butterfly milkweed and black-eyed Susans. Among the refuge's wildlife denizens are buffalo, elk, white-tailed deer, pheasants, wild turkey, badgers, skunks, rabbits, raccoons, gophers, turtles, bats, cowbirds, red-tailed hawks, falcons, meadowlarks and monarch butterflies.

Budget issues that emerged late in the process resulted in the modification of some features. But the design's central essence was preserved, blending an entry road, auto tour loop, several miles of interpretive trails and signage, outlying environmental education sites, operations facilities and the visitor center into the restored prairie environment.

The site was renamed the Neal Smith National Wildlife Refuge in 1998.

PROJECT CREDITS

PLANNING/DESIGN: Design Workshop, Inc.
  PIC: Gregory Ochis
  Landscape Architects: Nancy Locke,
  Scott Chomiak

CLIENT: U.S. Fish & Wildlife Service

Collaborators: Dave Schaeffer, Mark Marxen,
U.S. Fish & Wildlife Service

Exhibit Design: Gerald Hilferty and Associates

Architecture: OZ Architecture

Civil Engineering: Butts Engineering Company

Landscape Consultant: Dunbar-Jones

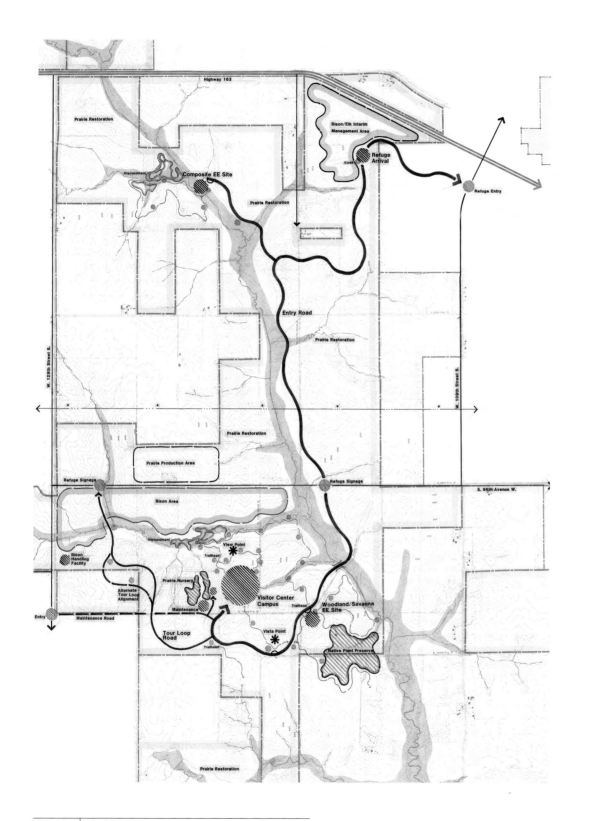

Highway 163

Prairie Restoration

Bison/Elk Interim
Management Area

Composite EE Site

Impoundment

Kiosk

Refuge
Arrival

Refuge Entry

Prairie Restoration

W. 129th Street S.

Entry Road

Prairie Restoration

W. 109th Street S.

Prairie Restoration

Prairie Production Area

Refuge Signage

Refuge Signage

S. 96th Avenue W.

Bison Area

Impoundment

View Point

Bison
Handling
Facility

Trailhead

Prairie Nursery

Visitor Center
Campus

Trailhead

Woodland/Savanna
EE Site

Alternate
Tour Loop
Alignment

Maintenance

Trailhead

Entry

Maintenance Road

Tour Loop
Road

Vista Point

Trailhead

Native Plant Preserve

Prairie Restoration

(at left) Congress approved the purchase of more than 8,000 acres to create the refuge, which is currently about 5,000 acres in size (outlined in yellow). Officials continue to acquire land to fill out the site, which encompasses areas along Walnut Creek (shown in gray).

(opposite top) Educational displays dot the walking trails near the visitor center, explaining the phases of transformation from agricultural lands to prairie.

(opposite left to right) The experience of spending several weeks on site allowed the team to design educational gathering spots that immerse people in the life of the prairie. During the design process, drawings helped people envision what the area around the visitor center would be like and what shape the outdoor classrooms would take.

Development was encroaching on the spectacular environs along the urban corridor between Colorado's two largest cities. A series of innovative tools and strategies allowed a consortium of conservation groups to preserve more than 30,000 acres of wildlife habitat and a series of iconic vistas.

PROJECT DISCUSSION:
INTERSTATE-25 CONSERVATION CORRIDOR

Douglas County, Colorado

New land conservation methods protect a region's natural and scenic resources

Scenery in the 65-mile-long corridor along Interstate 25 between Denver and Colorado Springs is some of the most spectacular in the world, from rolling grasslands to views of Pikes Peak. This is the southern part of Douglas County, which has been one of the fastest-growing counties in the nation since the early 1980s. From 1990 to 1995 alone, its growth rate soared to 45.8 percent, with a great deal of land consumed by road-building and subdivisions.

In the mid-1990s, The Conservation Fund, a national land conservation organization, became involved in efforts to preserve the area after concerns arose that continued unplanned growth could ruin the region's scenic qualities and result in an unbroken strip of development between the two cities. In 1994, Design Workshop began a study of a 50-square-mile area along a relatively undeveloped 15-mile stretch of highway with the goal of protecting the most important lands in this unique Colorado landscape. The area was a transition zone between the mountains and the plains, encompassing historic vistas, working cattle ranches, habitat for a wide array of wildlife, critical ecosystems and significant recreation opportunities, as well as passage for more than 50,000 commuters and travelers a day.

Investigations revealed that Douglas County had had more than 140 real estate transactions in the most recent three years and that the value of the land had doubled in response. Most of these were purchases of parcels that were 35 acres or larger, which, under the county's agricultural zoning, could be used for single-family residences, a trend that scattered development across the land.

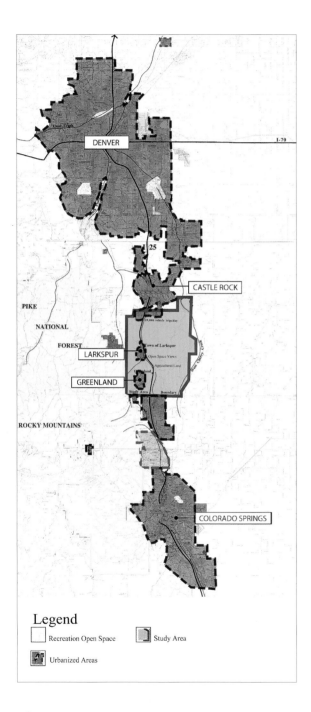

Legend

☐ Recreation Open Space ▦ Study Area

▦ Urbanized Areas

The planners helped create a coalition with environmental groups and state and county officials, including then-governor Roy Romer and representatives of the Colorado Division of Wildlife and the state parks department. Acknowledging the limited resources at their disposal and the high rate and degree of change in the situation, the team created a unique analysis tool to pinpoint the most important places to preserve and the places where conflict was most likely to occur. They collected data on such attributes as topography, land cover, natural hazards, zoning, land ownership, transportation, elements critical to the health of the ecosystems and wildlife habitat, view sheds from the interstate highway, the limits of existing zoning and public policy, water rights, funding options and recreation needs. They mapped the area, setting priorities: Lands with complex vegetation, a high wildlife count and important views took precedence over simple grasslands. They used historic patterns to create a model that showed where development would probably occur and matched it against the sites with the most natural resources to reveal potential conflicts and establish preservation priorities.

The analysis identified the tracts most vulnerable to development, the most significant scenic values, the places where new public open space would matter most and the wisest use of money and resources. With this information, the team created a plan to protect the most critical lands, recommending permanent protection of a core area of 25,000 acres, including 12 miles of highway corridor, by outright purchase or conservation easement. The goal was to use limited development schemes, by creating a zone to buffer development and clustering development to support conservation efforts. By locating limited development in places where it minimized the impact on the land, didn't harm habitat and didn't encroach on views, it was possible to preserve land around development, which in turn would increase the value of the land.

In 1996, Conservation Fund officials asked for and received a multimillion-dollar Legacy Initiative grant from the state lottery-funded Great Outdoors Colorado trust fund to begin acquiring these lands. In the course of a 10-year process, development itself became an important method for preserving lands. The coalition purchased land zoned for intensive development and then developed only a fraction of the land, tucking houses back away from public views and placing the remainder of the land in conservation easements, preserving both

NATURAL RESOURCES

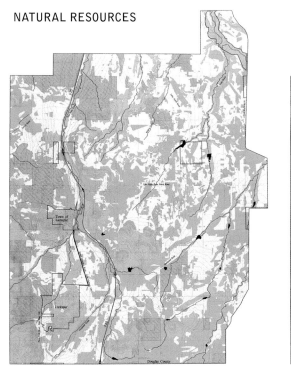

SENSITIVE HABITAT

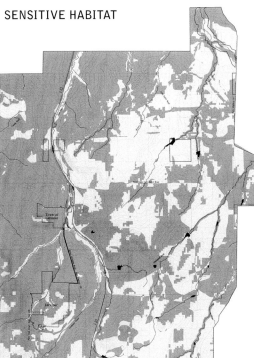

NATURAL AREAS

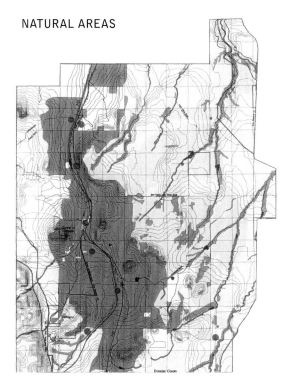

OWNERSHIP

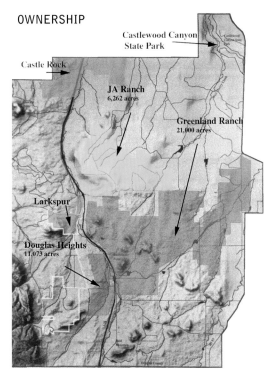

Castlewood Canyon
State Park

Castle Rock

JA Ranch
6,262 acres

Greenland Ranch
21,000 acres

Larkspur

Douglas Heights
11,073 acres

(opposite) The metropolitan areas of Denver
and Colorado Springs, with a combined population of more than 2 million, were beginning to grow toward each other into a single
megalopolis. The team of collaborators identified an area that had the greatest potential
for preserving a scenic corridor between the
two cities (in green).

ANALYSIS MAPS
Natural Resources (upper left) The site's
natural resources allowed the corridor to
qualify for a conservation easement. Limited
or no development suitability is indicated by
blue and green, with moderate to high suitability in the yellow and orange areas.

Sensitive Habitat (upper right) The team
found sensitive habitat at the center of the
site (in pink), with low sensitivity in surrounding areas (gray).

Natural Areas (lower left) Undeveloped areas alongside the highway were given a high
preservation priority (green).

Ownership (lower right) Several large land-
holdings were key to the eventual success of
the preservation process.

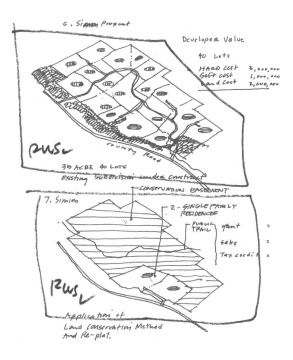

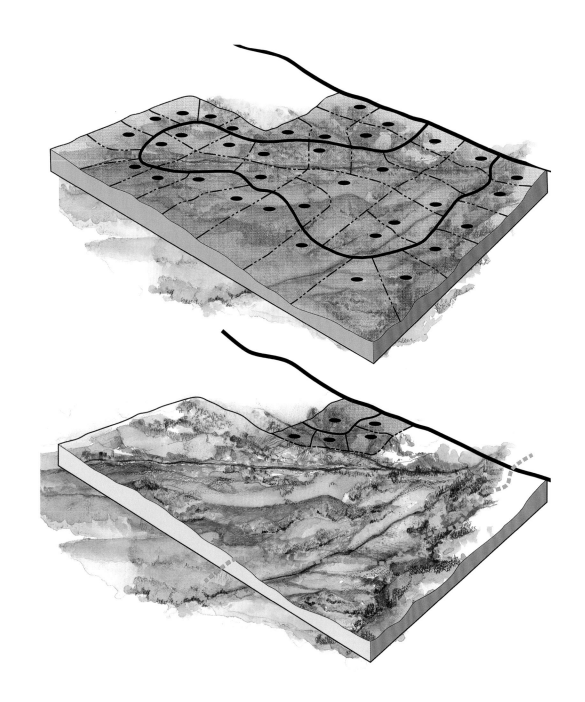

Intricate negotiations allowed limited development that was tucked out of view, leaving most land in conservation easements. The sketches and drawings show how a single parcel along a county road could have been used for full development and how it was preserved under a conservation easement, with limited development.

open space and views in perpetuity and conferring tax benefits on the future owners. The plan identified where the lands richest in resources overlapped those that had the lowest appraised costs, so that funds could be spent where they would have the greatest effect. This formed the basis for decision-making, consensus-building, negotiation and acquisition of the lands deemed most valuable for conservation. The plan also encouraged developers to consider natural and aesthetic values in addition to economic return and helped conservationists understand that appropriate development can support land conservation.

Most of the transactions were extremely complex. The designers played a key role on the team that resolved each of the 11 conservation-based land transactions. The most dramatic was the preservation of Douglas Heights, where, in an 11-hour intervention, The Conservation Fund used a special grant to secure most of a 1,300-acre property on which road-building and grading had already begun. The deal reduced the number of homes on the site and relocated them to preserve scenic views. Another coup was acquisition in 2000 of a conservation easement on the 17,000-acre Greenland Ranch, which was considered the linchpin parcel of the project, an agreement that required several years of negotiation. The final parcel, True Mountain, was acquired in December 2003.

Through conservation-based development and a variety of other land-protection techniques, the group was able to protect 34,000 acres at a cost of only $32 million on land valued at three times that amount. These mechanisms also kept 80 percent of the land in private hands, significantly reducing the role that had been anticipated for the Division of Wildlife.

This unprecedented conservation success in an area facing such acute development pressures used limited development coupled with strategic grants and minimal public resources to help shape urban growth and recreation development and preserve scenic views and open-space trails and greenways. The plan protected wildlife habitat for deer, elk, mountain lion, bear, bobcat, prairie falcon and one of only two herds of bighorn sheep known to exist east of I-25 in Colorado, as well as such land types as prairie, riparian corridors, grasslands, buttes, pine forests and foothills. The project stands as a model for how to keep metro areas from merging into continuous urban sprawl by guaranteeing preservation of a scenic corridor.

PROJECT CREDITS

PLANNING/DESIGN: Design Workshop, Inc.
  PIC: Richard Shaw
  Project manager: Suzanne Richman
  Landscape Architects: Sarah Chase, David Lendon

CLIENT: The Conservation Fund
  Project Coordinator: Sidney Macy

Collaborators: Douglas County Planning Department, Great Outdoors Colorado (GOCO)

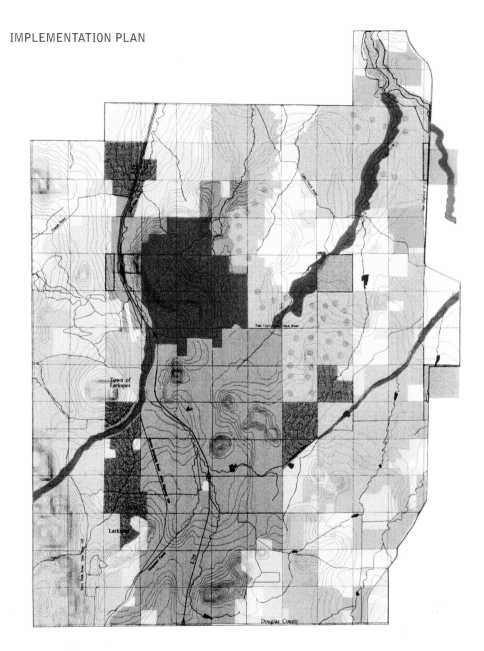

Protection and Implementation Concept Plan

1st Priority Permanent Protection	Conservation Easement/Openspace Corridor	Existing Development	Cluster at 1 Unit per 35 Acres
2nd Priority Permanent Protection	Hillside Development Control	Approved Subdivision	Limited Development Site
County Permanent Protection	State Owned Land	Recent Land Sale	Existing 35 Acre Lots

I-25 CONSERVATION CORRIDOR PLAN

The implementation plan at left identified areas that needed immediate protection (in olive green), already protected areas (black) and existing public and private ownership and controls. Final negotiations preserved the rolling countryside and views to the mountains along a 12-mile stretch of Interstate 25, shown at right beneath Pikes Peak.

Tamarron was a true mountain golf course, but it was aging and dated. New owners added nine holes and remodeled the existing 18-hole course, going to extraordinary lengths to preserve the environment and create a memorable golfing experience on the steep, spectacular site.

PROJECT DISCUSSION:
GLACIER CLUB

Durango, Colorado

Golf course honors the ecology of a majestic mountain setting

Tamarron, which opened in the early 1970s in the San Juan Mountains of southwestern Colorado, was master-minded by golf-course builders Stan and Brent Wadsworth and designed by Arthur Hills. Only 300 acres of the 750-acre site were used for the golf course and resort condominiums, leaving a large, challenging parcel on the back of the property.

Tamarron's setting was spectacular, with picture postcard views in every direction, but over the years the facilities — including the irrigation system, cart path, condominiums, lodge and the course itself — had begun to deteriorate. The resort changed hands many times over 25 years, but no owner had the necessary resources for rehabilitation and it began losing a substantial amount of money. In late 2001, Tamarron was purchased by new owners, who decided

to add a new private nine-hole golf course, re-design the old course and master-plan new accommodations.

Except for such places as Banff Springs, most so-called mountain courses are actually in valleys at the base of mountains. Tamarron's original 18 holes were a true mountain course, with the obstacles typical of such a place. But the new 450-acre site on the back of the ridge where the owners wanted to create a new course was more challenging yet — steep, rocky and heavily forested, with narrow meadows and abundant wetlands. Many stretches had no topsoil at all.

The terrain and its ecosystem guided the course design. The team crafted a holistic vision balancing all of the uses on the site, while also minimizing the removal of vegetation, preserving as much of the site's forests as

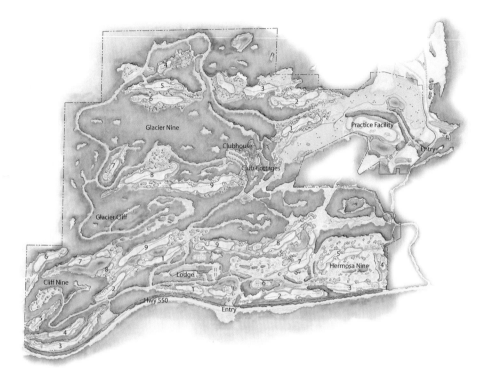

possible and working hard not to displace its wetlands. For environmental and aesthetic reasons, the designers rejected conventional storm-water management systems of culverts and piping, structuring the entire course instead with an underlayment of 8 inches of sand and a natural filtration system of constructed wetlands. They configured irrigation with reclaimed water and disturbed less than a half acre of the site's total 14 acres of wetlands.

The project's first phase produced the new course and remodeling of the existing 150-room lodge, including the addition of a new restaurant and conference facilities. Opened in July 2004, the new par-35 Glacier Nine is 3,583 yards long and takes the golfer through an elevation change of 400 feet.

The careful fitting of the course to its alpine context gives golfers a true experience of playing in rugged mountain terrain. The generous landing areas are flanked by conifer-lined fairways and the existing topography enhances the risk-reward strategies for each hole, many of which carry over wetlands. The course offers scenic views to Missionary Ridge to the east and south, the Hermosa Cliffs to the west and the Needles Range and Engineer's Peak to the north. The designers worked to infuse the existing course with the character of the

new one in the redesign of the original 18 holes. The courses, which feature five sets of tee boxes to accommodate players of all abilities, have been earning rave reviews from golfers.

The master plan for The Glacier Club, which sited parcels for town homes, single-family lots and swimming facilities, also incorporated more than 8 miles of trails for hiking and mountain-biking. These weave through the canyons and ridgelines of the site and connect to extensive trails on adjacent Bureau of Land Management lands.

PROJECT CREDITS

MASTER PLAN, GOLF COURSE DESIGN, LANDSCAPE ARCHITECTURE:
Design Workshop, Inc.
  PIC: Jeff Zimmermann
  Golf architect: Todd Schoeder
  Landscape architect: Jamie Fogle

CLIENT: Tamarron Development Corporation/ Mal Dunlevie

Golf course contractor: Golf Works, Inc.

Irrigation design: Harvey Mills Design

Golf course superintendent: Mark Hanson

Director of golf: Patric Flinn

Management company: Troon Golf

Engineering: Russell Engineering

Environmental engineering: Sugnet Environmental

Water engineer: Wright Water Engineering

Site construction: Rathjen Construction

Landscape contractor: High Country

Land-use attorney: Shand, Newbold, Chapman

(above) The master plan added residential uses, redesigned the former Tamarron course and added nine new holes on the steep, tight parcel at the back of the site, at the top of the drawing.

(opposite) The design features carry over both existing and manmade wetlands, which are also integral parts of the course's bio-filtration system. In lieu of conventional piping drainage, the course was constructed with an underlayment of eight inches of sand and a hierarchy of bio-filtration swales and wetlands that cleanse the water before it rejoins the nearby Animas River.

To protect wetlands and streams, the entire site was graded to collect and filter all storm-water runoff before it reaches a natural environment.

1. FILTRATION PLATING. The entire course is plated with 8 inches of coarse drainage sand, which also provides an excellent growing medium for turf. Rainfall either infiltrates through the sand or, in the case of major rainfall events, is directed to biofilter collectors that have been constructed throughout the site.

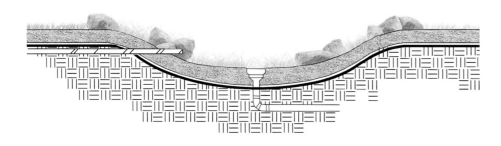

2. BIOFILTER COLLECTOR. The biofilter system is a series of about 60 basins and swales, up to 100 yards across, where rainfall collects in the event of unusual levels of precipitation. Filter fabric (heavy black line) underlies the collectors and allows water to permeate into the ground but keeps debris from entering the constructed system. From these basins, any water that did not seep into the ground is transferred through a pipe into biofilter basins.

3. BIOFILTER SWALE. The swale is a constructed system of native grasses over sand, ranging in width from 30 feet to 300 feet. The water from the swale flows into an undisturbed native berm of grasses (at center) that is a minimum of 50 feet wide. At the far end of the swale, filtered water finally flows into wetlands, ponds, a stream or a lake.

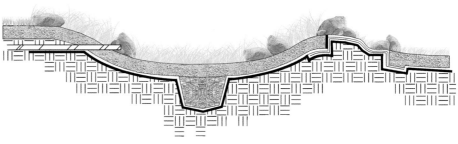

4. BIOFILTER DETENTION BASIN. Filter fabric allows water to infiltrate back into native soil through the biofilter basins. In the event of major weather events, most water will flow into a 6-foot-square sump of drainage rock. Any overflow will pass across a non-permeable liner into a biofilter swale.

(opposite) The design preserved as much forest as possible, combining it with the tight, steep mountain topography to create unique risk-and-reward strategies.

(at left) The new course is tucked up next to the steep rise of the Hermosa Cliffs, with eight of the nine new holes playing downhill.

(above) The clubhouse sits at the top of the site with views to fairways in three directions, with the ridgeline of the San Juan Mountains behind it.

CASE STUDY

DILEMMA: Wastewater and storm water had created lush habitat in the desert, but uncontrolled runoff and flooding were destroying it. This neglected land, which had once been a gathering spot for wildlife observation, had deteriorated and become the domain of vagrants and dirt bikers.

LEGACY GOALS:

Community
With community input and support, thread the 12-mile-long wash with trails and furnish it with shelters and educational displays to transform it into a haven from city life and desert surroundings for residents and visitors.

Environment
Use erosion control on damaged lands and reintroduce indigenous plants in derelict areas to restore and stabilize wetlands, which in turn will draw wildlife back to the area and rejuvenate bird habitat on a major flyway.

Economics
Protect the wetlands and the newly created trails with a visitors' center, research facilities for educational institutions and tourism attractions and recreational uses that are compatible with restoration of the wash.

Art
Create a tranquil space that frames views to surrounding mountains and that draws people to trails and shading structures that invite exploration, give people a sense of discovery and connect them with wildlife and nature.

THESIS: Erosion control will stabilize the land so that it can be transformed into a nature preserve and a serene refuge from nearby city life.

CLARK COUNTY WETLANDS PARK

Clark County, Nevada

Healing wounded land creates a refuge in an urban setting

Overview

For many years, the Las Vegas Wash thrived on the city's growth, until the runoff reached overwhelming proportions and wetlands were damaged or swept away in a series of floods. Uncared for, the land deteriorated, but in the early 1990s, voters approved more than $13 million in state funding to rehabilitate the area and transform it into a regional park.

This project, which transformed the Las Vegas Wash into a regional park, was an effort to rescue a wilderness that was created and then nearly ruined within the space of 40 years. This 2,900-acre oasis exists in the middle of the eastern Mojave Desert on the edge of Las Vegas. Its wetlands were created out of the former Las Vegas Wash, originally a dry streambed that prospered from urban runoff and treated wastewater discharges. As growth in the area began to soar in the 1970s, surging wastewater and storm flows gouged out the wash along its length. The master plan outlined a strategy for rehabilitating the wash and restoring and protecting the wetlands, adding a system of trails, picnic areas, interpretive exhibits, visiting points and protected zones to create a coherent landscape that could serve as a retreat from the city and the desert.

History/Context

The Las Vegas Wash and its tributaries produce perennial stream flow that drains the entire Las Vegas Valley, about 1,600 square miles, sending groundwater, storm water and treated wastewater to the Colorado River by way of Lake Mead and the Hoover

CASE STUDY

Las Vegas

Las Vegas Wash

Lake Mead

(above) The Las Vegas Wash, which lies southeast of the city, drains the 1,600-square-mile Las Vegas Valley and is the main channel for urban runoff that flows from Las Vegas into Lake Mead.

(opposite) Aerial images of the Las Vegas Wash show its evolution from a mostly dry streambed to wetlands and finally to a badly eroded floodplain. Population growth in Las Vegas over 40 years produced ever increasing urban runoff, which first created and nurtured the wetlands in the wash and then devastated them with flooding. Floods cut deep channels out of the wetlands, which can be seen in the image from 1984.

Dam, 20 miles southeast of the city. This area south of the city had been designated as a park but had no security, no signage and no formal trails. It is subject to extensive flooding during seasonal storms. It had grown lush over several decades because of the city's increased runoff, which had transformed the wash into a rich 2,000-acre marshland of cattails that drew and sheltered abundant wildlife and many species of birds. But as fierce, sustained growth hit the Las Vegas area, the 12-mile wash began to suffer from the intensified runoff, which scoured its edges, gouging the land, denuding hillsides and eroding several hundred thousand tons of soil each year. As wastewater discharge surged to 110 million gallons daily, channels eroded as much as 25 vertical feet in some locations, killing wetland plants by taking most of the water out of their reach. More than half the wetlands were destroyed in only a few years. The area is an active flyway for many species of migrating birds and had been a significant center for bird-watching, but the destruction in the wash had a serious impact on habitat, which in turn affected wildlife and those who took pleasure in observing it. This situation was compounded over several years as the urban communities crept closer and the area deteriorated and attracted dirt bikers and vagrants and was used for

trash dumping. Campfires set by transients frequently burned out of control, occasionally threatening nearby homes and public facilities. In 1991, in acknowledgment of the problem and the opportunity to develop the site into a passive recreational area, Nevada voters approved a wildlife and parks bond, earmarking $13.3 million for a project that would institute erosion control and create a park in the Las Vegas Wash.

Process

The study area encompassed more than 5,000 acres. Work began on several fronts at once. Design Workshop led a team of 11 consultants to create innovative engineering solutions and scientifically sound recommendations for the site, including an environmental impact statement for the park and an environmental assessment for the first erosion control structure. Working with 22 local, state and federal agencies, the project team created a dozen inventory maps in a GIS database to analyze soil and geologic suitability, scenic resources and vegetation communities. These would serve as a foundation for local officials to track changes in the area, help educate the public about the land's value and shape consensus for the restoration of the area and protection of the proposed wetlands park.

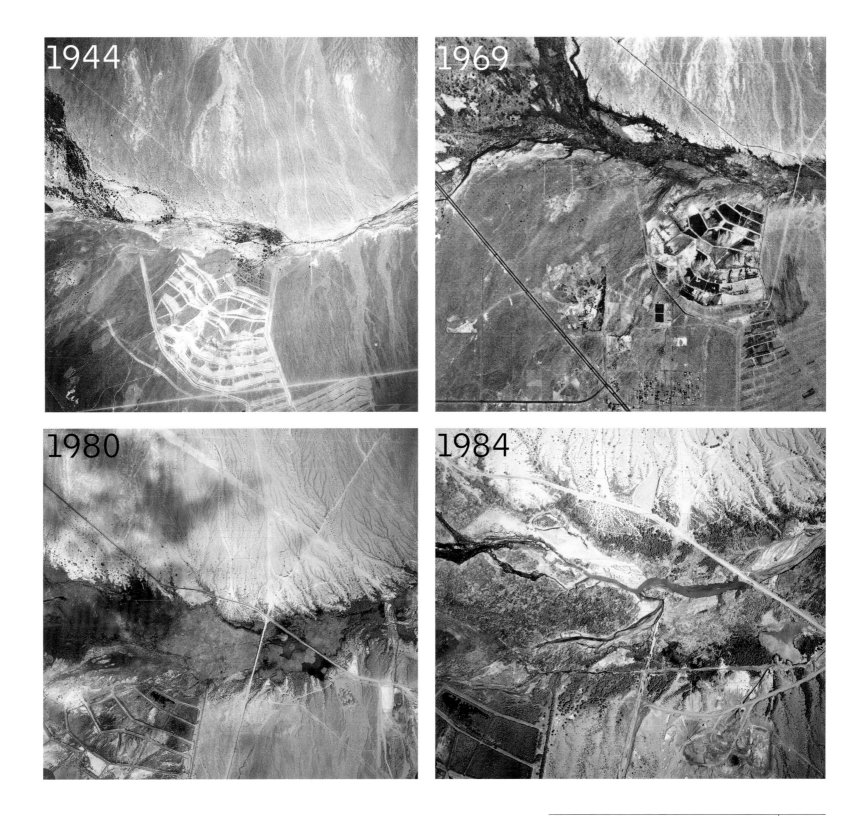

1944

1969

1980

1984

CASE STUDY

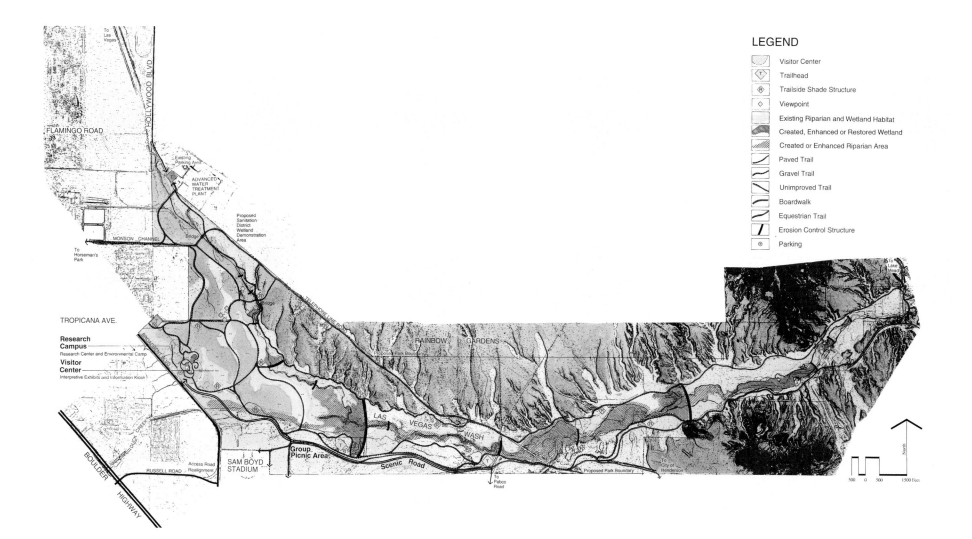

LEGEND

- Visitor Center
- Trailhead
- Trailside Shade Structure
- Viewpoint
- Existing Riparian and Wetland Habitat
- Created, Enhanced or Restored Wetland
- Created or Enhanced Riparian Area
- Paved Trail
- Gravel Trail
- Unimproved Trail
- Boardwalk
- Equestrian Trail
- Erosion Control Structure
- Parking

A series of erosion control structures stabilized the wash to allow for wetland enhancements, as well as creation of a 100-acre nature preserve at the western end of the park and trails that wind along the park's length as it approaches Lake Mead.

(above) Starting with a sharp, sustained spike in growth in the 1970s, wetland areas in the wash were regularly gouged out by flood events and the ever-increasing runoff from the city. In places, the water cut down as far as 25 vertical feet, washing away large swaths of wetlands and leaving the roots of surviving plants without access to water.

The designers used a series of newsletters to keep all stakeholders informed about the master planning process, outlining the input that would be solicited at upcoming public meetings. A wide range of residents, interest groups and officials participated in six public workshops to determine what the park was best suited for. Alternatives included four plans: one that would cater to recreation, one to conservation, one to full development and a plan that integrated the three alternatives, matching uses to land types — the alternative favored by most people. The master plan that emerged from this public process set the boundaries of the park at 2,900 acres and integrated it with 4,000 acres of the Rainbow Gardens, managed by the Bureau of Land Management (BLM). To ensure that it would thrive past its founding, the process included an inventory of the physical features of the site, strategies for land acquisition, financing and fund-raising to make improvements and guidelines for its management and operation. As a culmination of the process, the team created a poster describing the plan, using a style that spoke to a wide range of interests, from groups like the Sierra Club to government officials and adjacent landowners.

The plan was unanimously adopted by the Clark County Board of Supervisors in November 1995 and received support from the local chapters of the Sierra Club and the Audubon Society, as well as the BLM and the National Park Service. The cost of all three phases was set at $32 million.

Outcome

Initial efforts focused on improvements that would shift people's perception of the area. Because the area is within a floodplain, public gathering places had to be carefully sited. The park is organized around a series of gateways, each of which expresses a unique quality of the site. The $13 million first phase created an erosion control structure, a trail system and outlook areas, a special interpretive site, a group picnic facility, habitat enhancement and a temporary visitor center that is home to the wetlands park volunteers.

The design changes the image of the wash and transforms it into a safe, beautiful public park, an oasis alive with wildlife, waterfowl and wetland plants unlike any other habitat in southern Nevada. The centerpiece is a 100-acre nature preserve positioned where the wash meets the city — a gathering place that would also serve as a gateway into the park. The preserve's first interpretive pavilion connects the natural and cultural resources of the wetlands to

CASE STUDY

the life experiences and interests of park visitors, helping them to enjoy, understand, appreciate and help preserve the park. A group picnic area, nestled next to a mesquite bosque and salt-grass meadow, features a pavilion, tables and benches, parking for 30 vehicles, waterless toilets and trailhead access.

Habitat support has focused on the riparian and wetland habitats in this desert ecosystem, which constitute a very small percentage of land cover but support an inordinate proportion of the area's wildlife. Enhancements have consisted primarily of replacing invasive plants such as tamarisk with more desirable riparian tree species such as mesquite, desert willow, acacia, willow and cottonwood, where soil and water-table conditions allowed.

Future phases will create a comprehensive visitor and interpretive center, expansion of the trail system and park interpretive programs and continued construction of additional erosion control structures. The visitor center is intended to become a regional education center, constructed at a central viewing area that will allow people to observe the various habitats in the wash. The

building will be sited to give visitors an entry sequence that takes advantage of the striking views of the surroundings. Officials anticipate adding research facilities to host people from educational institutions, government agencies and nonprofit special-interest groups who wish to conduct research on particular characteristics of the wash system.

The Las Vegas Wash is now home to more than 300 fish and wildlife species and almost as many species of upland, riparian and wetland plants. Almost $60 million has been approved for park amenities, facilities and enhancements, mostly through the Southern Nevada Public Lands Management Act, which permits selling off developable federal lands to support the area's more environmentally sensitive lands. Future phases of the park are to expand the nature preserve to 280 acres, create 20 miles of trails and visitor facilities at four trailheads, build three bridges over the wash, and enhance and revegetate habitat in the park and in channels that flow into the wash. Officials anticipate that erosion control will ultimately require funding of $100 million, of which about $27 million has been

approved so far. Completion of the wetlands park is expected in 2008. Clark County Wetlands Park was a featured project at the 2001 and 2005 Brownfield and Graywater Symposiums held by the Graduate School of Design at Harvard University.

PROJECT CREDITS

MASTER PLAN: Design Workshop, Inc.
  PIC: Rebecca Zimmermann
  Project Design: Mark Soden, Jim MacRae

CLIENT: Clark County Parks and Recreation

Environmental engineering: SWCA Environmental Consultants

Engineering: Montgomery Watson

Planning Consultation: University of Nevada – Las Vegas

CASE STUDY

(above and at right) Shelters and blinds, along with interpretive displays, give visitors a full experience of the varied ecosystems in the preserve and the wetlands park.

(opposite) The preserved and refurbished wetlands provide a scenic foreground to Lone Mountain in the distance.

LEGACY

Places

ESSAY

Terrall Budge, a partner since 2003, explores the dangers of franchising spaces and the need for insightful intervention to create a platform from which people can create the meaning of a place. The projects that follow show how using the history, context and environmental conditions of a site creates distinctive places — places with strong appeal and documented drawing power.

PROJECT DISCUSSIONS

Rio Grande Botanical Garden: A dangerous park finds new life as a botanical and cultural history of the Rio Grande.

Blackcomb Ski Resort: A vision for the future turns Blackcomb Mountain into one of the world's top resorts.

Inn on Biltmore Estate: The Vanderbilt family replicates the turn-of-the-century experience at this national landmark.

Gardens on El Paseo: A lush desert setting broadens the mission of a retail hub to include community events.

La Posada: New purpose and design reverse the decline of a historic Santa Fe inn, creating a destination resort and spa.

IN-DEPTH ACCOUNT

Pittsburgh World War II Memorial: Creating a war memorial in Pittsburgh honors home-front efforts as well as the fight.

To have deeper meaning in our lives, we need real places — places that teach us about how we are connected to nature and to each other

AN ESSAY BY TERRALL BUDGE

It was dark and cold when we arrived at the beach. It was January 1, 1985, on the eastern edge of Honshu, Japan. I had come with friends to watch the sun rise on the New Year over the steel-gray sea. Innumerable bonfires were visible up and down the coast, like a flickering constellation outlining the edge of the known world. The smell of strange, exotic foods wafted through the humid air. The predawn light steadily intensified, and thousands upon thousands of human silhouettes began to emerge from the dissipating darkness. The beach was filled as far as the eye could see.

My toes were chilled by the damp sand underfoot and a cold offshore wind cut through my clothes. We huddled around a shared fire to stay warm and sampled traditional foods from bubbling pots. The sky overhead was turning pink and the horizon on the sea was a deep and glowing red. Boats were now discernible and groups of people swimming broke the calm surface of the water.

Suddenly, the blood-red sun broke the horizon line and illuminated the beach. I was quickly and unexpectedly overwhelmed by emotion. In that moment, I was directly connected to the symbolic abstraction of the Japanese flag, which symbolizes the red morning sun, and to the pictorial written characters that constitute the national name — the Land of the Rising Sun. I was directly connected to the spectacular daily rhythms of sun, sky, sea and land and the natural phenomena of wind, cold, moisture and warmth. I was directly connected to the people who had gathered on this beach, in this place, down through the generations, to witness this same simple, yet profound moment. I was directly connected to something much bigger than myself — a wider context, a larger culture, a great continuity of human action. I was connected to this place.

Making Places

Real places provide deep, timeless connections to culture and nature, like those I experienced on the beach in Japan. They connect people with people, people with nature or both. They link people with the history of a location while leaving traces of contemporary culture for future generations, thus becoming a part of the great palimpsest of human existence. They may be consciously designed and constructed within a relatively short

Places become possible at the intersection of nature and culture, when people are linked with the inherent forces at work in a location. Above, a bicyclist rides on salt flats recently wetted with rain on the Salar de Uyuni before Mount Thunupa in the Bolivian Andes. Opposite, a Shinto shrine decorated with white flags of the New Year nestles in the forest on the edge of the town of Akizuki on Kyushu Island in Japan.

Both art and science come into play in creating and maintaining places, whether they are active spaces, habitations, work environments or contemplative spaces, such as the garden at Ryoan-ji Temple in Kyoto, Japan.

time period or they may be the result of a long evolution of incremental decisions and adjustments made over centuries. They may be wholly man-made constructions or they may be carefully preserved natural environments. But while real places range widely in form, function and scale, they have one unifying and distinguishing characteristic: their capacity to link people with the fundamental, authentic forces at work in a particular location. Without such essential linkages, sites never become places. They remain mere spaces — generic, meaningless and devoid of lasting interest.

Creating real places is not rocket science. It is more complicated. Transmuting spaces into meaningful, relevant places requires a sort of alchemy and a deep understanding and balanced application of the arts and sciences of both nature and culture. True place-makers must always search and learn in order to decipher the essential cues embedded in a particular location. When these cues are sensitively acknowledged, calibrated and tuned, meaning can arise at the delicate interface between scientific process and aesthetic apprehension. And it is meaning that gives power and efficacy to a place by creating emotional and/or intellectual attachments. Places that give rise to meaning have the power to produce cultural change and become sites of resistance to globalization, digital displacement and sprawling placelessness.

The job of the place-maker is to create the circumstances from which meaning can begin to flow and the locations to which it can accrue over time, as Marc Treib has noted in his essay "Must Landscapes Mean?" Place-makers must integrate both scientific knowledge and artistic interpretation of culture and nature in their work to create the platforms that will allow meaning to be discovered or created. Through the fusion of the scientific and artistic aspects of nature and culture in a space, multiple "readings" can occur, multiple experiences can be had and multiple attachments can be made.

Interestingly, meaning generally cannot be dictated or imposed by the designer. It must arise from the users of a place as they make their own connections to culture and nature in that location. Therefore, the would-be place-maker must approach his or her work with a combination of boldness and humility. Boldness is required to determine and

declare what cues are important to reveal, acknowledge or make visible in the design of a new place, while humility is necessary to accept, and even celebrate, interpretations and uses that were neither intended nor anticipated. These are acts of local appropriation that bind a space to its cultural and natural context and help transform it into an authentic, meaningful place for its users.

The Art and Science of Nature

It is in vain to dream of a wildness far distant from ourselves. There is none such. It is the bog in our brain and bowels, the primitive vigor of Nature in us, that inspires that dream. — *Henry D. Thoreau,* The Natural History Essays

The idea of Nature is a human construction. It is a cultural construct we use to identify that which is Other, that which we believe to be separate from and independent of human action. But this idea of nature as something standing apart from that which is human may be coming to an end. As William Cronon has argued in *Uncommon Ground: Rethinking the Human Place in Nature,* with the advent of global warming, acid rain, air pollution and expanding populations, virtually every climate and location has been affected and altered in some way by human action. These effects and alterations on natural systems are now being vigorously measured and documented by science. Temperature change, parts per million of mercury traces and net losses of wetlands acreage are just three examples of these measurements. As scientists identify problems and propose and implement remedies, we will learn about the technical aspects of these systems and their associated phenomena and will add to our existing understanding of the complex connections, interdependence and delicate balance needed for responsible, sustainable human existence. Traditionally engineered storm-water management systems will be replaced with on-surface bioswales, subsurface catchment and reuse systems, constructed wetlands and infiltration galleries that capture water where it falls. Renewable energy sources will replace outdated systems that pollute air and water. Waste streams will be converted to raw inputs for other systems. All of these and many more technical advances will happen. But they will not be enough to regain our disappearing ground.

Far less understood than the scientifically quantifiable impacts of a loss of natural systems on the physical makeup of a place are the impacts of a loss of nature on our cultural and aesthetic sensibilities. As the natural systems of specific locations are damaged, obliterated or replaced with global placelessness, their ability to provide deep, authentic connections to aboriginal contexts are lost. Light pollution blocks out the night sky. Naturally occurring precipitation is replaced with unnatural irrigation regimes. Exotic plants replace the native. The environmental signifiers that may have led to an understanding of the natural context of the place and how to live responsibly within it are replaced with artificial systems found throughout the industrialized world. These systems negate the location, context, connections and environmental conditions of the place. Somewhere becomes Anywhere. A synthetic climate stands in for the real. People are separated from the land. This separation leads to generations of people who do not understand where food comes from or how water appears at their taps, who have never experienced the wonder of a starry night and who do not have any contact with the natural processes occurring in their world. They have lost their place on Earth.

There are many who have argued that manmade interventions in the greater landscape must look "natural" — that the best landscapes are those that look as if humans have never been there. But simulating or attempting to replicate nature has its own inherent set of problems. After all, these are still manmade constructions. This approach to landscapes and places denies their true character as human creations. More importantly, it robs them of the chance of producing what theorist Jean Baudrillard calls in *Simulacra and Simulation* "the charm of the abstraction." A thoughtful, sensitive, abstract intervention is honest and can create a dialogue between nature and culture, mediating between the two. Merely replicating or simulating nature cannot create opportunities for learning, understanding and appreciating this dialectical relationship present in every place touched by humankind.

Instead we need an aesthetic sensibility and intervention ethos that can interpret, explicate and create emotional connections to natural processes rather than natural forms. When the aesthetic properties of natural systems are revealed in artful, intentional and straightforward ways, they have the potential to inspire us through their inherent poetry, beauty and emotional power. They can elicit a great appreciation and deep love for the unique and authentic properties found only in that particular place. This can ground us, root us and ultimately bind us to the land and its systems. It can provide the strong emotional attachments that are required to create and maintain a responsible, sustainable human existence in that place.

When combined with the scientific knowledge of natural systems, this aesthetic sensibility will lead to places that not only function in a sustainable manner, but will also remain and grow more powerful over time as emotional attachments deepen and broaden.

The Art and Science of Culture

The Internet is great, but it ain't the Piazza Navona: free association and chance encounter still demand the meeting of bodies in space. Embodiment is the condition of accident, and accident is a motor of democracy.

— *Michael Sorkin,* Some Assembly Required

Just as in the realm of nature, an understanding and an interpretation of culture require a combination of art and science. And the application of both is necessary for the creation of meaningful places for people. The science of culture and social systems has much to teach us about creating places for human interaction and social production by explaining the importance of our connections to one another and to our surrounding natural systems. Scientific study can reveal how and under what circumstances peoples have interacted and prospered over the millennia. It can instruct us on ergonomic optimums for human comfort and leisure. Psychology can help predict how spaces will be used and what sorts of interactions between groups we might expect to see under differing proposed design configurations. Market studies and marketing plans can direct design decisions toward economic sustainability. The importance of these types of studies increases as world cultures blur and become increasingly global, digital and uniform. The art of culture, by contrast, interprets the human condition and attempts to reveal its value and

Places generate energy at the interface of order and chaos, illustrated above in a huge
gathering in the Piazza del Duomo in Milan,
Italy, where the formality of the soaring
façade of the cathedral contrasts with the
tangle of human gathering. Meaning will accrue to a real place; no veneer of style can
give it life. Robert M. Pirsig said in *Zen and
the Art of Motorcycle Maintenance,* "Quality
isn't something you lay on top of subjects and
objects like tinsel on a Christmas tree. Real
Quality must be the source of the subjects and
objects, the cone from which the tree must
start."

meaning. Dance, music, painting, landscapes, architecture and other artistic practices provide commentaries on the ways we live and can inspire us to greater heights.

In the emerging global economy, people are connected to the greater world by digital links via the Internet, telephones, satellite radio and/or television, which continually feed us a global pop culture. We learn about the world through a digital conduit rather than through direct human contact. The more universal and pervasive this digital culture becomes, the more people may become disconnected from local realities and lose their sense of grounding. Anonymous people meet anonymous people under conditions where both time and space have collapsed. Communications take the same amount of time, whether the spatial distance between communicators is 3 feet or 3,000 miles. Because face-to-face interactions in time and space are no longer necessary or even desirable, we become isolated from traditional human interaction. As cultural critic Guy Debord describes in his landmark book *The Society of the Spectacle*, since we all now communicate and interact in this manner in this culture, we have become unified in our isolation. We now live remotely through digital connections but without shared, lived experience. In this world, spectacle and surface are valued and privileged over substance and depth. This is the "society of the spectacle," where traditional symbols, music and images are reused, combined in nontraditional ways or even digitally altered to become completely detached from their original contexts. Original meanings are lost through a process of decontextualization, as discussed by Neil Leach in *The Anaesthetics of Architecture*, because signifiers no longer indicate traditional signifieds. Meaning is fleeting, superficial and shallow in the midst of floating and ever-changing signifiers. There are no anchors, no truths to keep us grounded.

Places can suffer the same fate as communications. They can be completely constructed by global mass culture and thus become totally decontextualized from their locale. Nuanced and sensitive aesthetic responses to local context are subsumed in a miasma of mass-produced commercial signifiers. A place devolves to become a superficial space — a thin image of popular culture, bereft of tangible, real meaning and plagued by a placelessness that alienates its users from authentic experience. Its potential meaning is negated by a dull sameness that pervades the environment. In many such cases, it is no longer easy to determine if one is in suburban New York, California or Iowa. Globalization leads to a sort of placelessness whereby no authentic ties to local culture are discernible.

In such cultural circumstances, people have no ability to connect with places and people in any meaningful way. This disconnection leads us to increased alienation and feelings of isolation from the local culture and/or the natural environment. The greater landscape no longer gives opportunities for a shared, lived experience but rather substitutes superficial encounters based on the latest cultural fad, object or image. Public discourse and interaction devolve to conversations without depth centered on the latest meanings attached to the ever-changing signifiers that are portrayed in the virtual world of television and the Internet. But this is a world of surfaces, of the outer skins of things, of superficial meaning and tenuous attachments rather than a world of depth, substance and deep connection.

By contrast, authentic landscapes — real places — are alive and meaningful, subject to nature's rhythms and seasons, dependent upon local contexts of culture and nature, and requiring time to reach full maturity. They depend upon authentic human interaction in time and space where social justice, freedom and democracy have a chance to blossom. They have the potential to bring us out of our isolation, connect us to one another and resist globalization.

The Value of Real Places

We live in a world where there is more and more information and less and less meaning. — *Jean Baudrillard,* Simulacra and Simulation

More than ever before, we need real places, places that teach us about who we are, where we have come from, how we are connected to nature and each other and how we can live in a meaningful way. We need a vision that fuses nature to culture and that integrates the art and science of each. For place-makers, it will be a fully integrated combination of art and science that will fuse nature and culture inextricably and meaningfully to the places we design. Science will teach us how it works and art will explain why it is important. A thorough understanding of science will lead to new aesthetic interpretations while new interpretations will lead scientists to further investigations and questions. One realm of understanding will inform the other. This will lead to systems and processes that are made visible in new and inspiring ways — whereby the apprehension of goodness, wholeness and beauty will be possible and real meaning, value and connection will arise. This will be the means of creating a synthesis, a symbiotic relationship between humans and nature. In essence, the duality — the opposites — will cease to operate as such and will become part of a larger dialectic cycle in which one realm explicates the other.

Through deeply holistic, combinatory and integrative interventions informed by the broadest range of human experience, action, cultures, values and site-specific environmental conditions, places unfold, arise, come into being. These places are rooted (literally and metaphorically), enduring, meaningful and intensely local. They consist of both science and intuition, intellect and emotion, prose and poetry. Achieving the proper balance is difficult, often elusive, and requires patience, practice and perseverance.

In the end, our place in the greater landscape is everything. It dictates how we live our lives, spend our time, interact with one another, connect with nature, recreate and re-create ourselves. It is the fundamental stage upon which life's events take place — events such as a New Year's sunrise on a beach in Japan where a whole new way of understanding my own place in the world was opened to me. True places connect people with the real, the tangible, the whole and the essential in this way. They can reach our souls. The transformation of space to place requires an alchemy of culture and nature. As human beings, it is our mission to pursue this alchemy, however imperfectly. This is what we are and, more importantly, this is why we are.

Gang warfare had turned an Albuquerque park into a dangerous place. A civic initiative reinvented the site along the Rio Grande to become a center for regional attractions, including a botanical garden that teaches people about the area's cultural and natural history.

PROJECT DISCUSSION:
RIO GRANDE BOTANICAL GARDEN
Albuquerque, New Mexico

Beauty connects people to the heritage of the land

A large park in Albuquerque's oldest district became a center for gang activity in the 1980s, deteriorating to the point that authorities installed a 12-foot-high, 200-foot-long metal wall along one edge to protect the adjacent neighborhood from gunfire. The park and its surrounding lands had cultural and environmental significance: It was the first section of town to be settled and it lay in the Rio Grande Bosque, the forest of cottonwood trees that grows along the river's edge.

In 1991, city officials undertook an ambitious campaign to reclaim and rehabilitate the area with a series of hallmark civic and cultural facilities to be called the Albuquerque Biological Park complex. This project would upgrade the city's small but celebrated zoo, expand an urban fishing venue, add an aquarium and clear away the troubled park to create New Mexico's first botanical garden. The designers led a team that master-planned and designed the botanical garden, which includes a conservatory, a visitor center, an educational building, a large space for public events and numerous garden exhibits.

Albuquerque officials had originally imagined the botanical garden as a kind of plant archive where people would be educated about unusual species, but early in the process the design team recognized that the garden needed to be more dynamic if it was to ensure return visits and earn the interest and support of local citizens. The designers began the master-plan process by bringing together several directors of botanical gardens from around the country with community members and future staff. The group turned to the story of the land and the river and the people living

the park was neglected land that lay along the Rio Grande

on it to craft a vision and a narrative for the garden.

The Rio Grande corridor is the longest continually cultivated area in the United States, having served as an agricultural resource for many different cultures for more than 1,000 years. Its ecosystem is exceptionally diverse, flowing from the high alpine valleys of the Rocky Mountains through fertile valleys and across dry deserts in its journey to the Gulf of Mexico. The design of the botanical garden uses this history as a foundation, focusing on how plants have contributed to the lives of people who have lived along the river, and how, in turn, people have affected its ecology.

A manmade representation of the river, fed with waters from the Rio Grande, serves as the central spine of the design, running from the far reaches of the site to end in a large pond representing the Gulf of Mexico. Along it, the designers created landscapes representing the river's different ecozones, interspersing these with demonstrations and displays of how different cultures have used the waters of the Rio Grande, from ancient Anasazi croplands to Zuni walled gardens, from the irrigation channels pioneered by Spanish settlers to modern societies. The gardens also address the urban, desert environment of Albuquerque through demonstration

displays that educate people on how to foster the river's well-being and how to use xeric principles to grow gardens appropriate to the local ecosystem. The site includes a large community gathering area, which the designers kept out of flood range by building an elevated "stage" and grassy seating area using the pond's excavated soil.

One of the project's innovative environmental measures was to make the large pond near the conservatory into functional wetlands that would illustrate the cleansing function of riparian wetlands by processing the facilities' wastewater. Although liability and management issues forced the team to use traditional engineering instead, the pond is lined to separate it from the river water and is designed to support reinclusion of this cleansing wetlands feature in a future phase as environmental regulations evolve.

The irregular shape of the 50-acre parcel presented a special challenge. It has a generous entry area that narrows precipitously before widening into a larger portion at the back. The primary design dilemma was how to draw people through the constricted area and into the main ethnobotanical exhibits. The design solved the problem of the site constriction by locating the conservatory at the junction of the two

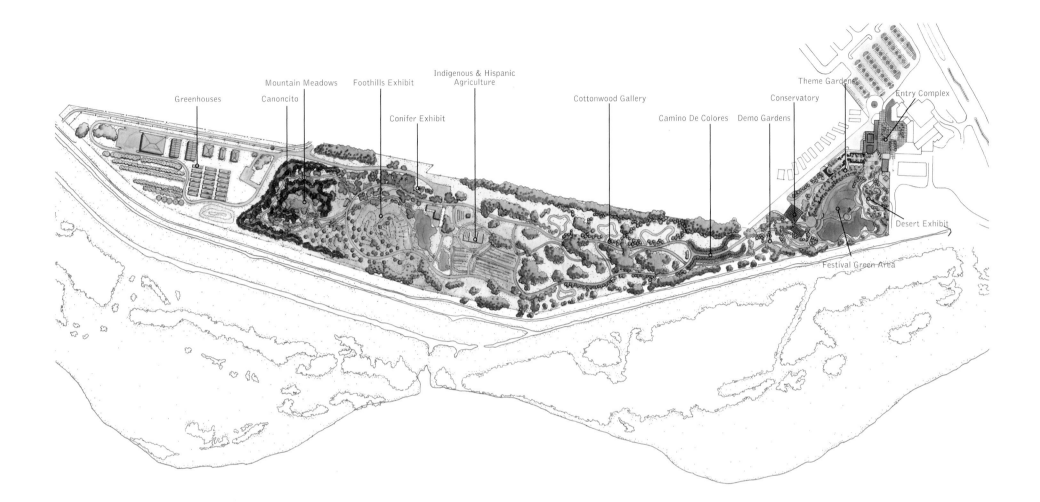

Greenhouses
Canoncito
Mountain Meadows
Foothills Exhibit
Conifer Exhibit
Indigenous & Hispanic Agriculture
Cottonwood Gallery
Camino De Colores
Demo Gardens
Theme Gardens
Conservatory
Entry Complex
Desert Exhibit
Festival Green Area

(above) The master plan's manmade waterway, representing the Rio Grande, is shown crossing through a series of crafted ecosystems, from high mountain canyons, foothills and agricultural lands to tree, shrub and garden galleries, finally emptying into the pond that symbolizes the Gulf of Mexico near the festival green, at right.

(right) An aerial photograph of the existing site shows the agricultural canals that separate it from the bosque and the river. The site's narrow "neck" presented the greatest challenge for designing the botanical garden.

(opposite) Large-scale community events bring people to the festival green for presentations staged in the band shelter "floating" in the wetlands.

(above) Urban horticulture demonstration gardens educate people about what grows well in the local arid landscape and how to care for plants, the soil and the river.

(right) A palette of indigenous plants and images of plants and animals, some imaginary, enliven the children's garden.

wedges, using it as a hub through which people could pass to get from the more public side of the site to the more intimate gardens at the back. Created by architect Ed Mazria, the glass conservatory was designed as a solar building that would house plants from desert and Mediterranean ecosystems as well as free-flying North American butterflies. It was designed to function without the use of any mechanical systems for heating or cooling — the major expense for most buildings of this type. City officials, uncertain of its viability, required the team to spend an extra $60,000 to install backup mechanical systems, which have never been used. The building itself has become a landmark for the city and is frequently used on promotional materials for Albuquerque.

Budget constraints, combined with land title issues on the federal land grant portion at the back of the site, have allowed development of only the front 15 acres so far. In this space, the team created the garden's main constituents: the Gulf of Mexico pond, the glass conservatory, the visitor center and an associated educational building, water features and the festival green for community gatherings, plus urban demonstration gardens and special themed displays related to the area's culture and history, such as a Spanish-Moorish

garden. These give the garden a platform to engage visitors in an ongoing relationship and to raise funds for the specialty gardens of the second phase.

PROJECT CREDITS

MASTER PLAN LEAD: Campbell Okuma Perkins Associates
Master plan PIC: Craig Campbell

DESIGN/IMPLEMENTATION: Design Workshop, Inc.
PIC: Bill Perkins
Designers: Faith Okuma, Mimi Burns, Jim Alsup, Allison Mulhouland, Bruce Trujillo, Rick Borkovetz

CLIENT: City of Albuquerque

Conservatory architects: Ed Mazria/Mazria Associates

Entry facility architects: Holmes Sabatini Edds Architects

Civil engineers: Bohannon Huston

In 1977, Blackcomb was a vacant piece of land at the foot of the hill. An astute vision and master plan gave an inspired developer the tools to create a new kind of resort that embraces the mountain and gives visitors a rich experience year-round.

PROJECT DISCUSSION:
BLACKCOMB SKI RESORT

Whistler, British Columbia

Setting the right framework fosters destination resort success

Whistler, British Columbia, was originally settled by trappers in the late 19th century and became a popular summer retreat in the early decades of the 1900s. Half a century later, four Vancouver businessmen began developing a ski area at Whistler Mountain, which opened in 1966. The Canadian government declared Whistler its first resort municipality in 1975, giving it land to create a town center.

Like Whistler, many North American ski areas that got their start in the 1970s faced major challenges in creating these new places. They had to come to terms with agencies dedicated to the preservation of forest lands and had to grapple with the economic realities of seasonally limited attractions and the challenges of transforming steep, scenic topography into recreational venues that could draw enough interest to survive.

In 1977, when the director of skiing for British Columbia began to promote development of a new ski mountain adjacent to Whistler, he contacted the most experienced ski-area developer in the world, the Aspen Skiing Company (ASC), which in turn commissioned Design Workshop to create a master plan for the mountain and its base.

At the time, Whistler comprised about 2,000 cabins and a few ski lifts, while Blackcomb was just two trailers at the bottom of a ski hill. The project placed equal emphasis on economic development of both Blackcomb Mountain and a resort at its base. Design Workshop's broad and holistic approach combined its experience in ski resorts and new communities. The team began to imagine the area as a year-round international destination resort and formulated plans, designs and recommendations

based on this vision, including suggestions to form a resort association and create a golf course and other year-round facilities.

The master plan for the ski mountain took advantage of the two resorts' proximity, configuring the area so that the lifts for both rise from a single point between Whistler and Blackcomb mountains, making it possible to ski either one. Once these plans were approved locally, they were submitted to the government and, in 1978, Canada awarded development rights to ASC.

Blackcomb's lifts opened in 1980, creating one of the largest ski complexes in the world. Four years later, after the mountain was purchased by Intrawest, Design Workshop configured the planning and design of the base village, including site plans for a hotel complex, plans for the first phase of residential development, design of the first site plan for condominiums and design of the connections between Blackcomb and Whistler.

The framework established by these plans set the stage for Blackcomb to achieve major successes over many years. Since its creation, it has been consistently voted among the world's top resorts by ski and travel magazines, including *Skiing*, *Ski*, *Snow Country*, *Condé Nast Traveler* and *Travel + Leisure*

Golf. In 1998, the two mountains merged and five years later, Whistler/Blackcomb (with Vancouver) won the bid to host the 2010 Olympic Winter Games. In recent years, Design Workshop has helped support the resort's efforts to become the first sustainable resort community in the world.

PROJECT CREDITS

PLANNING/DESIGN: Design Workshop, Inc
PICs: Joe Porter, Bill Kane, Richard Shaw, Don Ensign
Landscape Architects: Bob Nevins, Pat Carroll, Bob Chipman

CLIENTS:
The Aspen Skiing Company
Twentieth Century Fox Real Estate
Intrawest Corporation

(above) The ski resorts of Blackcomb and Whistler were developed simultaneously. In 1977, the place that would become Blackcomb was just two trailers at the base of a mountain with spectacular potential for skiing. The entire area was called Whistler, after the sleepy village at the base of the adjacent mountain. Blackcomb was renamed after the ski mountain was developed and opened in 1980.

(opposite) The master plan fosters the growth of both ski areas by giving skiers access to both Whistler and Blackcomb mountains by way of a connection through the Whistler town center, which was designed by Eldon Beck.

Glacier Access

Lost
Lake

Fitzsimmons Creek

Town
Center

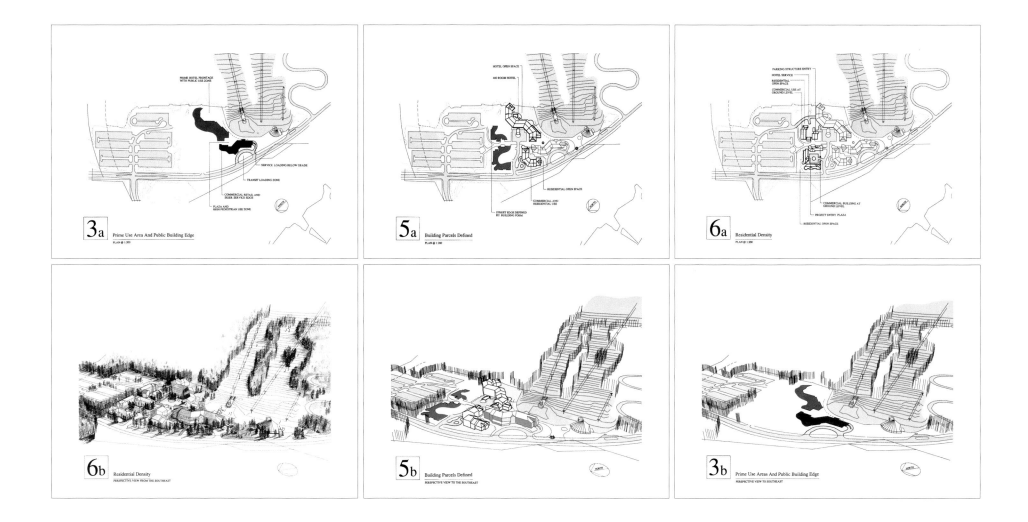

Early computerized analysis diagrams of Blackcomb base village phased the development in order to keep the ski area open and accessible throughout the creation of parking, public spaces and residential accommodations.

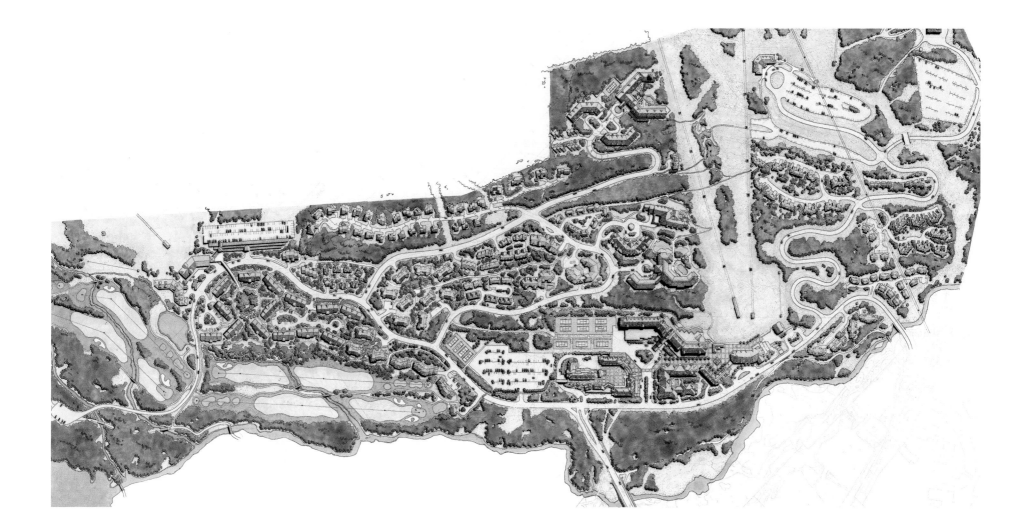

The base village was configured to give ready access to the mountain in both snowy weather and warmer seasons.

Blackcomb was planned to function as a year-round resort, its attractions, programming, accommodations and public spaces designed to engage visitors in all seasons.

(opposite) Blackcomb's base village embraces the ski runs at the bottom of the hill. Whistler's town center lies in the foreground.

(left) The village is seen through the ski lift at the bottom of hill.

(above) Summer visitors to the base village find options such as concerts on the mountainside, golf, bicycling, fishing, a spa and mountaintop barbecues.

When the Vanderbilt family decided to locate an inn on the grounds of Biltmore Estate, they wanted to replicate the experience of turn-of-the-century guests. The original design principles of Frederick Law Olmsted served as the basis for locating and designing the new accommodations for this Southern landmark.

PROJECT DISCUSSION:
INN ON BILTMORE ESTATE

Asheville, North Carolina

Careful siting of a new inn preserves an icon's sense of seclusion

In 1890, George Vanderbilt purchased 120,000 acres to build a lodge in the Blue Ridge Mountains, land that had been denuded of its forests by settlers. Vanderbilt hired Frederick Law Olmsted, the nation's premier landscape architect, to develop the estate and manage the forests, and architect Richard Morris Hunt to design a 250-room house modeled after three 16th-century French Renaissance châteaux. Eventually, the family would deed 90,000 acres of the site to the federal government to create nearby Pisgah National Forest.

Forty years later, Biltmore House opened to the public in the midst of the Depression. The Asheville economy had been hit hard and local officials asked the family to invite visitors in order to encourage tourism to the area. In the years since, studies have estimated Biltmore's economic value to the region at hundreds of millions of dollars.

The Biltmore Estate has been managed in recent decades by a for-profit cooperative of heirs with overall objectives of sustainability and preservation. The extensive estate lands were divided among family members in the 1970s, leaving the 8,000 acres containing Biltmore House and the designed landscape, farms and forests around it. As development increased nearby, low-end accommodations grew up around the estate, a stark contrast to Biltmore's beauty and refinement. At that time, Biltmore counted about 350,000 visitors annually. The family worked to create amenities and programs to encourage longer visits, and visitation increased dramatically. In 1996, after a 10-year debate, they decided to build an inn that would evoke the original experience of staying at Biltmore House,

Visitors approach both Biltmore House and the Inn on Biltmore Estate by winding roads through forest canopy, which allows the buildings to be suddenly revealed.

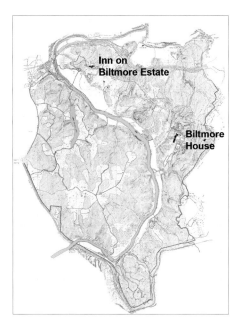

Both the inn and Biltmore House sit on the crests of hills above the French Broad River about 3 miles distant from each other.

giving visitors a seamless experience of this national historic landmark and augmenting the estate's revenues. Design Workshop collaborated with Biltmore Estate management to lead a team of engineers, architects, preservation landscape architects and a landscape historian to create a site design that would also embrace and integrate Olmsted's principles of design for beauty, self-sufficiency and sustainability.

The designers helped site the inn, using extensive computerized visual assessments and careful site analysis so that it would emulate the way the grand residence is situated on the land. Both sit on the crest of a hill and both are approached through highly controlled landscapes that are by turns pastoral and forested and that conceal the building until the last turn. But the siting of the inn was crucial for another reason: It was located so that it has controlled views of Biltmore House with limited views back to the inn and careful integration into the surrounding landscape. The inn was also designed to reference Biltmore House in its forms, rooflines, materials and detailing.

The site chosen for the inn was a parcel of former dairy complex and pasture that lay upslope from the Biltmore Estate Winery. The design transformed it using the inspiration of the great

house, with formal terraces close to the building and naturalistic landscapes farther away, including the Deer Park. Inspired by the pastoral and picturesque styles of Olmsted's work at Biltmore, the designers positioned carefully calculated scenery over pasture and woodland and views to the vast forested hills beyond. The inn's landscape of 25 acres includes an entry drive, several informal gardens, swimming pool gardens and terrace, a new 5-acre demonstration vineyard, converted meadows with native grasses, and heavily planted, terraced guest and employee parking. The demonstration vineyard, which grows wine varietals, is connected by a pathway to the estate's winery.

Since it opened in 2001, Inn on Biltmore Estate has earned numerous accolades, including a four-diamond rating by AAA and four stars from the *Mobil Travel Guide*, as well as placement on *Condé Nast Traveler's* 2005 Gold List. The carefully designed setting of approach and the inn's landscape are pivotal elements in this praise. The inn has also been featured in articles in *Travel + Leisure* and *National Geographic* and on NBC's *Today Show*. Annually, nearly a million people now visit Biltmore Estate, which is self-sustaining with no subsidies from government or national historic organizations. In keeping with

the original principles of self-sufficiency and sustainability, the estate grows much of its own vegetables, grapes, lamb, beef and fish, and bottles its own wine.

Following its work on siting the inn and designing its landscape, the firm created a 20-year master plan for Biltmore Estate, which aims to reinvigorate the forest preserve and the agricultural and livestock operations, and worked with the family to plan new programming and amenities such as river-rafting tours.

PROJECT CREDITS

PLANNING/DESIGN: Design Workshop, Inc.
PICs: Kurt Culbertson, Bruce Hazzard
Landscape Architects: Amy Capron, Daisuke Yoshimura

CLIENT: The Biltmore Company

Preservation Landscape Architects: Patricia O'Donnell, FASLA/Heritage Landscapes

Olmsted Historian: Charles E. Beveridge, F.L. Olmsted Papers/ American University

Architects: Scott Sickler/Thompson, Ventulett, Stainback & Associates (TVS)

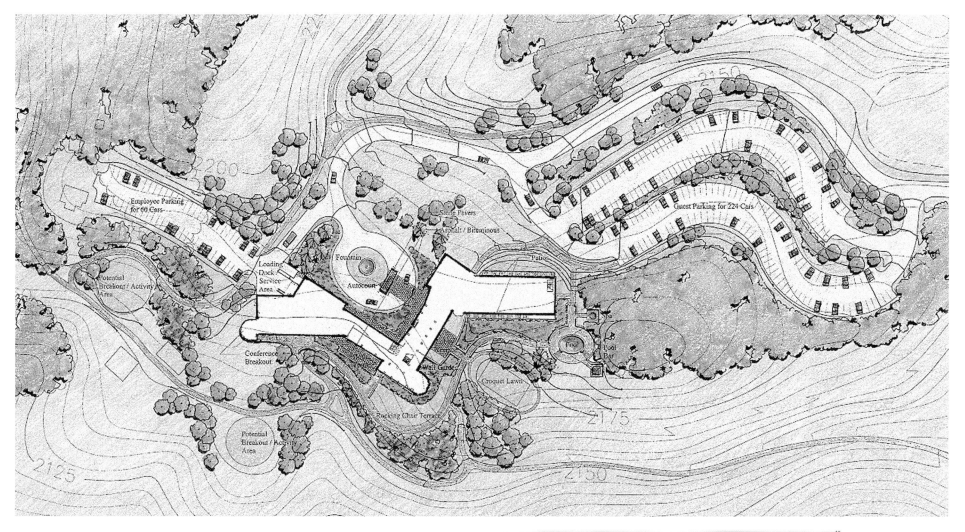

The grounds of the inn and its approach were calculated to emulate those of Biltmore House. The inn is oriented to give full attention to the grand house in the distance.

(above top) The inn, like Biltmore House, sits squarely on the crest of the hill, dominating its surroundings.

(above center, bottom) The inn's round pool was carefully situated in a setting that gives visitors a sense of both seclusion and serenity.

(above right) An image taken with a telephoto lens from the back patio of the inn shows the rooftop of Biltmore House 3 miles away, as well as several intervening ridgelines. The inn cannot be seen from the grand house except from its top floors, which are off-limits to the public. In the foreground is a pastoral setting designed to evoke vistas of an earlier age.

The siting of the inn frames views so that it appears to be surrounded by open countryside rather than the development of the city of Asheville. Views from the inn's grand terrace evoke the turn-of-the-century experience of Biltmore Estate, when it covered 120,000 acres.

When Palm Desert suffered a significant drop in sales tax revenues, local officials began to explore the idea of creating a year-round retail destination. An imaginative team responded by creating beautiful gardens where people could not only shop year-round but also come together for community events.

PROJECT DISCUSSION:
GARDENS ON EL PASEO

Palm Desert, California

Desert retail complex draws people for more than just shopping

During the late 1980s, the city of Palm Desert was hit hard by a decline in retail sales revenues in the El Paseo commercial district, which made it difficult for the city to keep up with services for a steadily growing population. City officials wanted to create a new year-round shopping destination to generate revenue, but they faced financing difficulties because summer temperatures have historically kept shoppers away and reduced retail sales performance. A creative developer purchased a parcel in the district in the early 1990s to make a new kind of place that would be environmentally friendly and comfortable in all seasons.

The 10-acre site is centrally located along El Paseo, Palm Desert's main street, which is lined with small boutiques and commercial offices in the heart of the city. Engaging city representatives and key neighborhood groups in discussions of site-plan alternatives, the design team put an emphasis on giving tourists and residents of Palm Desert a vibrant, upscale retail space in a unique, outdoor garden setting that would bring visitors from around the region — and also be a venue for local activities.

In order to draw people on a year-round basis, the first hurdle was to create comfort, which the design team did with several layers of shading devices, including freestanding architectural trellises, large awnings, date palms and canopy trees, as well as misting systems. The team also oriented buildings to maximize shade on public spaces and pathways and used sand-set permeable paving that can be wetted down in the morning to create a cooling, evaporative effect during the day.

The landscape is the project's primary focus. The design arrays the buildings around a central lawn and a lush desert arroyo garden. The lawn is used throughout the year for events like outdoor concerts, fashion shows and family activities such as Easter egg hunts and the city's annual golf-cart parade on El Paseo. A long central rill separates this lawn from the desert garden and brings a cascade of water into a pool at its head. This quarter-acre centerpiece garden embodies the environmental history of the region and is designed to recall the verdant landscapes of the neighboring mountain arroyos, whose native fan palms provided food, shelter and clothing to Native Americans centuries ago. The garden contains a mixture of indigenous and exotic desert plants reminiscent of the surrounding Coachella Valley, including fan palms; zahedi and medjool date palms, which are grown locally; along with museum palo verde, a thornless desert tree; and a variety of succulents. The ground is seeded with native wildflowers that emerge in the spring to provide a show of color for people who pass by along El Paseo. Embedded in the desert garden's floor are native hand-picked stones and arroyo cobble, which, along with plant forms and patterns in the decorative gravel and sand, evoke sinuous water patterns. The designers collaborated with California sculptor Mineko Grimmer to create the public art at the far end of the garden, an environmental water feature that is formed by five large, hand-sculpted boulders, down which water gently cascades, making light and shadow patterns on the public plaza that surrounds it.

During the design process, Design Workshop brought together the developer and officials of The College of the Desert to plan a work/study program for local horticultural students. The goal was to give students the chance to apply their knowledge and skills in the working world and use the desert garden as a living laboratory to propagate rare or endangered desert plant species. The developer also prepared educational brochures for visitors about the historical and cultural aspects of the gardens' design and contents.

Gardens on El Paseo has become a showpiece for the developer and for the city of Palm Desert, as well as a resounding economic success. Opened in late 1998, the project is fully leased and enjoys some of the highest sales tax of any retail center in the region. Officials give the project much credit for the increase from $65 million to $173 million in the city's sales tax revenue over the last six years. They also believe that the project attracts patrons and visitors from the larger region because of its appealing retail tenants and unique retail shopping environment. In 2004, it was named a great public space by the Project for Public Spaces.

PROJECT CREDITS

LANDSCAPE ARCHITECTURE:
Design Workshop, Inc.
 PIC: Bruce Hazzard
 Project Manager: Jim MacRae
 Landscape Architect: Jim MacRae

CLIENT: Madison Marquette Realty Services
 Project Coordinator: Mary Dolden-Veale

Sculptor: Mineko Grimmer

Architect: Altoon + Porter Architects

Evening events extend the day beyond typical shopping hours.

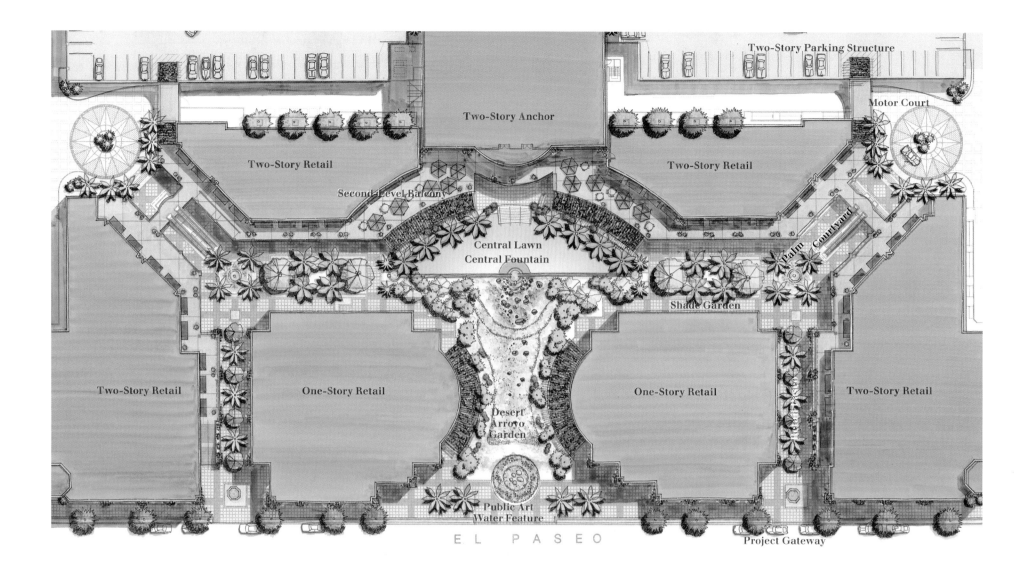

Two-Story Parking Structure

Two-Story Anchor

Motor Court

Two-Story Retail

Two-Story Retail

Second-Level Balcony

Central Lawn
Central Fountain

Palm Courtyard

Shade Garden

Two-Story Retail

One-Story Retail

Desert
Arroyo
Garden

One-Story Retail

Two-Story Retail

Public Art
Water Feature

E L   P A S E O

Project Gateway

(above) The central garden was created as the main space that welcomes pedestrians into the complex. At its far end is the lawn that serves as a gathering place for community events.

(opposite) The garden is planted at all scales, from towering palms and thornless desert trees to the spines of desert plants and indigenous wildflowers, which keep the space colorful year-round.

sketch @ Paseo
3 24 98
OPT #1

The design of the auto courts brings elements of the landscape out into dropoff areas to create gateways that herald the lush and comfortable surroundings of the complex itself.

(left) The sheltered entryways, which lead toward the central garden and lawn, give visitors gathering places that are layered with desert palms and drought-tolerant plants.

(above) An architectural rill runs across the middle of the project's central space, dividing the main lawn from the desert arroyo garden.

The 1890s Staab Mansion on the historic La Posada Hotel site in Santa Fe had served as a destination inn since the early 1930s, but it had become rundown and cluttered with "improvements." A transformative renovation has re-established it as a premier destination resort and spa.

PROJECT DISCUSSION: LA POSADA

Santa Fe, New Mexico

Reviving the landscape brings new beauty and life to an old inn

La Posada de Santa Fe sits in an impressive historical context that includes such landmarks as the early 17th-century plaza and Palace of the Governors and the magisterial 19th-century St. Francis Cathedral. The site, dotted with springs fed by subterranean streams, has been inhabited over several centuries. Native Americans grew crops on it starting in the 13th century and Spaniards raised orchards on it after arriving in the early 1600s, irrigating it with the acequia canals they built throughout much of northern New Mexico. In 1882, a prosperous merchant built a three-story, mansard-roofed mansion in the Second Empire style on the property, using materials imported from Europe, but when he died in 1913, his heirs sold the house. In the 1920s, the third story of the home was destroyed by fire and the home was later clad in adobe-like

stucco. During that time, annexes were added and converted into guesthouses to make a motor lodge that was called La Posada ("the inn"). During the early 1940s, dozens of adobe-style casitas, or "little houses," were built in the orchard behind the mansion to house artists and art students who were part of Santa Fe's flourishing arts community. But over several decades, the motor inn, with its hodgepodge of styles, fell into disrepair. A new owner bought the site in the 1990s with plans to transform it into a resort and spa that would be a tranquil retreat from the tourist frenzy of the city's famed plaza.

The designers began by creating a vision and a master plan that would rejuvenate the entire 6-acre site. The plan's goal was to pull together this eccentric and neglected 1940s adobe-style motor lodge by shaping the

A clustering of Pueblo-style casitas creates enclosed courtyards for social gatherings, intimate nooks and walking corridors that allow people to explore the grounds.

buildings around newly created, serene public spaces and intimate, colorful gardens. The design preserved the best of the historic landscape and transformed the previously auto-dominated site into a pedestrian environment by adding a parking structure, new guestrooms and a convention center, as well as spa and pool facilities. In lieu of the driveways and parking lots that once overwhelmed the site, the designers interlaced a tracery of stone and concrete paths among courtyards, fountains, lawns and flower-sprinkled terraces.

Design Workshop led the site planning for a team that included architects and interior designers in a process that emphasized sustainable strategies. The new plan blends new facilities into the surrounding landscape of huge trees and expansive gardens, retaining the old, undulating walls of the original motor inn casitas. The new buildings were carefully sited to fit comfortably with the historic buildings and the trees that shade this walled refuge. The original Victorian globe streetlights were preserved to light the paths that wind among the gardens and courtyards.

The design preserved the healthiest portions of the remnant formal Victorian plantings, including boxwood, yew, juniper, lilac, holly, forsythia, privet, blue spruce, birch, horse chestnut, pear,

apricot and apple trees and hybrid tea rose, adjacent to beds of sage, aspen, yarrow, lilac and overgrown juniper. It added drip irrigation throughout the site, a water-harvesting system and new plantings to reduce water use and enhance the seasonal color palette. These include eastern redbud, hawthorn, crabapple, New Mexico plum, lilac, butterfly bush, cotoneaster, shrub rose, dwarf juniper, barberry, catmint, sheep fescue, blue avena grass, delphinium, yarrow, valerian, salvia, rudbeckia, artemisia, Russian sage, penstemon, daylily and trumpet vine. To provide fresh herbs for the resort's kitchen, the designers created a formal herb garden in a Victorian style with a curving lavender parterre that edges the stone walk with plantings of thyme, sage, chive, angelica, rosemary, oregano, mint and other local herbs. The new herb and rose garden, the dining courtyard and other small patio areas are intimate in scale and comprise a dynamic mix of textures, seasonal colors and forms throughout the year.

Stone and brick materials from the original site were reset or reused, including original paving bricks that now edge the historic drive along the southernmost casitas. The private stone-paved courtyards were left intact, except where the existing entry steps did not

(above) Vegetation at many scales adds texture and depth to the site.

(left) The spa and swimming pool took the place of a large portion of the former motel's asphalt parking lot. Other former parking areas were transformed into gardens and courtyards.

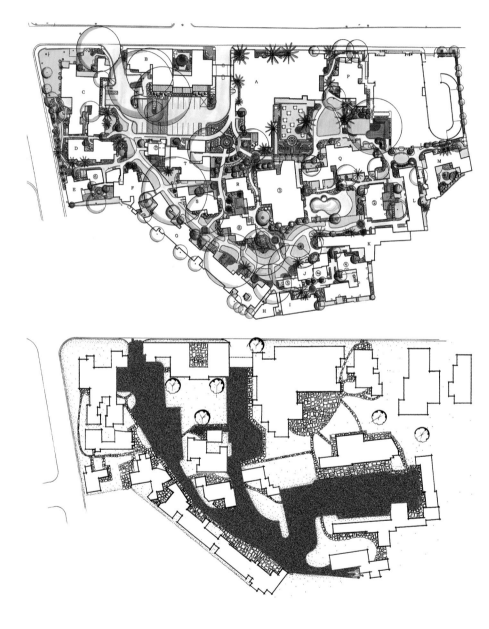

Much of the motel site was taken up by asphalt for parking, which the new design transformed into gardens and courtyards.

meet current code standards or where drainage issues needed to be resolved. New steps and ramps were matched to historic materials while low-maintenance stucco and flagstone garden walls contributed to the Southwestern flavor. Mexican porphyry stone served as paving accents and patio surfaces because of its compatibility with the hues of the existing materials, its rich color and texture and its durability.

The design reconciled the buildings' eclectic styles by infusing the public spaces with traditional New Mexico influences. The gardens and courtyards feature decorative tiles, stone paving, adobe-style walls and wooden beams, easing the transition from the original Victorian mansion to the adobe Pueblo style of the rest of the compound. The theme is restated more casually in the updated casitas, where the adobe walls and hand-hewn cedar beams are accented with local art, paving and gardens in warm Southwestern hues. The resort grounds also harbor subtle settings for both monumental and small sculptures to accent the gardens, reflecting the site's history as a home to artists and the artistic culture of Santa Fe, and to convey a sense of quiet luxury.

After a yearlong overhaul, the resort reopened in the summer of 1999 with 159 adobe-style suites and rooms, many of which feature original works of art from Santa Fe's most prestigious galleries. La Posada has been featured in numerous magazines, including *Architectural Digest*, *National Geographic Traveler* and *Sunset*. In 2004, it was listed as one of *Travel + Leisure*'s 500 Greatest Hotels in the World and selected by the readers of *Condé Nast Traveler* for the Gold List Reserve.

PROJECT CREDITS

PLANNING/DESIGN: Design Workshop, Inc./ Campbell Okuma Perkins (COPA)
  Master Plan PIC: Faith Okuma
  Design team: Todd Johnson, Michael Larson
  Implementation PIC: Kathleen Bogaski, Faith Okuma
  Design team: Michael Larson, Eddie Chau

CLIENT: Metro Hotels /BKG Management

Fountain consultants: Dave Schneider, Nature's Creation

Architect consultant: Wayne Lloyd, Lloyd Tryk Associates

Interior design: Bob Zimmer, Zimmer Hundley Associates

(above) Walking paths now take guests deep into the site through lush gardens that are dotted with artwork from some of Santa Fe's finest galleries.

(left) Rustic screens, plantings, stone and adobe lend a rich character to intimate spaces.

DILEMMA: Pittsburgh has monuments to several wars, but none to World War II, which has a deep and enduring meaning for the city. The region needs a place that will anchor the collective memory of the war and educate new generations by honoring combat veterans and those whose service on the home front were critical to winning the war.

LEGACY GOALS:

Community
Tell the story of the war efforts, both at home and abroad, to honor a generation and teach people about this era of the city's history; link to the River Walk trail system to make the memorial part of a larger contemplative experience.

Environment
Let the land and the river speak through the design, conveying a sense of timelessness by framing views to the water, integrating land and memorial with dignity and using native plant materials to ensure the longevity of the landscape.

Economics
Create an icon to draw new visitors to the city and integrate the memorial with the surrounding urban fabric to make a seamless transition from one to the other and mark the site with a beacon that will signal this new destination.

Art
Craft the memorial from materials that went into the manufacture of the war's armaments and use the five-pointed star of the United States military tradition to honor those who served, evoke respect and inspire people.

THESIS: The memorial will foster deeper meaning for residents, visitors, combatants and their descendants if it is structured as an outdoor museum that balances formal, symbolic gestures with the story of the war and a roster of the fallen.

PITTSBURGH WORLD WAR II MEMORIAL
Pittsburgh, Pennsylvania

City history enriches the remembrance of war-time efforts

Overview

World War II had a profound effect on Pittsburgh, not only because of the extraordinary sacrifice of its younger generation, but also because it played such an important role in war production. Like many American cities, Pittsburgh has no memorial to that struggle: The significance of the war is simply taken for granted. But as the ranks of veterans thin, many feel it is time to retell the story and honor the combatants. In 2002, Pittsburgh officials and veterans groups began that process by mounting a design competition for a memorial to Allegheny County citizens who had served, both in battle and at home. The winning design was a memorial that focuses as much on home-front efforts as on the fight itself.

History/Context

Pittsburgh was at the heart of war production, with an output of armaments, airplanes, and munitions that was seriously underestimated by the Germans. The city was pivotal to helping win World War II, with its manufacture of steel, glass and aluminum and the scientific and technological expertise of such institutions as Carnegie Mellon University, Westinghouse Electric Company and the H.J. Heinz Company. Pittsburgh and Allegheny County also contributed a substantial force to the fight itself, enduring the loss of more than 4,000 soldiers to the war.

Allegheny County boasts more military veterans than any other urban area in the nation, and they have been active and prominent in the city's civic life. Though Pittsburgh is home to monuments to the Korean and Vietnam wars, there is none to

Two Pittsburgh veterans spearheaded the campaign to build the memorial: the Honorable John G. Brosky (left) and Stanley J. Roman (right). They are shown in 2005 in the top photo, above images taken in 1942 in the course of duty, Brosky in Bora Bora in the Pacific and Roman in training at Fort Chaffee, Arkansas, before being shipped to the European Theater of Operations.

CASE STUDY

The site, circled in red at right, lies on the north shore of the Allegheny River across from downtown, with connections into the city's River-Walk trail system.

In an intensive three-week design charrette, the landscape architects collaborated with sculptors to design the individual elements that convey the memorial's central values of duty, honor and country. Pictured here is the tower, which serves as a beacon, calling people to the site.

World War II. City officials felt that recognition was long overdue and worked with veterans for three years to site the memorial in its new River Walk development along the north shore of the Allegheny River. The project got its first major boost in early 2001, when Mayor Tom Murphy contributed $50,000 to begin planning a design competition. Competitors included Julie and Omri Amrany, De L'Esprie with David Spellerberg, Beverly Pepper, Allan Cottrill with Gerald Morosco and Susan Wagner. In June 2002, the team of Design Workshop and sculptor Larry Kirkland was named the winner.

Process

Several on the team felt a personal investment in the project because their fathers had fought in the war. In their view, the central task of the memorial was to keep alive the story of the war and the principles for which it had been fought, a concept the team used to expand the idea of a monument into an outdoor museum. During the design charrette process, members of the team overheard a rebroadcast of General Douglas MacArthur's famous 1962 speech "Duty, Honor, Country" and knew immediately that these values were the structure they had been seeking, values that stood at the center of the war

efforts and marked a generation. They would be the heart of the memorial.

Design

The site is on the north shore of the Allegheny River between the Clemente and Seventh Street bridges. To convey the importance the war holds for Pittsburgh, the design needed to give visitors a context for the fight and show how these values manifested — in heroic actions, in daily life, in dedication. With the help of a university historian, they found letters home, personal memoirs, news stories and anecdotes not only about battles and global events but also about the home-front's prodigious war production, including such stories as the H.J. Heinz Company retooling its packing crate operations to make wooden airplane gliders that couldn't be detected by radar.

As the simplest visual incarnation of American values, the design team chose the five-pointed star. They began with the idea of Duty, which they embodied at the western end of the sloping site with a star-shaped plaza centered on an open, 65-foot-high steel tower that acts as a beacon, calling people to the site. The tower's arching shafts form a rising latticework that, when viewed from below, make the shape of a star. The plaza's walls, which are etched with

CASE STUDY

timelines, photography and text, are steel where they meet the hillside and glass where they face the river, two locally produced materials that were crucial to winning the war.

A walkway from this outdoor museum leads to the memorial's other, more contemplative spaces, proceeding eastward and passing glass panels carved with the names of the fallen. This roll of honor is framed against the river to give a sense of the flow of time and the ephemeral nature of life. At the eastern end of the walkway, the principle of Country is embodied in an imposing silver star sculpture pitched at an angle to reflect the American flag flying above. Under the edges of the star are steel panels inscribed with the enduring principles for which the United States stands — principles of Country such as courage and respect, which were tested

and challenged by the obligations of Duty and Honor.

Outcome
The team's design was chosen unanimously by the selection committee and fund-raising for the memorial began in late 2002, with a total cost estimated at $2.5 million. Supporters are hoping to begin construction by 2006.

PROJECT CREDITS

PLANNING/DESIGN: Design Workshop, Inc./ Kirkland Studios
  PIC: Todd Johnson
  Designers: Kirby Hoyt, Nino Pero, Zac Boggs, Elin Tidbeck, Matt Shawaker

CLIENT: Pittsburgh World War II Memorial Fund

Collaborators: Larry Kirkland/Kirkland Studios, Bruce Janacek/North Central College (Illinois)

(above) Diaries of the charrette tracked the evolution of ideas for each of the three elements of the final design. The symbol of the five-pointed star came early in the process, its use evolving through multiple iterations.

(opposite) Models, drawings and renderings all played a part in helping the team envision the memorial and allow the values of Duty, Honor and Country to inform the design.

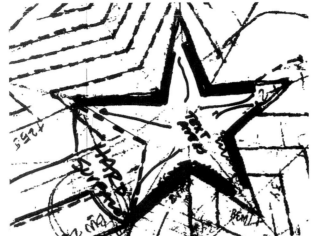

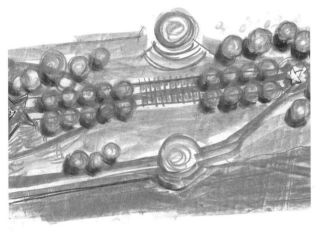

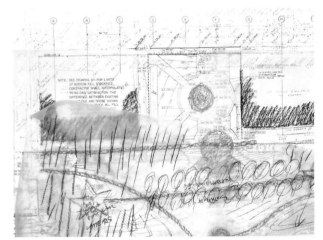

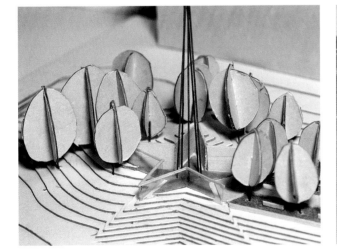

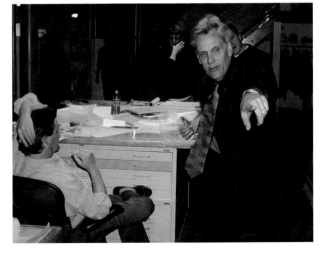

DUTY

HONOR

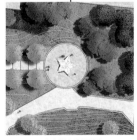

COUNTRY

(opposite) Visitors move from the memorial's beacon and its interpretive walls past a roster of the fallen and through an allee of trees.

(above) Each of the three elements reflects one of the values highlighted in MacArthur's speech.

Duty, honor, country . . . are your rallying points: to build courage when courage seems to fail; to regain faith when there seems to be little cause for faith; to create hope when hope becomes forlorn.

— Douglas MacArthur, West Point, N.Y., May 12, 1962

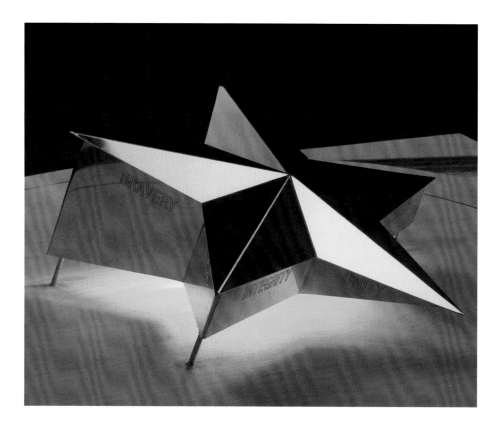

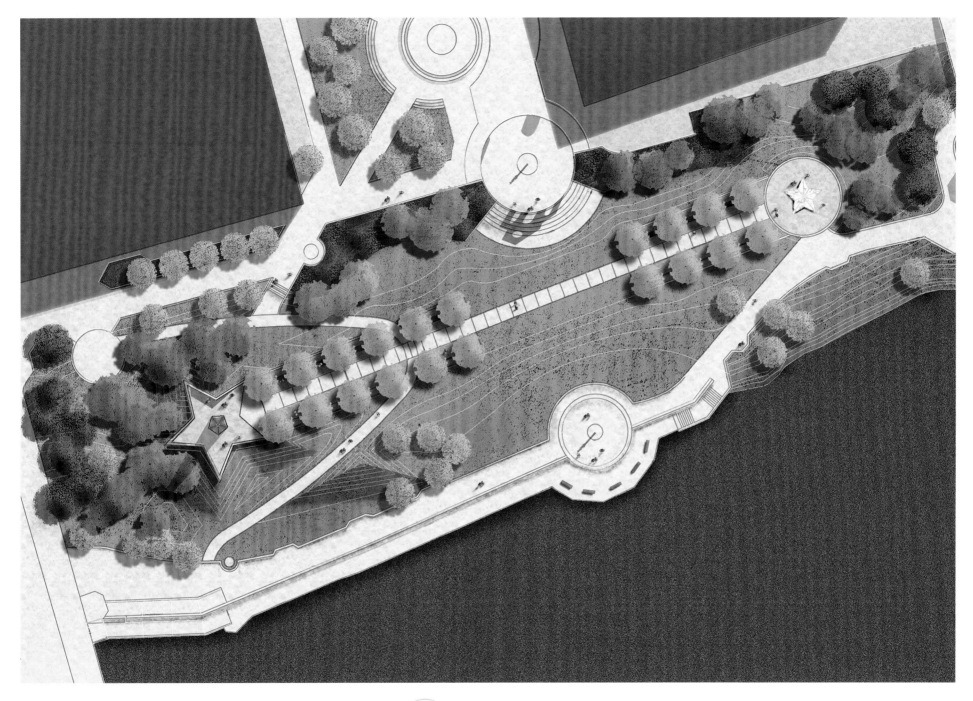

LEGACY

3 Community

ESSAY

Joe Porter, a founding partner of Design Workshop, shares a history of community-making and his experience of creating communities through a process that integrates all elements of community at all scales. The projects that follow illustrate the complex and often messy process by which a community is brought into being, with the need to meet conditions imposed by the economics, aesthetics and environment of specific sites, sometimes over a long period of time.

PROJECT DISCUSSIONS

High Desert: A school builds its endowment and keeps faith with its values by creating a community based on the ecology of the land.

Arbolera de Vida: A successful environmental battle lets a neighborhood expand — and stay affordable.

RidgeGate: Proximity to open lands and transit creates an edge city that offers the pleasures of nature and access to urban amenities.

IN-DEPTH ACCOUNT

Rancho Viejo de Santa Fe: Officials and developers collaborate to build villages that preserve the land and conserve natural resources.

We have seen the good old days of suburban sprawl and New Urbanism. Where do we go from here?

AN ESSAY BY JOE PORTER

For three-quarters of a century, we have abandoned the quest to create whole communities. We learned how to efficiently engineer, construct, regulate, finance and develop vast residential areas and how to produce houses, commercial buildings, roads, infrastructure, schools, parks and churches as individual elements, but we lost the capacity to bring all those things together in a way that harnesses their collective energies and creates community.

Social connection is a basic human need. In our modern society, it has been disrupted by changes in generational values, technology and mass media, sprawl and pressures of time and money. These trends make communities and neighborhoods more important than ever as social havens. The movements that have emerged in recent years — including smart growth, livable communities, New Urbanism and sustainability — are a call to reintegrate the fragments of development into neighborhoods, towns and cities to create whole communities.

History and Trends

In the early 20th century, town planners and landscape architects were writing about and striving to design whole communities based on integrative town-planning principles, as Susan L. Klaus recounts in *A Modern Arcadia*. In the borough of Queens, New York, the Russell Sage Foundation, in its mission to help ameliorate social and living conditions, applied these principles to a suburban setting to create Forest Hills Gardens. The foundation established a holistic development process that was driven by landscape architect and town planner Frederick Law Olmsted and architect Grosvenor Atterbury, who shared the philosophy that the designed environment could improve the lives of individuals and society as a whole. Olmsted and Atterbury designed Forest Hills Gardens as a walking community, configuring it around a sequence of parks and gardens, with an urban center and a great variety of building types, 15 minutes from Manhattan via the Long Island Railroad. In today's terms, it would be a transit-oriented development with a jewel of a train station forming one side of Station Square, the gateway to the community. The success of Forest Hills Gardens in fostering social organizations and community

(opposite) Levittown, Pennsylvania, is viewed as the prototype mass-produced suburb of the 1950s and 1960s.

(above) Forest Hills Village, created in 1909, is an early example of transit-oriented development. It is a walking community created around a sequence of parks and gardens, with an urban center, a great variety of building types that together have created a context for community institutions and events for nearly 100 years.

Developer Jim Rouse called on an array of disciplines to create community at Columbia, Maryland.

traditions demonstrates the success of the process and the design it created.

The efforts of Olmsted, Atterbury and other town planners were cut short, according to Klaus, by several factors, including abandonment of the City Beautiful movement as too expensive, the massive flight from the city and accompanying advances in the mass production of housing. Town planning and urban design were replaced with laws, administrative policies and engineering that heavily influenced city management, the development industry and the engineering professions, helping to create a development process focused on operational efficiency. The upshot is production-line development that continues to forge the American suburbs, the evolution and implications of which are well-documented by authors like James Howard Kunstler in *The Geography of Nowhere*.

It appears that the opportunity now exists to resurrect the quest to create whole communities. Clues to where this opportunity might lead and what may come next can be found in the evolution of new communities, which in the past have introduced development trends, both good and bad. Levittown on Long Island, famous for introducing mass-produced housing, was actually a new community with a small commercial center, a village green and sites for schools and churches. Columbia, Maryland, and Reston, Virginia, led the New Town movement of the 1960s and provided a paradigm that has been refined by the southern California planned communities of Woodbridge, Rancho Margarita and Ladera Ranch. In recent years, New Urbanism's Seaside, Florida, and Disney's Celebration have introduced a return to urbanism in the suburbs.

The future of urbanism, social equity, efficient uses of natural resources and developing with nature is being tested and developed incrementally in a variety of new communities across the United States. The next stage is to integrate these emerging innovations. This integration will require government, citizens and developers to collaborate to create an integrative development process that the public trusts and respects.

Process

Development isn't a collection of things but rather a process that yields things.
— *Jane Jacobs,* The Nature of Economies

The physical form of our communities is a manifestation of the process that creates them. Changing the form of the suburbs requires changing this process. The production-efficiency era isolated the physical elements of communities and the professionals who create them. It has led to a development process that is confrontational and expensive, produces enormous negative energy, exhausts its participants and is directed at achieving minimum standards instead of maximizing opportunities. The process has isolated developers from government and citizens and, as an industry, they have been content with that isolation.

The future will be in reintegrating the parts of community. The question is how to develop, and part of the answer is that no individual sector can do it alone. The most difficult challenge in creating an integrative development process will be for government, citizens and developers to overcome the distrust and disrespect of the past 80 years and collaborate in creating a new model for how to develop.

In her book, *Systems of Survival*, Jane Jacobs suggests that the role of government, as guardian of the public interest, is to decree what should be and the role of the commercial sector is to determine the ways and means to make it happen. Government must engage citizens in creating a clearer vision of the future and what should be. Developers must participate as citizens in the envisioning process, then acknowledge the vision and finally lead in its execution. Where government is the developer of community elements like transportation systems and public buildings, the public investment must be directed to creating community. Regional transit should stimulate efficient urban growth patterns, and public buildings should demonstrate how public spaces and architecture create community identity, culture and pride.

Community and Commerce

Design Workshop was first exposed to the extraordinary power of developers and the private sector in 1969 when the firm began working with The Rouse Company on Columbia, Maryland. The holistic thinking and process that Rouse applied to developing Columbia exemplifies the power that developers have to make positive change and subverts the negative view of the development industry. Jim Rouse was a visionary entrepreneur who believed that community could be created through commerce.

The inherent conflicts of combining commerce and community are epitomized in a story from Rouse's biography, *Better Places, Better Lives*. Before planning began, Rouse assembled a team of 13 leading community experts to establish the social vision for the community. He asked them to do this without concern for profits, which he indicated was his problem. The advisors were to determine what the community should be, with Rouse and his company responsible for finding the ways and means to make it happen. The difficulty was evident in Rouse's comments at the conclusion of their first day of vague academic discussions. He told the group, "I am going to be a very rude host, but I have got to tell you this is the most disastrous evening I've ever spent. You've all been invited to participate in this. Everyone we asked agreed to do it. You're all being paid. You all professed that you believe in this idea, and right around the table, you all said it's impossible." The group continued its work and built a vision around an idea that both they and Rouse embraced, a vision that Jim Rouse's town should be planned to nourish love. The result was a community with mixed-use village centers close to neighborhoods clustered around elementary schools, with interfaith religious centers, the Columbia Health Care System, employment centers and the Columbia Association, which is still a model for community associations.

Jim Rouse was interested in creating social equity, ethnic and economic diversity, affordable community facilities and services available to everyone, and the means for people to participate in determining the future of their community. These are the same challenges that face the community development industry and government today.

Environment

The community development process begins with the land, which is typically the most tangible element in programming and designing a new community. It remains consistent and measurable in the complex and changing economics, market and politics that affect the development of a community. Each landscape is different. Fitting a community to the land

requires observing, mapping and understanding the land at each scale of community design. In the past 80 years, many areas of ecologic and amenity value have been needlessly destroyed in the development process because people charged with reducing costs and those responsible for creating value do not listen to each other and work together to integrate development and nature.

Working with the land extends beyond individual development sites to influence the entire planet. The term sustainability has gained popularity in recent years to express the idea of living within the limits of the Earth's natural resources. As described by economist Herman Daly in *Beyond Growth*, sustainable development does not exceed the capacity of the ecosystem to regenerate raw materials and absorb the world's waste. In community development terms, this means creating transportation-efficient communities where densities, mixed uses and the opportunity to walk provide alternatives to the car. It means fitting development to the land to preserve sensitive ecosystems, capturing the energy of the sun and wind to heat and cool spaces, applying the cleansing power of plants to clean the air and water and using "green" building processes and materials that reduce waste and energy. These are emerging aspirations for community development, but the design and engineering professions have barely touched on what is required to achieve them and to develop in balance with nature.

The Art of New Communities

The art of community has not been seriously considered since early in the last century, when those engaged in designing towns thought of them as art. This thinking is reflected in Hegemann and Peet's *The American Vitruvius: An Architects' Handbook of Civic Art* (1922) and in the work of Olmsted and Atterbury at Forest Hills Gardens and other town planners of the time.

Beauty influences the joy and pride people take in the places they live and is an important factor in creating the culture of a community. The art of community can be seen at many scales. It may begin with the way the community sits on an open landscape. It may be expressed in the shape of public spaces or in the way that development fits the land. It may create amenity from infrastructure or by integrating nature into the community. It may be the art in a detailed bridge railing, the design of a park pavilion or a tree-lined neighborhood street enclosed by homes of tasteful and varied architecture.

Community art is not about style but about form and content. More and more, in the United States, it is about urbanism. The pressures of population growth, land costs, development and transportation costs are requiring people to live in urban environments, making the current challenge one of creating artful community in dense, urbanized surroundings. New Urbanism has made a significant contribution by introducing design that urbanizes the suburbs.

The process of the future will acknowledge that art plays a crucial role in creating community, that it enriches the lives of those who live there, brings people together, cares for the environment and contributes to the economic success of a community. It will also apply the enormously underutilized potential of design and the design process to bring people with different perspectives together to visualize and experience the possibilities of the future. Drawings can communicate values that are difficult to describe with words or numbers. The nature of the design process is integrative and tangible and has the potential to combine values of community, environment, economics and art in a single solution.

The Future

The private sector has enormous power to build capacity to develop in a more sustainable manner. The inevitable question is, "What's in it for the developer?" The answer is: the opportunity for the industry to control its own destiny.

The terms whole communities and sustainability express ideals of balance and comprehensiveness. They are vague because the ideals are so foreign to community development that there are few familiar words to describe them. Daly writes in *Beyond Growth*, "Sustainable development is a term that everybody likes but nobody understands" and he argues that whoever defines the term will politically influence our future. The

community development industry has an opportunity to help define this future through its actions — or it can leave the definition to those who see the industry as the problem rather than a potential solution. Daly takes the controversial position that sustainable development is qualitative, not quantitative, that it is ultimately development without growth. No one knows if society will ever reach this state but whatever the future, the call for change is clear and striving for quality development is the next logical step. It would be an ironic contribution for community developers and their designers, who at present rely on growth for their existence, to become leaders in the quest for whole communities and sustainable development.

(opposite) The new Daybreak community near Salt Lake City, Utah, is highly advanced in applying principles of sustainability. It reclaims a mining waste site, utilizes riparian vegetation spines to cleanse and return rainwater to the aquifer, supports wildlife habitat, integrates jobs and commercial services and will ultimately connect to downtown Salt Lake City by light rail.

When Albuquerque Academy decided to develop the final parcel of a land bequest, its board of trustees found their own strong environmental ethic pitted against the need to make the most of their endowment. A pioneering plan solved the dilemma by drawing on the land's ecology to create a beautiful place that has also proven to be highly popular.

PROJECT DISCUSSION:
HIGH DESERT

Albuquerque, New Mexico

Natural systems become the framework for a new community

As it considered the last piece of land in a decades-old bequest, Albuquerque Academy wanted to set a good example for its students by handling the land responsibly while still maximizing the economic return in order to insure the school's future. After school officials explored issues of community and environment, they decided to build a new community on the land, acting as their own developer. Design Workshop created the master plan for this community and guided them through the development and entitlement process.

The site encompasses 1,000 acres of open land at the foot of the Sandia Mountains, with typical suburban residential communities to the west. The community, environmental, business and educational components of the plan were integrated through close collaboration among school officials, students,

teachers and the design team. Faculty and students were involved in the planning process to ensure that there was buy-in from all of the academy's constituencies. A thorough land analysis was the basis for a plan that would use the landscape's deeper character to blend 2,000 homes into this fragile desert landscape.

One focus of the plan became managing the drainage of these arid lands without destroying the beautiful high-desert landscape, which is cut by numerous arroyos that drain the property and the foothills of the Sandias. The plan transforms this existing natural framework into an open-space system and network of trails, clustering neighborhoods around this basic community structure. Before High Desert, arroyos within developed areas of the city were made into concrete-lined V-ditches,

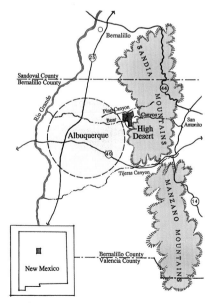

High Desert's site is flanked on three sides by suburban subdivisions, and on the fourth by the Sandia Mountains.

devoid of any aesthetic value or natural vegetation. The design convinced city engineers that by leaving the floodplains of these dry gulches as open space (with an additional prudent setback to accommodate arroyo migration), these drainages could serve as habitat, flood control and scenic open space. By crafting a design that would enhance the natural drainage system, the community could harvest water to irrigate open space, reduce the costs of drainage improvements and preserve the property's ecology and views.

The plan sited development between the arroyos, armoring portions of them with native stone to accept urban runoff and creating detention "ponds," then restoring all areas with an indigenous plan palette. The school dedicated some of the arroyos to the city as open space and placed the balance under conservation easements — the first such use by a private developer in New Mexico. The open-space system includes paved and unpaved trails, some with interpretive signage, as well as a community center with a 10-acre neighborhood park.

The design guidelines for High Desert included other environmental measures, such as a water-conservation policy of low-flow plumbing fixtures and native plant materials, and ground-breaking light-pollution efforts. Five years later, the city used these same guidelines as a model for a citywide water-conservation ordinance and the state instituted very similar night-sky protection measures.

The project is known for its popularity and absorption rate in the local real estate market and its features are touted as a model for future development. The impressive economic success of the development, which far exceeded the school's expectations, appeared to demonstrate the high value that local residents place on ecology. To signify the project's care for the environment, High Desert is identified by a stylized image of blue grama grass, a drought-tolerant plant native to the area.

PROJECT CREDITS

PLANNING/DESIGN: Design Workshop, Inc.
PIC: Kurt Culbertson
Designers/Planners: Mark Soden, Keith Simon, Jeff McMenimen, Jeff Zimmermann

CLIENT: High Desert Investment Corporation/ Albuquerque Academy

Civil Engineers: Bohannan Huston Inc.

Community Governance: Hyatt & Stubblefield

Environmental Consultants: SWCA

DEVELOPABILITY

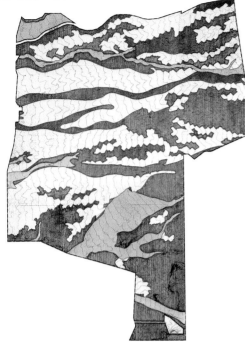

HYDROLOGY

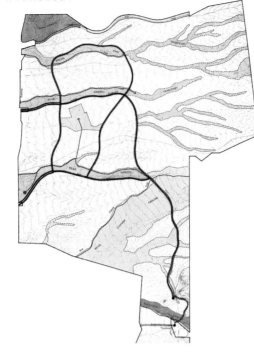

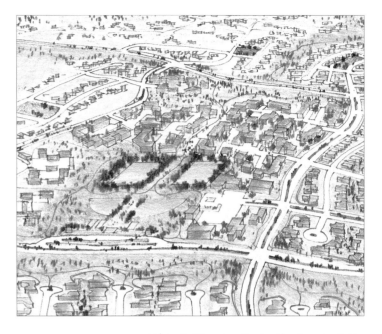

(above) The density in the heart of the community was designed to transition toward the Sandias without interrupting the arroyos and the functional and amenity value they provide the community.

DEVELOPABILITY (upper left) — Early assessments of the land identified areas to be preserved (blue), areas that could be developed (ivory) and those that could be developed only with extremely sensitive handling (red).

EARLY CONCEPT

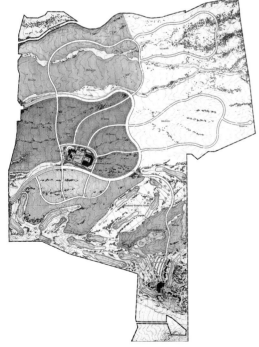

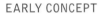

FINAL ILLUSTRATIVE PLAN

HYDROLOGY (upper right) — This diagram of open space and trails also shows the arroyos and washes that drain rainwater off the mountains, a system that became the framework for the community of High Desert.

EVOLUTION OF THE PLAN (lower right) — A variety of programs and circulation options tested the blending of the development and landscape values (lower left), before producing an integrated plan with a dense village core and a system of parks and open-space trails shaped around the land's natural systems.

(far left) Natural arroyos were armored with stone and replanted with indigenous plants so they can carry higher post-development runoff without compromising the ecosystem or the area's scenic views.

(above) A sandstone-slab bench is typical of furnishings for the trail system, which are done in a style that blends in easily with the community's desert surroundings.

(left) An entry monument in stainless steel is one of several stylized images of blue grama grass, a drought-tolerant plant native to the area, which signifies the project's care for the environment.

The design engages people with nature through its system of open space and trails, which are configured around the land's fragile arroyos.

After a grassroots movement rid a neighborhood of toxic dust from a lumber mill, residents set their sights on expanding and redeveloping their neighborhood. Teaming with professional collaborators, they helped design a plan, housing and public spaces that grow from their own cultural and economic resources.

PROJECT DISCUSSION:
ARBOLERA DE VIDA

Albuquerque, New Mexico

Citizen-driven collaboration augments an affordable community

Albuquerque's Sawmill neighborhood near the Rio Grande and the city's Old Town was originally settled with family gardens, orchards and livestock, all supported by the acequias, or irrigation canals, created by Spanish settlers in the 17th century. The neighborhood took its name from the mill established on the site by the Duke City Lumber Company and is home to one of Albuquerque's longest-standing Hispanic enclaves, with 80 percent of its 2,500 residents of Hispanic descent. It is a community of modest means: When the project began in 1998, median annual income was $19,500 and one-third of residents lived below the poverty level.

In the 1980s, alarmed by a surge in respiratory illnesses, residents near the lumber mill lobbied for better enforcement of air-quality regulations at the mill — a grassroots advocacy effort that

ultimately led to its closure. Fearing that another polluting industry would take its place, residents persuaded city officials to buy the vacant site and rezone it for mixed uses and affordable housing. Federal, state and city funds were used to clean up the 27-acre parcel. By 1997, the neighborhood's advocacy group formed its own development corporation.

Bringing residents together with architects, environmental experts and financial advisors, Design Workshop worked with residents to plan a future for the new neighborhood of Arbolera de Vida ("orchard of life"). The main objectives were to foster community and use environmentally sound design to keep costs down. The final master plan achieved this with two primary components: (1) an unusual financial model that guards against gentrification, ensuring that resale homes will remain

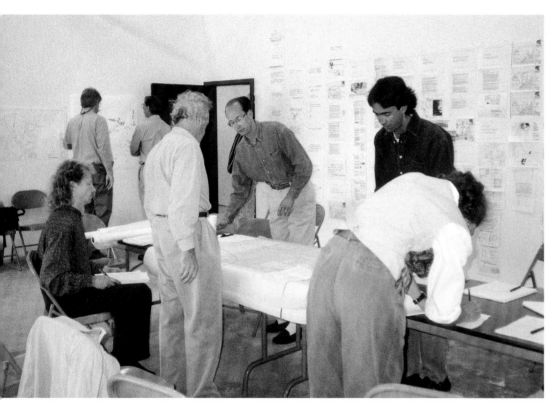

(**this page**) The extensive public process engaged the entire community, including children in neighborhood schools, in determining what form the neighborhood should take as it expanded onto the old sawmill site.

(**opposite**) In the spirit of traditional New Mexican towns, the expansion creates a mix of community uses around a plaza, adding such elements as a restored acequia, or irrigation channel, community gardens and an orchard to honor the new name of the expanded neighborhood.

affordable; and (2) application of sustainable design principles that will keep housing prices and operating costs low.

In 1998, residents formed a community land trust that leases the land to keep homes in the area permanently affordable for low- to moderate-income families, a system that allows Arbolera to offer homes with as many as four bedrooms at prices ranging from $54,000 to $104,000. Each home is sited to maximize passive solar heating and harvest water for domestic irrigation, in order to take advantage of the long-range economic benefits of environmentally sustainable design. Plan guidelines require later phases to incorporate recycled or renewable building materials. Ultimately, 105 homes will be added to the neighborhood, ranging from about 1,000 to 1,800 square feet and featuring such "green" building elements as xeriscaping and water-saving fixtures.

To recapture the green space and sense of community lost when the site became industrial, the neighborhood expansion clustered around a central plaza and is graced with an orchard, a restored acequia and a community garden. Other features include senior housing, pedestrian and bike paths, green spaces, retail, new commercial uses and employment centers that buffer the neighborhood from existing industrial sites.

Comments from the first homebuyers were used to streamline the home-buying process. Feedback from homeowner education classes is being used to improve course content and services to prospective homebuyers. Trust officials are also organizing health services, an environmental advocacy program, an outdoor education program and a tool bank.

PROJECT CREDITS

PLANNING/DESIGN: Design Workshop, Inc.
   PIC: Keith Simon
   Project Manager: Mimi Burns
   Project Advisor: Joe Porter

CLIENT: Sawmill Advisory Council

Architect: Eric Naslund, AIA/Studio E Architects

Engineer: Bohannon Huston, Ike Benton, AIA, Van Der Ryn Architects

General Contractor: Vigil Construction

Land trust consultants: Burlington Associates in Community Development, LLC, Institute for Community Economics

Creation of a land trust to guide the neighborhood development corporation was critical to developing protocols that would protect Arbolera de Vida's affordable housing from being exploited for profit.

Lush vines grace the trellis and shade picnic tables on the community's central gathering plaza. The plaza, public gardens and community facilities are all positioned to be central to the existing neighborhood and the new community.

Communities south of Denver are spread out in a pattern typical of suburban growth. But on one large open parcel, proximity to both transit and open space allows the creation of a dense edge city where people can have one foot in the city and one foot in nature.

PROJECT DISCUSSION: RIDGEGATE

Lone Tree, Colorado

An edge city changes the pattern of typical suburban development

This 3,500-acre parcel is strategically positioned to become an urban center that is the nexus between suburban Denver to the north and rural areas to the south. The site is on the southern fringe of the metropolitan area, straddling Interstate 25. Taking shape over the next 50 years, this proposed high-density edge city is designed to balance jobs, homes and nature, with more than 12,000 dwellings, 20 million square feet of mixed-use commercial space and more than 1,200 acres of open space.

Several factors combined to make the project possible, including timing, the right government support, a connection with regional transportation and application of urban design principles to create density in a suburban setting.

The owners of the land bought the site in the 1970s, when it lay far outside the urban area, and then waited until development reached it before exploring what the land and surrounding communities could support. When they decided to develop an edge city, they found that county officials, who were accustomed to scattered rural development and low-density communities, couldn't embrace the idea. The planning team approached a nearby municipality, Lone Tree, and explored the possible benefits of annexing the site and proceeding with the project, including generation of new jobs, tax revenues and housing supply. Together, they forged a strategy that would lay the foundation for RidgeGate. The shift brought both tangible and moral support for the project and offered Lone Tree the means to guide its own future. With the master plan and entitlement process complete, the town's voters approved annexation in 2000.

Early on, the team recognized the importance of transit. At the time, Denver's Regional Transportation District (RTD) was in the process of constructing a light-rail system that was to come to within a half mile of the northern edge of the property. The planning team persuaded RTD to extend the I-25 light-rail system into RidgeGate, with a special station at the new RidgeGate Parkway interchange and two transit stations within the development, all part of a $4.7 billion package approved by Colorado voters in late 2004. A public-private partnership was also forged with the Colorado Department of Transportation to locate and design a new highway interchange on donated RidgeGate property that would alleviate regional transportation congestion and give the new development better highway access.

RidgeGate is designed with a framework of high-density, mixed-use centers and urbanized edges supported by both regional transit and a strong network of open-space corridors and trails, including a permanently preserved southern boundary of spectacular bluffs.

The dominant feature of RidgeGate will be its city center, a mixed-use downtown area east of the highway that will come to fruition in 20 to 30 years as the development of smaller centers and residential neighborhoods reaches critical mass. Development of this city center is expected to begin sometime after 2010.

The initial phase of the project has already begun on the west side of the highway. The building of Sky Ridge Medical Center, which brought 1,000 jobs to the site, has helped support the development's first phase. Plans and designs for this area concentrate development in order to preserve the highly scenic qualities of the land, introducing dense design by placing familiar suburban stores in a pedestrian-oriented urban pattern within walking distance of metro light-rail stations. The anchor of the west side's mixed-use center is the first suburban SuperTarget in the nation with structured parking. Changing its design from a typical surface-parking configuration to a mixed-use, transit-oriented center significantly reduced the parking footprint and allowed a higher

concentration of commercial uses.

Residential neighborhoods will border the natural drainages and the bluffs to take advantage of both scenic assets and regional open-space trails and parks. Circulation systems feature narrowed streets to slow cars and foster a pedestrian-friendly atmosphere in residential and commercial districts and in office development along I-25. Linear urban parks are designed along the natural drainage corridors that run through the development to provide relief for the dense, mixed-use districts that front them. An urban feel will be created by the intensity of detail in public spaces, promenades and pedestrian underpasses within the linear parks.

This new urbanization strategy is designed to make the first phase three times as compact as typical suburban communities. The project has already had success, as evidenced by market prices and demand for homes, office and retail space that are as high or higher than other development in the suburban Denver metro region.

PROJECT CREDITS

URBAN DESIGN/MASTER PLAN: Design Workshop, Inc.
PIC: Todd Johnson
Managing Principals: Keith Simon, Jim MacRae
Project Managers: Jeff McMenimen, Allyson Mendenhall, Jamie Fogle
Landscape Architects: Bret Frk, Geoff Gerring, Chad Klever, Kirby Hoyt, Jeremy Alden, Todd Wenskoski

CLIENTS: Coventry Development Corporation Colorado as agent for Colony Investments, Inc., and Rampart Range Metropolitan District

Civil Engineer: Carroll & Lange

Traffic Engineer: LSC, FHU

Legal representatives: Holme Roberts & Owen LLP

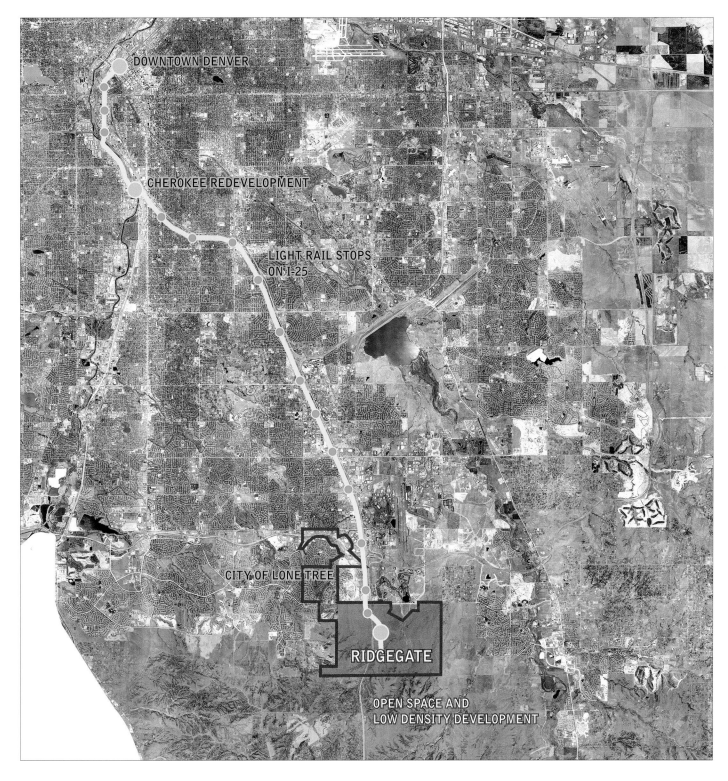

The mixed-use edge city of RidgeGate lies at the interface of rural Douglas County (in green) and the Denver metropolitan area, served by planned light-rail stations along Interstate 25. Plans overlaid on an aerial view show the light-rail connection between Denver's urban core and the RidgeGate site (red-screened shape). Major transit hubs are shown by orange dots, with Union Station at the top, the Gates intermodal center below downtown Denver and RidgeGate's transit parking hub near the end of the light-rail line.

DOWNTOWN DENVER

CHEROKEE REDEVELOPMENT

LIGHT RAIL STOPS
ON I-25

CITY OF LONE TREE

RIDGEGATE

OPEN SPACE AND
LOW DENSITY DEVELOPMENT

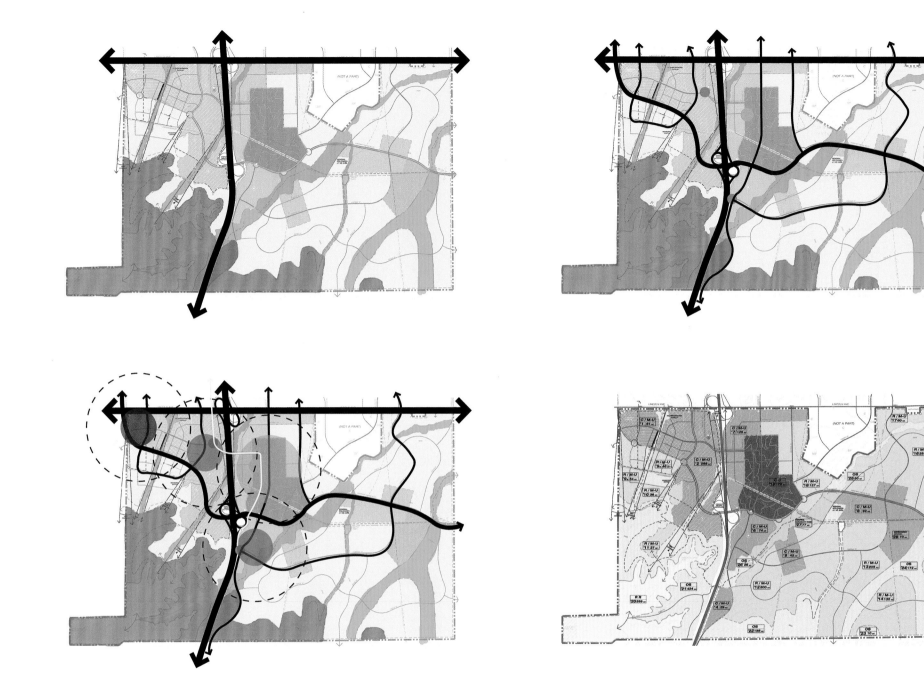

The plan was based on the natural open-space bluffs and drainages (top left) and the existing transportation corridors (top right). To relieve the burden on the site's two major roadways, the design layers in an extensive network of internal vehicular roadways that is fitted to the land but urban in character (bottom left), distributing circulation throughout the site and incorporating a new interchange to pull people off the interstate highway onto RidgeGate's main spine. This network of roadways, along with three stops on the light-rail extensions, which is shown in yellow, nurtures several centers that are within a 10-minute walk of each other.

(bottom right) The project's zoning map shows that the community's densest development (in dark orange) will be on the east side of Interstate 25, anticipated to occur between 2020 and 2030. Development has already begun on the west side of the highway, with the first mixed-use, transit-oriented district.

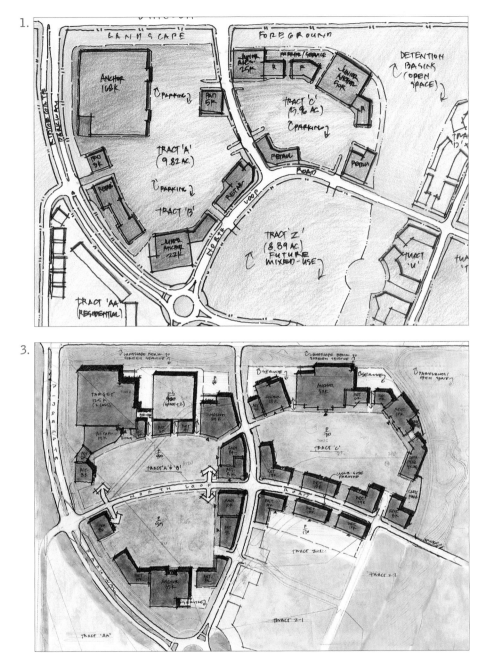

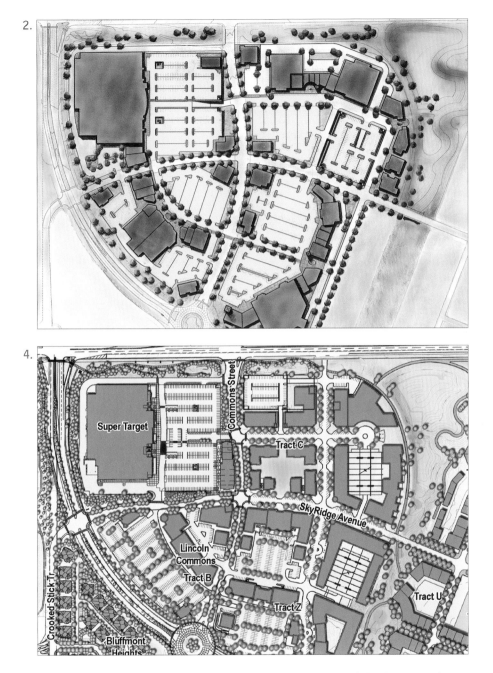

It took two years of testing, planning and negotiation for commercial developers to absorb and accept the potential value of combining structured parking, transit, pedestrian streets and a mix of uses in the project's first phase, a significant step in implementing the vision of RidgeGate as an edge city. This sequence of diagrams shows the evolution of plans. (1) The starting point of the original plan was a typical suburban shopping center. (2) The next phase of the design moved the district toward a Main Street ambiance by cutting an east-west street through it, fronting stores along it and persuading Target to build a two-level parking structure (gray square at top) that will integrate it with a planned lifestyle retail center. (3) The pedestrian feel was deepened with an expansion of the district and a re-orientation of the stores to the streets instead of to the parking lots. (4) The final design integrates retail with institutions, urban parks and plazas and orients walkways to light rail, creating a true mixed-use district.

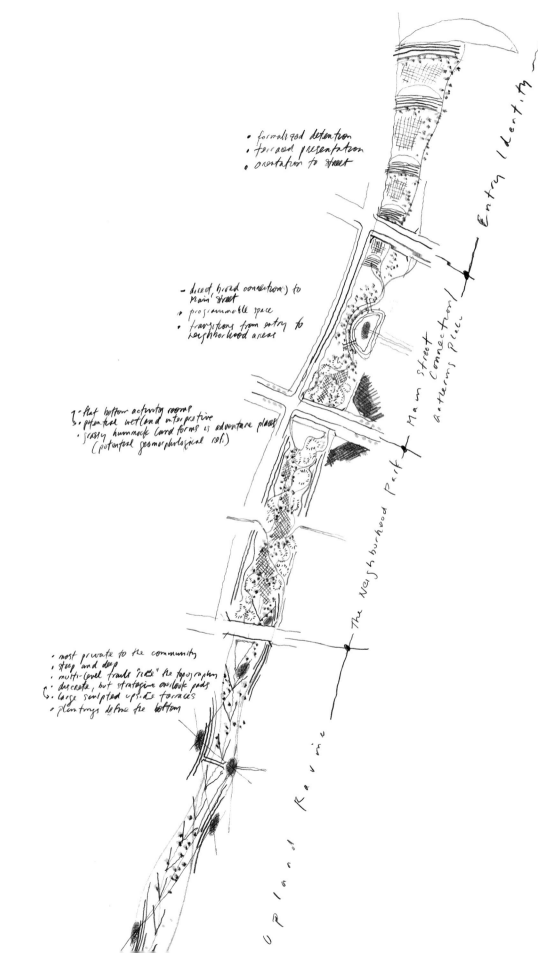

- formalized detention
- terraced presentation
- orientation to street

Entry Identity

- direct hard connection(s) to Main Street
- programmable space
- transitions from entry to neighborhood areas

Main Street Connection
Anthems Place

3. flat bottom activity rooms
3. potential wetland interpretive
- grassy hummock land forms as adventure places
(potential geomorphological ref.)

The Neighborhood Park

- most private to the community
- steep and deep
- multi-level trails "into" the topography
- discrete, but strategic overlook pads
3. large sculpted upside terraces
- plantings define the bottom

Upland Ravine

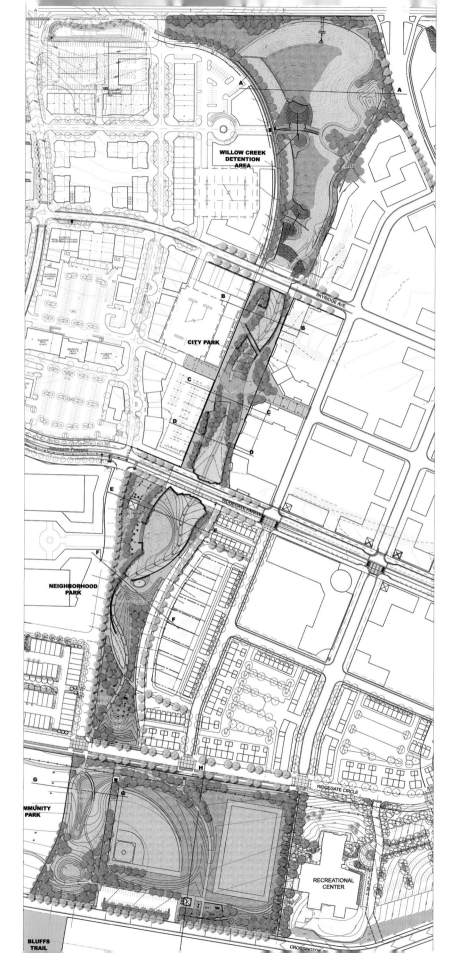

WILLOW CREEK DETENTION AREA

SKYRIDGE AVE

CITY PARK

RIDGEGATE PARKWAY

NEIGHBORHOOD PARK

COMMUNITY PARK

RIDGEGATE CIRCLE

RECREATIONAL CENTER

BLUFFS TRAIL

CROSSINGTON

a progression of architectural, programmed events

a progression of thematic landscape settings

The Willow Creek urban park is an amenity in the tradition of central city parks. It provides a promenade for commercial and residential buildings and active and passive recreation, and links the center to the bluffs' open space. Its core of riparian vegetation provides habitat for birds and small animals while it cleanses and returns surface water into the ground. High-density residential and ground-floor retail will both front directly on the park.

DILEMMA: Large-lot subdivisions with wells and septic tanks were destroying the environment, ambiance and sense of culture in Santa Fe County. No master plan existed to regulate or shape growth in the sector, which had continued uncontrolled over many years.

LEGACY GOALS:

Community
Collaborate with citizens, developers and officials to realize their common desire for smart growth, working together to set development guidelines for a large district and ensuring that residents will have the power to guide their own future.

Environment
Set aside half of the district as open space, preserving habitat and scenic assets and minimizing disruption of the land; conserve resources by harvesting runoff and using it to recharge groundwater and by orienting homes for solar heating in winter.

Economics
Negotiate a creative land deal that keeps housing prices low and use this to build a significantly dense and affordable mixed-use core for each village, optimizing land use and supporting the county with new tax revenue.

Art
Use natural systems for infrastructure, preserving the beauty of the arroyos and lining them with trails that make villages walkable; frame views to the distant mountains from village cores and the community's trails.

THESIS: By committing to the hard work of collaboration and bringing smart growth principles to fruition, citizens, government officials and developers can create a new pattern of development that will make wise use of the land and protect the local environment and culture.

CASE STUDY:
RANCHO VIEJO DE SANTA FE

Santa Fe, New Mexico

Unusual alliance sets a new course for development in Santa Fe

Overview

The "amenity migrants" drawn to Santa Fe have consumed the landscape with large homes on huge suburban lots. County officials and developers in the city's primary growth corridor challenged that trend when they teamed up to create a new pattern of villages that accommodate growth, preserve the landscape and conserve natural resources. A unique collaboration of developer, government and designers is producing a new settlement pattern guided by principles of community and sustainability on 11,000 acres in Santa Fe County. The design of Rancho Viejo allows the natural environment to determine the pattern of development and leaves half the land as open space for wildlife habitat, aquifer recharge and scenic value. Each of 10 proposed mixed-use villages is clustered around a central plaza in the tradition of early New Mexican settlements, and each includes affordable housing and promotes resource conservation.

History /Context

In recent decades, Santa Fe, New Mexico, has come under increasing growth pressures and fallen prey to indifferent suburban development. While the compact, traditional pattern of old Santa Fe has attracted many "amenity migrants," these transplants often choose to live on 2- to 10-acre lots in large suburban subdivisions — the very antithesis of what drew them to the area in the first place and a trend that is devastating the region's beauty, natural resources and culture.

CASE STUDY

The careful planning of this sensitive terrain perserved its essential character from un-managed growth.

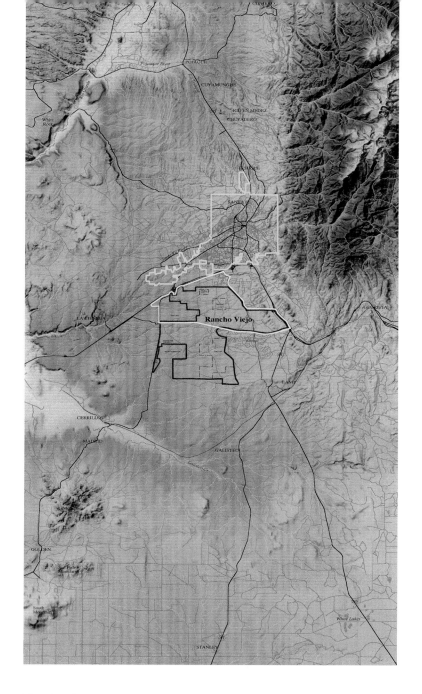

The city of Santa Fe (outlined in blue) is bordered on three sides by hilly and mountainous terrain, large-lot subdivisions and federal lands. The only land capable of accommodating Santa Fe's growth is the corridor to the south, where the Rancho Viejo landholding (outlined in red) and the Santa Fe Community College District (outlined in yellow) both lie.

In 1996, Santa Fe's city planning department proposed reducing growth pressures outside of the city by creating infill development within the city, but voters rejected the idea. Since mountains and suburban development embrace the city on three sides, its most suitable growth option was an open corridor to the south. Local smart-growth advocacy groups had long considered this area "the poster child for sprawl," since 2,000 acres of it had already been zoned for large lots with individual wells and septic tanks. In an effort to foster innovative development in the corridor, county planners had embarked on a new growth management plan for the area. About two-thirds of this area belonged to Rancho Viejo de Santa Fe, a group of landowners who had considered developing for several years but who loved the land and wanted to make sure it would be well cared for.

Process

"Collaboration" was the watchword for the project from the beginning. The longtime owners of the land had talked informally with a developer, SunCor of Phoenix, for several years about how they might work together to maximize the special potential of Rancho Viejo. They finally agreed to proceed. In 1996,

to ensure the development would meet their goals for the environment and community, the owners asked Design Workshop to lead a workshop with the developer to establish a vision for the site, which they would then use as the basis for the contract to sell the land and begin development. The collaboration broadened significantly when planner Jack Kolkmeyer of Santa Fe County visited the vision workshop. In the chaos of tracing-paper plans, sketches and idea cards, he recognized the same emphases on the land system and village pattern that had been initial ideas in the county's new growth management plan. This early recognition of common vision spurred a commitment to collaborate in lieu of the typically adversarial relationship between developers and government.

The weeklong workshop produced a vision plan that protected the aesthetic and environmental values of the land, clustered development in villages in the tradition of New Mexican settlements, made a priority of affordable housing and designed a native landscape that conserved water. It also created an innovative business deal that made the project possible.

The owners realized that they faced many hurdles, including hefty front-end investment, a small market, a difficult political environment and high commu-

CASE STUDY

nity expectations for affordability, economic development and sustainability. They realized the futility of trying to force the pace of development beyond what the market could comfortably support or what was politically acceptable. To mitigate the potentially heavy initial development costs, the owners and developer crafted an agreement that priced the value of the land based on the number of units developed instead of the cost per acre. This allowed the land to be purchased and developed one village at a time, with the land purchase price figured as a percentage of each home and commercial parcel sold. SunCor would be able to reduce its early debt and carrying costs, which would help keep prices low and provide flexibility to respond to market and political changes. The Rancho Viejo partners would get a greater long-term return by participating in developed land values. By tying the land price to finished homes, the deal also eliminated the land cost for parks and open space.

The central question was how to make this happen in a skeptical political environment and untested market. The developer decided to create what was essentially a demonstration village that would test the practicality of this vision.

Rancho Viejo Village

A previously approved large-lot subdivision plan was consolidated to create the first 350-unit village. The county supported this change by granting administrative approval without requiring the surrounding Rancho Viejo property to be planned first. The village was designed and developed as a freestanding settlement with no guarantee of zoning for the entire property or future villages. Infrastructure was designed and financed to stand alone if necessary without income from future development phases.

The land determined the size and shape of the village. The Rancho Viejo landscape has three major landforms: flat meadows, hillsides and arroyos, or dry gulches. The arroyos are the heart of the area's beauty; they also serve as wildlife habitat corridors and their pervious soils help recharge the aquifer beneath the district. The design of the village left these usually dry drainages as open space, concentrating the highest density of village development on the flat meadows and allowing very limited development where it can be tucked into forested hillsides. This kept a large portion of the land as open space, which became a major village amenity.

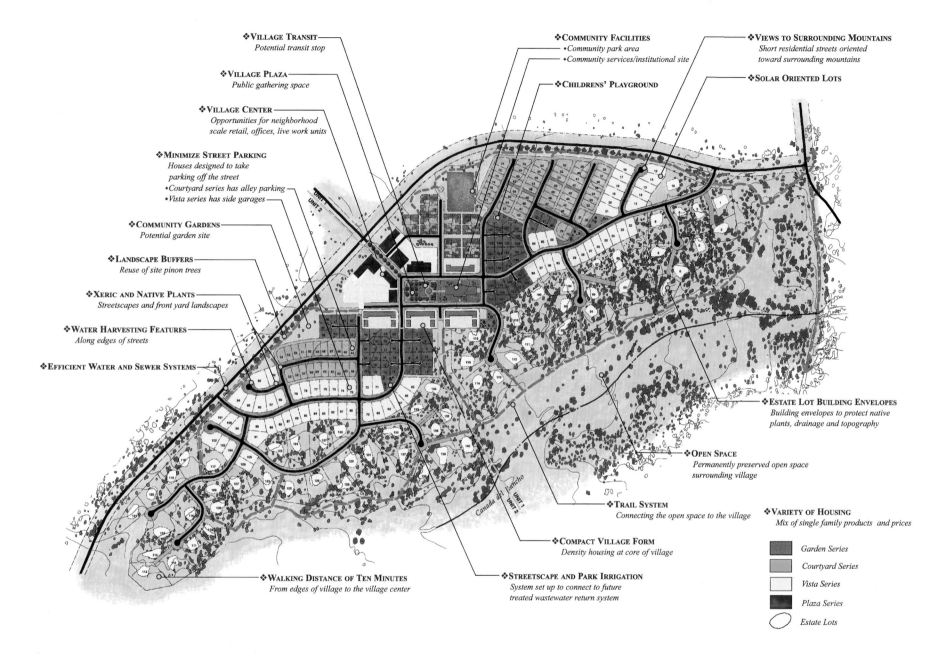

❖ **VILLAGE TRANSIT**
Potential transit stop

❖ **VILLAGE PLAZA**
Public gathering space

❖ **VILLAGE CENTER**
Opportunities for neighborhood scale retail, offices, live work units

❖ **MINIMIZE STREET PARKING**
Houses designed to take parking off the street
 • *Courtyard series has alley parking*
 • *Vista series has side garages*

❖ **COMMUNITY GARDENS**
Potential garden site

❖ **LANDSCAPE BUFFERS**
Reuse of site pinon trees

❖ **XERIC AND NATIVE PLANTS**
Streetscapes and front yard landscapes

❖ **WATER HARVESTING FEATURES**
Along edges of streets

❖ **EFFICIENT WATER AND SEWER SYSTEMS**

❖ **COMMUNITY FACILITIES**
 • *Community park area*
 • *Community services/institutional site*

❖ **CHILDRENS' PLAYGROUND**

❖ **VIEWS TO SURROUNDING MOUNTAINS**
Short residential streets oriented toward surrounding mountains

❖ **SOLAR ORIENTED LOTS**

❖ **ESTATE LOT BUILDING ENVELOPES**
Building envelopes to protect native plants, drainage and topography

❖ **OPEN SPACE**
Permanently preserved open space surrounding village

❖ **TRAIL SYSTEM**
Connecting the open space to the village

❖ **VARIETY OF HOUSING**
Mix of single family products and prices

Garden Series
Courtyard Series
Vista Series
Plaza Series
Estate Lots

❖ **COMPACT VILLAGE FORM**
Density housing at core of village

❖ **WALKING DISTANCE OF TEN MINUTES**
From edges of village to the village center

❖ **STREETSCAPE AND PARK IRRIGATION**
System set up to connect to future treated wastewater return system

(opposite) The Rancho Viejo land system consists of three primary land types (top to bottom): arroyos, or dry gulches, that are preserved in open space; wooded hillsides where low-density residential development is tucked into existing forests; and flat, upland meadows that are the primary village areas.

(above) The master plan for the first village transitions from a core density of apartments and town homes to single-family detached estate homes along the edges, where the land transitions to hillsides and arroyos. More than half the land is left as open space.

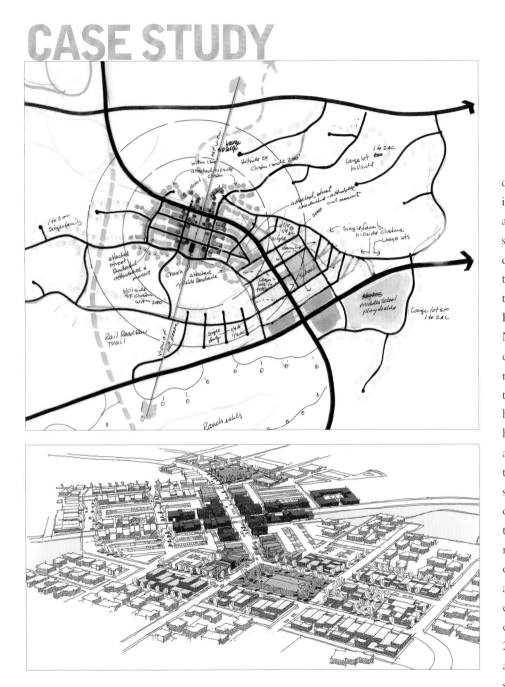

(top) An early diagram testing the Windmill Ridge Village program on the land.

(bottom) The Rancho Viejo Village center plans established a framework of plazas and pedestrian streets for commercial uses, live-work housing and high-density residential development that will be added as the community and market evolve.

The village was designed to create community and conserve resources. It is configured to save water and energy and to promote inclusion of a wide spectrum of economic levels. Its design draws on the centralizing features of traditional New Mexican settlements that evolved from the Law of the Indies, Philip II's manifesto for settling the New World. The village radiates from a central plaza surrounded by two-story residences and commercial and institutional uses. Density transitions from this high level in the village center to estate homes tucked into the wooded hillsides at the village edge. No home is more than a five-minute walk from the trail system that runs through the arroyo open space. Residential streets are positioned to offer both views of distant mountains and a solar orientation that optimizes energy conservation. Currently, about 70 percent of the homes have an energy-efficient orientation with no compromise to the community plan. In 2004, Rancho Viejo began constructing all homes to Build America energy standards. The village plan included eight different residence types, from townhouses, lofts and two-story live/work units to single-family residences of varying sizes. The cost of the first homes ranged from $100,000 to $450,000.

Construction of the first village began in 2001 and sales were so successful that a second village, Windmill Ridge, was begun in 2003. At full build-out over 20 years, the entire Rancho Viejo community is expected to provide as many as 19,000 new units of housing.

The College District Plan

The demonstration village did more than create a new community. It helped county planners persuade elected officials and the public to create the 17,000-acre Santa Fe Community College District and make a comprehensive master plan for it based on the fundamental principles at work in Rancho Viejo. Land analysis for the first village established the principles that would become the foundation for the College District Plan, the foremost of which was to preserve all of its arroyos and make half of the entire district open space.

Again, collaboration was the rule. Landowners, citizens, community and environmental advocates served on a district planning committee that worked together for 18 months to create the plan and its supporting development codes. Much of the money that developers would normally have spent planning their own individual projects was directed instead into forming the College District Plan. Four major developers in the district contributed planning, engi-

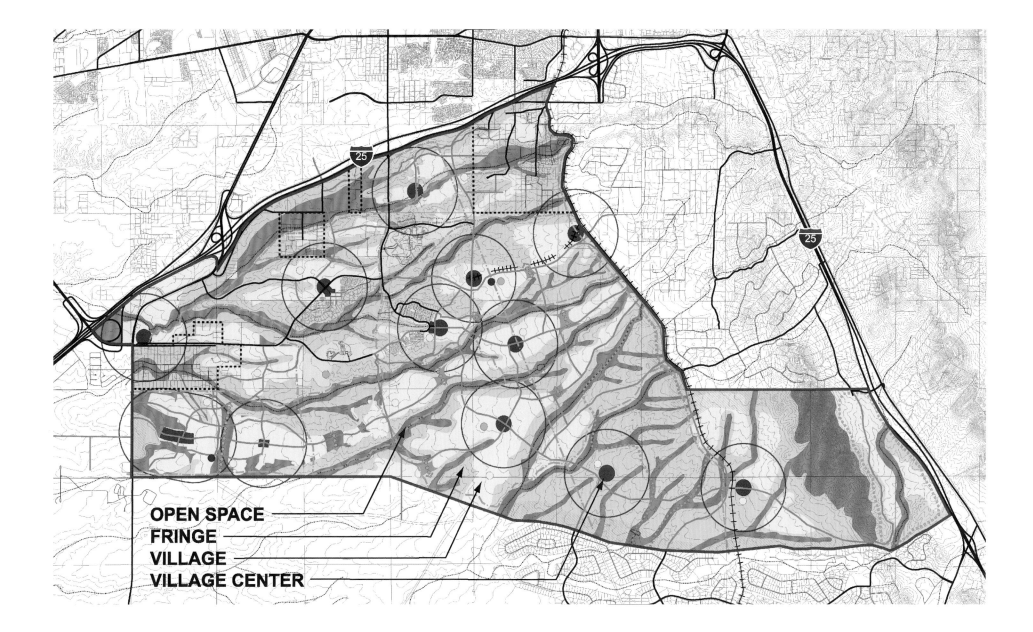

OPEN SPACE
FRINGE
VILLAGE
VILLAGE CENTER

The Santa Fe Community College District Plan, which serves as the master plan for Rancho Viejo, establishes the pattern of villages delineated by arroyo open-space corridors.

CASE STUDY

A water plan for future generations

Other Water Sources

open Space

Recycled Water

other uses

Construction Water Re-use

-ARROYO-
Natural Aquifer Re-charge zone

Advanced Treatment Plant

Water Tank

Rancho Viejo

Parks and Plazas Irrigation Re-use

well

Water re-use, re-charge and conservation
Santa Fe Community College District.

Return clean water to Aquifer

Clean water injection

Infiltration Ponds

SUSTAINABLE AQUIFER THROUGH RESOURCE MANAGEMENT

(opposite) Community development requires the kind of process thinking that characterized the creation of Columbia, Maryland. The Community Development Matrix is a visual representation to help keep track of progress, whether activities occur simultaneously or out of sequence. Elements of the process run across the top and are tracked through various scales of decisions along the left. This keeps the project solidly embedded in its largest-scale context at all times and also recognizes that the design process is similar at every level. Every square on the matrix represents a technical discipline operating in relative isolation; the lines between the drawings represent communication barriers. A process that recognizes these and integrates the elements and scales of design has the potential to remove these barriers. The drawings and images here help reveal and clarify the complexity of the Rancho Viejo process.

(above) The water-cycle drawing illustrates Rancho Viejo's holistic plan for water conservation, showing the cycle of water conservation and aquifer recharge and describing a vision for water use in non-technical, commonsense terms.

neering and legal services, master plans and working papers, with Rancho Viejo de Santa Fe, the developer of Rancho Viejo, leading these contributions.

The first village proved to other developers that land stewardship and village development can be profitable. It gave the county commissioners the confidence to require the new approach without fear of stifling economic growth. It also served as a tangible reference for the district planning committee during long debates on issues such as connectivity, density, floor-area ratios and mixed-use centers.

To keep the process as open and objective as possible, the county brought in a third party to lead the group through its collaborative decision-making process. This allowed county planners to shed the typical role as neutral mediators, openly advocate the planning principles in the comprehensive plan and sell the county's positions on issues like the environment, water conservation, affordable housing and creating density.

The result of the process was a plan for the College District that provides zoning for 12 villages on 17,000 acres, with the land determining the community pattern and land uses. Fifty percent of the district is dedicated to open space that preserves steep hillsides and arroyos, guarding the district's scenic value, hab-

itat and aquifer. Level, open meadows are zoned as village areas whose boundaries are delineated by arroyos and whose character emulates traditional New Mexican villages. The plan encourages density by establishing minimum residential densities in the village and minimum floor-area ratios to ensure building mass in village centers. The College District Plan also mandates affordable housing, water conservation and a balance of jobs with homes.

Rewards

Together, Rancho Viejo and the College District Plan demonstrate a process and product that are alternatives to sprawling large-lot subdivisions in the county. In the course of creating the district plan, planning committee members created a list of 84 sustainability principles that covered design, environment, resource conservation, economics and governance. At completion, the plan included principles, plans and standards that support 65 of these. Provisions are in place to address the remaining principles as infrastructure and human capacity allow.

Of the development's resource-sustaining practices, such as energy efficiency, "green" building practices and in-progress plans for public transit, Rancho Viejo's water-conservation plan

CASE STUDY

The drainage system at Rancho Viejo utilizes the natural cleaning power of nature to remove contaminants as water infiltrates into the ground and the aquifer. Drainage diagrams (upper right and lower right) served to educate the developer about the advantages of water harvesting and natural drainage, which are now standard operating procedure in the community.

(above) Cisterns that capture roof drainage for irrigation are provided as a standard feature for every new Rancho Viejo home.

(opposite) Irrigation from Rancho Viejo's household graywater systems combines with a palette of drought-tolerant grasses and flowers to produce lush domestic landscapes.

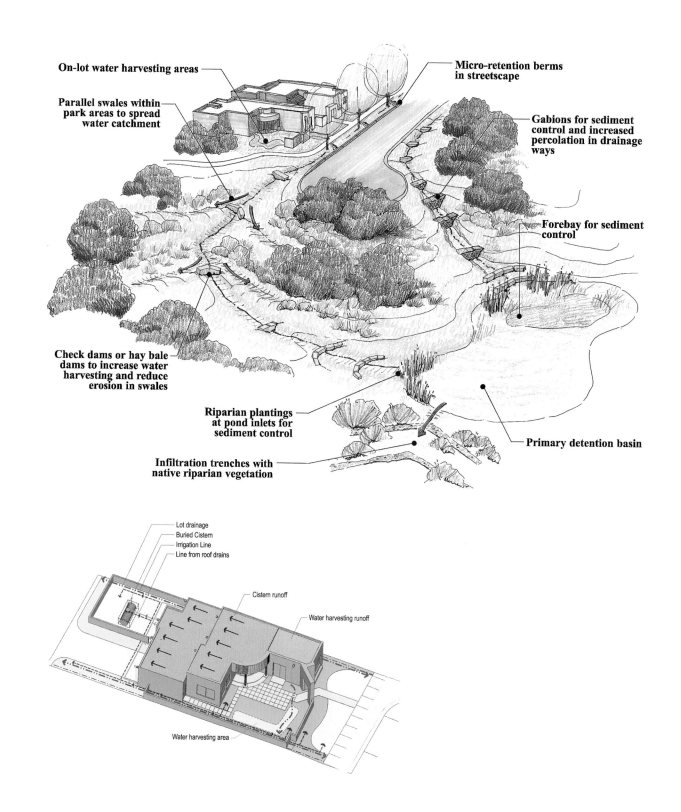

On-lot water harvesting areas

Micro-retention berms in streetscape

Parallel swales within park areas to spread water catchment

Gabions for sediment control and increased percolation in drainage ways

Forebay for sediment control

Check dams or hay bale dams to increase water harvesting and reduce erosion in swales

Riparian plantings at pond inlets for sediment control

Primary detention basin

Infiltration trenches with native riparian vegetation

Lot drainage
Buried Cistern
Irrigation Line
Line from roof drains

Cistern runoff

Water harvesting runoff

Water harvesting area

has shown the most success so far. In 2002, domestic water conservation at Rancho Viejo alone realized a 33 percent savings over the county's already stringent water-use limits. Fully occupied homes at Rancho Viejo used an average of 0.18 acre-feet of water per year, as compared with the 0.25 acre-feet allocated to water users by Santa Fe County. (By comparison, the average home in Phoenix uses 0.71 acre-feet of water per year.) In March 2003, Rancho Viejo became the first major new community in the nation to provide, as a standard feature of every home, underground cisterns that capture roof runoff for irrigation and evaporative coolers. The plan also reduces water use through an innovative system of natural drainage and water harvesting and the planting of native landscapes that are nurtured by treated-effluent irrigation. The Rancho Viejo water-management plan and wastewater treatment system are designed to preserve the aquifer's current level for the next 100 years by reinjecting it with treated wastewater, which will be further cleansed by natural processes.

Rancho Viejo's success in water management has persuaded officials to consider groundwater recharge, and in 2004, the State of New Mexico awarded Rancho Viejo de Santa Fe $500,000 to test groundwater injection in the state's first injection well.

Conclusion

The experience at Rancho Viejo demonstrates that the creation of trust among people is fundamental to the community development process, and that building a culture of working together may be more important and more lasting than the resulting streets, buildings and villages. The process of an enduring relationship may make communities and the lives of residents better in a broader way than would simply making a single place.

PROJECT CREDITS

PLANNING/DESIGN: Design Workshop, Inc.
  PICs: Joe Porter, Faith Okuma, Kathy Bogaski, Greg Witherspoon
  Project team: Don Ensign, Charles Ware, Claudia Meyer-Horn, Michael Larson, Amanda Szot, Anna Mondragon-Metzger, Bruce Trujillo, Cameron Owen, Sara Lillyblade, Joseph Charles

CLIENT: Rancho Viejo de Santa Fe, Inc.

Residential architects: Eric Naslund (Studio E Architects), Terry Linderoth (Linderoth Architects)

Commerical architects: Nelson Architects

Signage consultant: Carlie Barnhart - CWH Graphics

CASE STUDY

Densities at Rancho Viejo transition from two-story town homes at the village core to neighborhoods of single-family residences, with estate homes tucked into hillsides at the periphery of the community. Reused domestic graywater is channeled into bioswales and other systems to irrigate the landscapes immediately around housing and village common areas.

CASE STUDY

(this page) Comprehensive water-conservation measures have allowed Rancho Viejo to use urban runoff for common area irrigation while beating Santa Fe's stringent water restrictions by a sizable percentage while still supporting lush and colorful domestic landscapes.

(opposite) Half the land is left as open space, which is threaded with an extensive system of trails.

LEGACY

4 Connection

ESSAY

Todd Johnson, Design Workshop's chief design officer, offers his insights into the importance of connecting the assets in and around a project in order to leverage its value to both the client and the community. The projects featured in this chapter cover a spectrum of types in which connection has proven to be the key to success and a foundation for nourishing towns and cities over the long term.

PROJECT DISCUSSIONS

Kierland Commons: Taking on Arizona's climate challenges, this plan creates a highly successful mixed-use complex.

Little Nell: Clearing away scattered buildings at the base of Aspen Mountain connects people with nature.

Lowry Parks: Five varied outdoor experiences foster social engagement and link residents to Lowry's town center.

Cherokee Redevelopment: Plans for a former industrial site envision a transit-oriented urban sector in the center of Denver.

IN-DEPTH ACCOUNT

Riverfront Park: Reconnecting a former rail yard to downtown and surrounding neighborhoods creates a dynamic new district.

Connection allows us to participate in the wider meaning of the place in which we live.

AN ESSAY BY TODD JOHNSON

The connection of people to each other and the mixing of their ideas and their collective inspiration is the strongest creative and problem-solving force in civilization. As in the carved circuits inside a silicon chip or the hallways and classrooms of a school, connections combine information and conduct operations that yield very useful outcomes. Connection creates newness: new experiences, new relationships, new perspectives.

Great towns and cities are built on systems of centers and connections that offer a wealth of experiences — natural and human-built, confining and expansive, sacred and profane, light and dark, social and desolate, rich and poor, humorous and sad. Great places to live embrace the natural world, draw people in with compelling forms, foster interaction, enliven encounters and create a broad range of value for a wide array of people.

When nature or opportunities compel us to travel through such a system, we help build the local culture. Meaning accrues from this movement and exchange, the weaving together of people and their experiences. For those who travel these paths, connectivity has a measurable value that is more than the sum of a single encounter. It allows us to construct meaning in our lives, to encounter the human in ourselves by seeing it in others and to participate in the wider meaning of the place in which we live. Great urban design creates the context for this to happen: It creates the structure of connections and centers from which the soul of the city evolves.

Connection and City-Building

People gather in order to exchange ideas and commodities. Seven thousand years of city-building have resulted from this desire to connect and exchange. Culture is the byproduct of this exchange, the coincidental cross-fertilization of ideas that results from gathering. The most fundamental activity within this public domain is the encounter of two people, an incident that builds the value of the city by creating a culture of trust between people bound by a common geography. From that meeting of just two people, the city houses progressively larger scales of gathering, drawing people together to stimulate institutions that focus cooperative activity and dialogue. Networks of information and systems of movement grow from the most basic encounters and these build the galaxy of

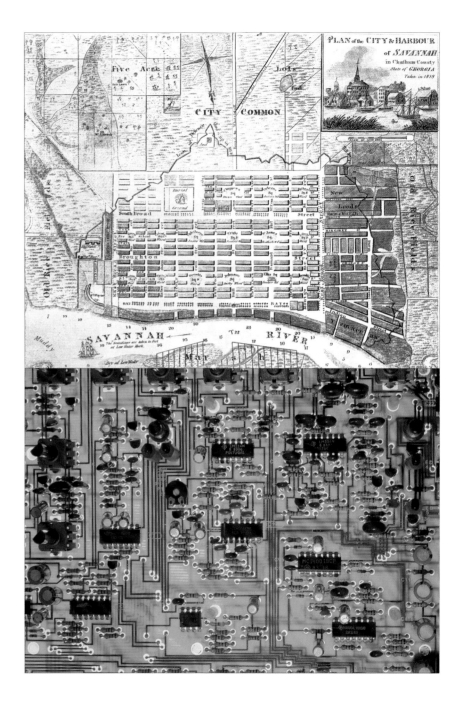

The grid of an early town plan for Savannah, Georgia, resonates with an image of a circuit board from a computer. They have in common a hierarchy of connections that feed and sustain the larger system.

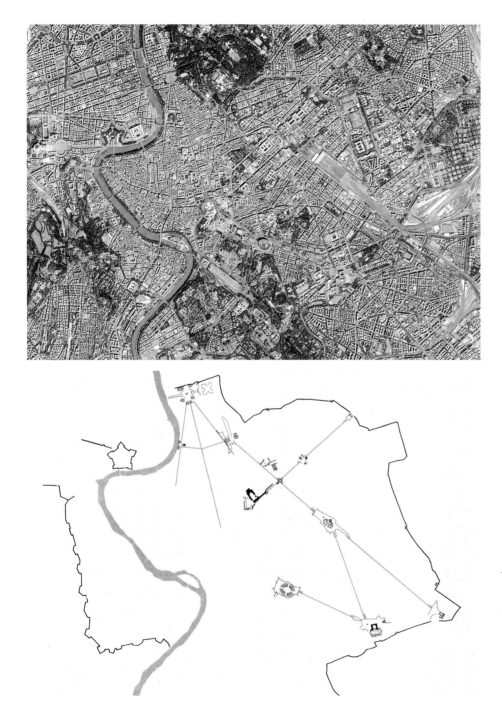

city life. The more choices that cities and towns offer, the more collisions of information they yield — the more conflicts, more stimulating gossip, more scientific discoveries, better art, stronger economies, a greater life presence and a greater production of social capital.

Pope Sixtus V understood the value of centers and connection when in the late 16th century he set out to restructure Rome to give additional value and meaning to districts and destinations within the city. Since the fall of the Roman Empire, the city had grown haphazardly, resulting in a lack of structure and identifiable form. The territory of the Vatican itself was disconnected from its surroundings and lacked the formal clarity that masters Bernini and Michelangelo would later give it. By adding a series of plazas, each one centered on an obelisk and connected to others, Sixtus gave people reasons to move, meet and make exchanges.

By today's standards, Sixtus' intervention would appear shallow, but it worked — by promoting new movement patterns and encouraging the creation of architecture responsive to these altered patterns. This would eventually serve as a foundation for such significant destinations and districts as the Piazza del Popolo and the Spanish Steps. These in turn developed and stimulated specialization and movement, ultimately resulting in more complex urban forms and one of the world's most layered cities.

Connection, Meaning and Value

In 1970, Mortimer Adler published *The Time of Our Lives* at a time when the groundwork for current urban thinking was being laid. Like Jane Jacobs and other writers and theoreticians in the 1960s and 1970s, he sought to identify the sources for meaning in a post-modern existence. Adler concluded that fulfillment can be achieved only through developing and integrating the compulsory and discretionary sides of our lives and that we suffer if we emphasize one over the other.

Cities are the same: Their public domain must interweave these two aspects in order to be places where people feel they can make something of their lives. The energy produced at the interface of these two forces is the fuel of success and this can be collected and circulated through the city's system of gathering places. This interplay between discretionary and compulsory can produce both the meaning and value that energize our day-to-day, week-to-week, year-to-year existence. When people consider changing their towns or cities, some people may automatically object to open space, plazas and parks (discretionary) as a luxury, while others will react negatively to compulsory (roadways, buildings, commercial and industrial districts). What both factions overlook is the richness that flows naturally from the co-mingling of the two.

Connections are the key: They are predictable contributors to high levels of activity, which in turn signify and foster conditions for business success and for the development of social capital. Of all factors in urban design, these are perhaps the most tangible and the most controllable. Just as a critical mass of mixed uses in the correct proportions is the most quantifiable measure for predictable success in place-making, just as traffic counts can be relied on for predicting retail success, we can use connection as a measure for the success of centers and destinations.

The Challenges to Urban Systems

Districts, towns and cities that achieve a high level of connectivity attract people and investment. Rather than collections of buildings, they are organisms that grow around the activities and value of the public domain, their ambience built on a framework of active links and hubs. But many obstacles stand in the way of creating such places.

Powers that finance or regulate such place-making efforts may be unwilling or unable to fund the weaving of the connections and creation of centers necessary to making great places. They may resort to standard solutions that are safe and easy to manage or wage a battle over greater or lesser amounts of open space relative to the size of development. There is also a propensity in the real estate community to invest in proven formulas that may not translate well from one application to the next, an impulse that ignores the pattern of destinations and links specific to that time and place. This desire to franchise successful models is futile, a risk almost guaranteed to fail, and one that works against the creation of meaning.

Those who care about and participate in place-making seek to better understand a rational approach to creating meaningful places, but the

(opposite) This comparison of an aerial photograph and Edmund Bacon's diagram of Rome sheds light on how the city of Rome is organized around destinations and connections established centuries ago by Pope Sixtus V.

(above) The chaos of human life is reflected in the layout of our most ancient cities, revealing the layers that were added incrementally or cleared and rebuilt in grand gestures. Because of their density, cities require the efficient channeling of people, but their underlying systems of gathering and linking are what energize them.

Hubs, like Grand Central Station, are critical
to the functioning of the city, but they also
bring beauty and a fleeting sense of community to the urban dweller's existence.

question of making a great city is not well-served by theory. Even ideas, if rigidly held, may work against making lively districts and towns. Efforts to predict, control or otherwise create static environments are bound to fail. Too much emphasis on issues of style or highly formalized patterns is unlikely to succeed without strategies that emphasize connection and meaning.

The task of shaping development through connectedness is complicated by how much information is available and the level of thought and open-mindedness. Many factors challenge the process of transforming a site into a meaningful place, including environmental, political, social, aesthetic and financial circumstances. Designers and developers encounter thousands of variables, not the least of which is the hundreds of individuals who participate in the making of a single place.

Complexity appears in deeper and more subtle forms as well. Connectivity refers not only to built systems but also to the links between galaxies of information that make up towns and cities. When a planner or designer intervenes in the life of a city or town, it must be done within the systems of connection that already exist. The synthesizing process of bringing these into relationship with each other is one of the most important steps in great design and place-making, and one of its most formidable. To be able to fashion an effective order out of this complexity requires the discipline of thinking simultaneously about aesthetics, the natural world, the people who live there and the investment in the place. A pattern that encourages highly active use balances the number of centers and connections against their character and aesthetics, requiring buildings to frame views, to put people on the street, to externalize their functions onto the sidewalk and to orient to the public domain in a responsible fashion, with sympathetic massing and scaling. Sometimes, it is possible to make an extraordinary difference with a single intervention. One ceremonial gesture may turn a neglected utilitarian object into an amenity. Or it may turn an activity like shopping into a civic experience and social capital that helps shape a sense of community. Or connection may push outward from a site to seek the assets of a city, whether those are destinations, physical features or more ephemeral qual-

ities. The challenge is to draw from the site and context as much energy as possible and to use it to enrich the spaces that make up a neighborhood, a district, a town or a city.

The Power of Connection

Urban life stimulates our minds, brings new things into our lives, melds diverse contributions and creates a forum for ideas and opportunities for discovery. Without the natural diversity of city life, dysfunctions abound, including civic self-centeredness or provincialism, which can result in racism, political aggression, non-critical thinking and limited cultural development. This is recognized in *The Death and Life of Great American Cities*, where Jane Jacobs quotes theologian Paul J. Tillich on the power of cities:

> *By its nature the metropolis provides what otherwise could be given only by traveling; namely, the strange. Since the strange leads to questions and undermines familiar tradition, it serves to elevate reason to ultimate significance…There is no better proof of this fact than the attempts of all totalitarian authorities to keep the strange from their subjects…The big city is sliced into pieces, each of which is observed, purged and equalized. The mystery of the strange and the critical rationality of men are both removed from the city.*

Great towns and cities continually give us new experiences, drawing people from many quarters to common destinations. In these migrations, we confront one another in all of our differences, a process that stimulates and challenges our humanity and our creativity.

The danger in landscape architecture has always been to confuse the composition of landscapes with their greater value for gathering people. Beauty cannot by itself connect us with others — design must also make it possible for us to engage with each other. It is the obligation of planning and design to maximize the building of social capital by configuring cities so that they stimulate the gathering and movement of people. When landscape and urban design achieve this, they have set the stage for the building of meaningful lives.

Stifling heat and an auto-dependent culture means that most shopping areas in the metro Phoenix area are indoor, air-conditioned environments. An unusual plan allowed the developer to create an exciting outdoor retail destination that is one of the most successful complexes in the country.

PROJECT DISCUSSION: KIERLAND COMMONS

Scottsdale, Arizona

An innovative district supports summer shopping in Scottsdale

In 1994, the designers began the process of creating the first truly successful outdoor shopping experience in the Valley of the Sun, on 40 acres set aside to create a commercial retail center in an exclusive 730-acre planned community that began development 25 years ago just northeast of Phoenix.

The team found the primary challenge in creating the development master plan, schematic design, design guidelines and entitlement documents was designing an outdoor shopping environment that could be used year-round, even during the fiercely hot Arizona summers. Formulating principles that would maximize comfort, the designers rejected typical suburban shopping-center style, with its large expanses of asphalt for wide streets and parking lots and instead embraced an urban configuration that would compress streets and

plazas and encourage outdoor use. They kept development dense to minimize walking distance and made streets narrow to fit both cars and people, fronting the streets with buildings but focusing the complex around a plaza that could serve as a social and cultural center for this suburban area. They also expanded the original idea of a destination retail complex to include a broad mix of uses, including retail, residential and offices, to create an urban district that had the power to reduce commuting.

The design's framework diagram supports compact, dense development as a pattern that fosters an animated, tightly spaced retail environs, while also cutting sun exposure to the street. The pedestrian-oriented setting positions the mix of uses within walking distance of each other. The district's pedestrian ambiance is further cultivated through

The central plaza at Kierland Commons is a quiet gathering place in the center of the complex, energized by active retail, office and residential uses in the surrounding spaces but far enough away from them to give visitors a peaceful sanctuary.

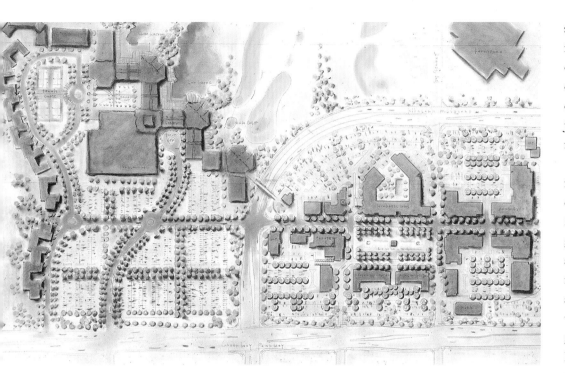

(above) Kierland Commons' central gathering space is the pop-jet fountain plaza, which lies at the center of this mixed-use complex along the lushly landscaped central spine. Prominent among the assets that support the project's success is its link to a nearby resort hotel, seen in the sketch master plan, which was improved upon to include strategies for structured parking.

(opposite) Narrowed streets reconcile auto and pedestrian uses, keeping the district lively but livable.

strict development controls and phased introduction of structured parking. To create a sense of destination within the complex, the designers centered the retail district on a plaza furnished with pop-jet fountains that would mitigate the region's harsh desert climate for visitors.

The result is an attractive and comfortable 38-acre, outdoor public-space destination that comprises a 535,000-square-foot mixed-use program, including a golf museum, a theater, a 130-room hotel, retail and restaurants, offices, residential units and a town center park. These are positioned within a traditional downtown setting graced with climate enhancement. Retailers are dispersed throughout the district in one-, two- and three-story buildings facing the project's main street and interior roadways. The fronting of shops and restaurants on the lushly landscaped central plaza helps create an intimate gathering place at the heart of the project. Varied architecture and public spaces evoke a Main Street ambiance unlike any other retail complex in the region. The project's carefully developed design guidelines ensure continuity of quality while encouraging a customized storefront for each tenant.

Retail expansion was completed in mid-2004, but residential sales had resounding success, substantially out-performing original expectations and prompting a second round of residential construction. Kierland Commons has won awards as a special destination commercial plaza that promotes pedestrian movement, reduces dependency on cars and connects with surrounding neighborhoods. The project has also been praised for its environmental excellence as a model for livable communities. The International Council of Shopping Centers, the global trade association of the shopping center industry, designated Kierland Commons Arizona's only "lifestyle center."

PROJECT CREDITS

PLANNING/ SCHEMATIC DESIGN:
Design Workshop, Inc.
  PIC: Todd Johnson
  Planner: Jeff McMenimen

CLIENT: Woodbine Southwest Corporation

Design/construction documents: EDAW

The urban feel of the Kierland complex has fueled highly successful residential sales and made it a popular destination for both shopping and dining.

In 1985, the base of Aspen Mountain was cluttered with aging buildings that hindered skiers' passage, confused visitors and diminished visitors' experience of the high-country environs. The Aspen Skiing Company's decision to build a gondola was the impetus for a design that connects people with the mountain, the town and each other.

PROJECT DISCUSSION:
LITTLE NELL

Aspen, Colorado

New public space joins a resort town with its ski mountain

Aspen evolved from a mining town at the turn of the century to a simple ski area in the 1950s and finally to a year-round resort community that now hosts 1.4 million skiers a year. But in 1985, the base of Aspen Mountain was cluttered with 1950s-vintage buildings, including ski-area maintenance shops, surface parking lots, public lockers and food and beverage facilities that acted as a barrier between skiers and the mountain. Though the area became uncomfortably clogged with people during peak ski season, it offered no outdoor gathering places for skiers or local residents. Aging ski lifts contributed to the problem by keeping skiers waiting at the bottom of the hill for a 45-minute ride to the top of the mountain.

As the ski area's owners began to work with Design Workshop to plan for a high-speed gondola and a five-star

hotel at the base, the designers broadened the project to look at how these new features could be used to integrate the town with the ski resort. Aspen was a typical western town with a 19th-century grid. The mountain, originally used for mineral extraction, had been transformed over decades into a world-class recreational sports venue — one of several skiing venues in the Aspen area. The design team recognized that the proposed upgrades could be an opportunity to create a focus for the town, both a hub for local residents and a gateway that would give visitors a sense of arrival.

At the time, Little Nells Saloon was the après-ski bar and its deck was the social place to be after a day on the slopes — a tiny setting that was often wild with activity during the winter months. But Little Nells was also the sole public gathering place at the base

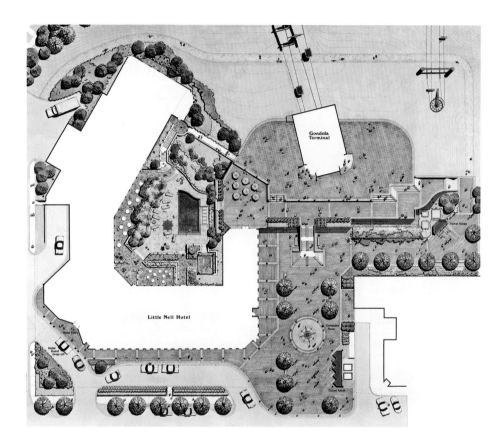

Gondola
Terminal

Ticket Kiosk

Little Nell Hotel

Hotel Entry

Hotel
Guest
Drop-off

Compass
Rose

Ticket Kiosk

(above) The master plan created a broad public plaza that directly connects the town with Aspen Mountain and its gondola, at top. The public spaces of the plaza and gondola were carefully positioned to separate them from the adjacent private spaces of the exclusive Little Nell Hotel.

(opposite) To create a larger site, the project pushed back the mountain, which used to end abruptly at the former Little Nells Saloon (upper left). The design team used early 3-D simulations (upper right) and illustratives (lower left) to allay residents' fears that the development would block views to Aspen Mountain. The design was approved with only minor adjustments (lower right).

of the mountain and was patronized by a very specific constituency, one that didn't necessarily include, appeal to or have room for families with children, for instance. There was a clear need for civic space that had a broader charm as well as a sense of permanence.

As the project evolved, the central design task of the Little Nell project became creating a public realm around the new gondola in a way that could be integrated with a private hotel and its proprietary outdoor spaces. The design would succeed if it could weave together the character and features of both sides through shared garden spaces, water elements, dining options, tempering of climate impact and the framing of views. But the design also needed to open the blocked access to the mountain with a progression of spaces that would both stimulate social interaction and link the town visually to the mountain.

Obstacles to success included both strong community sentiment and the severe constraints of the site itself. For two years, the designers worked hand-in-hand with residents and town officials to allay fears that the project would change the culture of Aspen or actually block views to the mountain. Anti-growth forces and an activist town council called for the plan to meet 25 stringent conditions to sustain the char-

acter of the town. This vigorous public input helped shape the design, whose final form makes about half the site public and half private, with the 92-room hotel on the east, the gondola terminal on the west and a broad central swath between them that directly links downtown with the ski area.

The program was so ambitious and the 2-acre property so steep that the design had to include excavating 100 feet of the toe of the slope and layering multiple uses on top of each other. The project's complexity is illustrated by its schematic design, which configured and integrated dozens of individual systems, including ski-trail grading, location of lift facilities, relocation of major utility infrastructure and building massing that preserves view corridors and access from the town to the mountain. The sequencing and layering of uses required that the hotel's private courtyard and swimming pool be created with rooftop construction above the hotel's conference space and parking structure. Ski-area maintenance facilities were also incorporated into the new structure, including a tunnel underneath the entire site from the hotel's loading docks to the gondola in order to get supplies to the Sun Deck restaurant at the top of the mountain. The newly created public space between the hotel

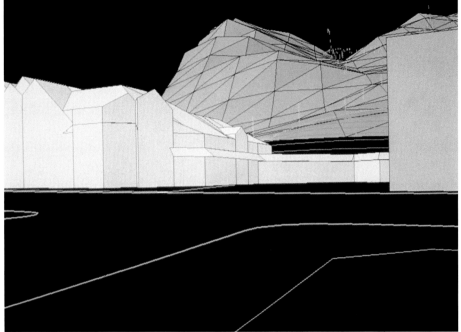

A model of the courtyard shows a view from the upper levels of the Little Nell Hotel, with green spaces separating it from the public spaces above and plantings that buffer the dining areas close to the building from the main pool area.

and gondola is car-free in order to foster a pedestrian ambience and is enlivened by such uses as restaurants and retail.

The success of the public plaza at Little Nell has helped define the qualities of public use for the resort industry. The design uses the central plaza to re-weave the urban fabric at this juncture of town and mountain, bringing the community into the space and easing the passage of as many as 2,000 skiers per hour at peak periods in winter, while maintaining a pedestrian scale appropriate for Aspen's lighter summer crowds. Cars, which formerly dominated the site, are excluded entirely, and in their place are pedestrian and skier amenities, including gondola access, food and beverage services, shopping, ski-lift ticket booths angled to keep lines out of the plaza and a large compass rose inset into the center of the plaza as a natural gathering spot that can be seen from the mountain. All spaces, as well as the stairs leading up to the gondola, are equipped with snow-melting technology, except for the gondola plaza where skiers need the snow as they come in off the hill. The high-speed gondola now brings skiers to the mountaintop in 12 minutes in an enclosed six-person car that can also be ridden to the bottom by skiers who want to avoid the tough terrain on the lower portion of the mountain.

The Little Nell Hotel is widely recognized in the industry as one of the most successful boutique hotels in the country, its courtyard amenities and its siting on the new public plaza a strong factor in this praise. In 2004, it earned Mobil's Five Star and the AAA Five Diamond awards, was named to the *Condé Nast Traveler* Gold List and was *Wine Spectator*'s Grand Award winner. It is the highest-rated ski resort on *Travel + Leisure*'s list of the 500 Greatest Hotels in the World and won the prestigious Andrew Harper's Award for best new small hotel.

PROJECT CREDITS

PLANNING/DESIGN: Design Workshop, Inc.
  PICs: Bill Kane (planning/approvals)
  Richard Shaw (design/landscape architecture)
  Project manager: Greg Ochis
  Landscape Architects: Scott Chomiak,
  Larry Hoetmer, Pat Carroll, Henry Thomas

CLIENT: Aspen Skiing Company

Water Feature Consultants: Howard Fields & Assoc.

Architect: Hagman Yaw Architects, Ltd.

Civil Engineer: Rea, Cassens & Associates, Inc.

Geotechnical Engineer: Chen and Associates

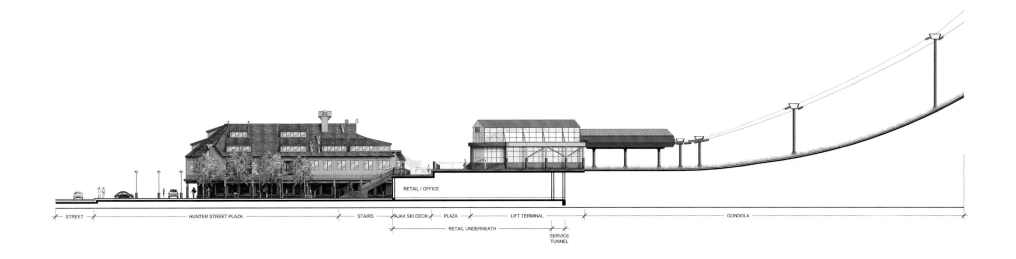

STREET — HUNTER STREET PLAZA — STAIRS — AJAX SKI DECK — PLAZA — LIFT TERMINAL — GONDOLA

RETAIL / OFFICE

RETAIL UNDERNEATH

SERVICE
TUNNEL

The complex layering of spaces on the tightly
constrained site was informed by numerous
studies, including cross-sections and 3-D
models, which show the relationship of the
private spaces of the hotel to the public
spaces of the plaza and gondola.

(this page) As the entrance to recreational skiing, the slope-side space is intensely public in contrast to the hotel courtyard, which is intended to be the private retreat domain of hotel guests. The design separates the two by level, orientation and landscaping, screening the courtyard from the active public spaces with full-grown conifers.

(opposite) At the bottom of the slope, skiers now have access to an après ski haven directly ahead, access to the Little Nell Hotel on the right and stairs down to the plaza and into town on the left.

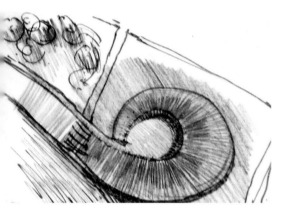

Redeveloped from a former air base, Lowry is a community with a commitment to creating interesting public spaces. The design of five different outdoor experiences offers a pedestrian network of destinations to draw people out of their homes and into the larger community.

PROJECT DISCUSSION:
LOWRY PARKS

Denver, Colorado

A system of provocative parks and public spaces fosters community

In 1994, Lowry Air Base, Denver's largest military site, was decommissioned after serving more than five decades as a training facility. A reuse plan devised for the 1,900-acre parcel proposed a diverse, mixed-use community complete with town center, schools, churches, a library, recreational amenities and housing that would emulate older neighborhoods nearby. Design Workshop implemented a 180-acre portion of the master plan for a proposed mixed-use development in the northwest quadrant, including creation of its parks.

To encourage movement, circulation and interaction in the newly created community, the designers revised block sizes, street hierarchies and parkways to promote pedestrian traffic to the town center. They then focused on creating a range of destinations, from expansive public spaces with active out-

door experiences to intimate nooks for passive uses. Though the two largest parks had been tentatively sited at neighborhood edges, the team repositioned them at the core of their respective residential areas and connected them with three fragments of land resulting from the overlap of urban grids, linking residential areas with the town center, offices, schools and retail.

PROJECT CREDITS

PLANNING/DESIGN: Design Workshop, Inc.
  PIC: Todd Johnson
  Project managers/designers: Kirby Hoyt, Heath Mizer, Elin Tidbeck, Isabel Fernandez, Allyson Mendenhall
  Landscape Architect: Kotchakorn Vora-Akhom

CLIENT: Lowry Redevelopment Authority
Master plan: Wenk Associates
Irrigation: Hydrosystem, Inc.
Civil engineer: URS
Structural engineer: Martin/Martin
Metal fabricator: NeoSource

CRESCENT PARK

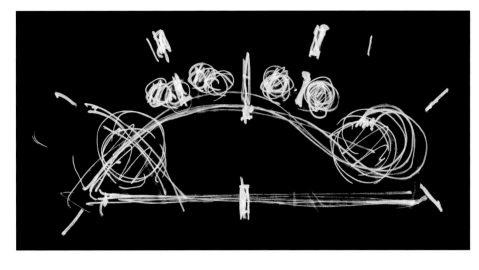

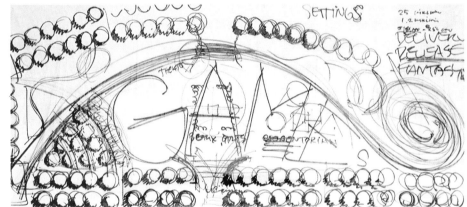

The initial design concept for this 8-acre space was an object-centered lawn with a pavilion in the center and separate "chambers" to either side. To create a more active and engaging space, the design positions a large open lawn for recreational uses at the heart of the park and surrounds it with a variety of experiences. An open plaza on the west contrasts sharply with a high contemplative mound on the east, while a promenade separates the lawn from a series of intimate settings along the north edge.

The western plaza features a playground and three pavilions for picnics, while the earthen mound is a naturalistic and contemplative setting with decomposed granite trails and native vegetation around a cluster of boulders, with views of the park, the neighborhood and the distant Rocky Mountains. Stone seating tiers on the north offer optimal sun exposure and views of the large central lawn, which is designed for sports activities.

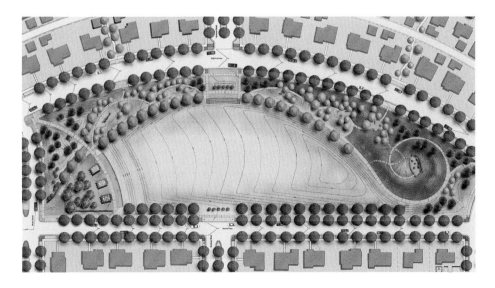

(left) Initial design concepts sought to break up the space and create a central destination, which people would be drawn to from many points of entry. The team evolved the design to allow community activities to serve as the space's focus instead. Small spaces were designed to edge the central sports lawn, with a high mound at one end commanding views into the distance.

(opposite, above) View from the park's eastern end shows the native grasses of the earthen mound in the foreground, with seating tiers for the game area at center and a small playground at upper left.

(opposite, bottom) Paths from the community intersect with the park's own pathways near the playground and picnic pavilions. From this area, visitors have views to the park's eastern mound.

SUNSET VILLAGE NEIGHBORHOOD PARK

This 2-acre park was sited a block away from the Lowry town center to serve both new and existing multifamily units and a scattering of new single-family homes. The rectangular tract was given a bottle shape by tapering the eastern end to form a gateway into the Sunset Village neighborhood. A high mound in native vegetation works with wide streetscape sections north and south of the taper to announce the entrance.

Because the park had to function as a detention pond in the event of a 100-year storm, the design slopes the space gradually as it moves west, using excavated material to create earthen mounds on the west and south. Native vegetation transitions to lawn for active play.

The western end of the park is formalized with a wide arc of stone stairs that acts as a retention wall and that is crowned by a semicircular, trellised plaza set against a backdrop of existing evergreens. From there, visitors can observe play in the grass below or look back across the park toward the entry mound. A traditional sidewalk runs along the north edge. On the south at the edge of an informal, narrow gravel path, the design tucks playground equipment under existing trees for shade.

An early plan (top) gives the general layout of the park, from the high mound of the narrow entrance to the semicircular plaza that overlooks a grassy bowl at the western end.

The park balances the formality of stone steps and the trellised pavilion with the intimacy of gravel paths and a palette of indigenous plants.

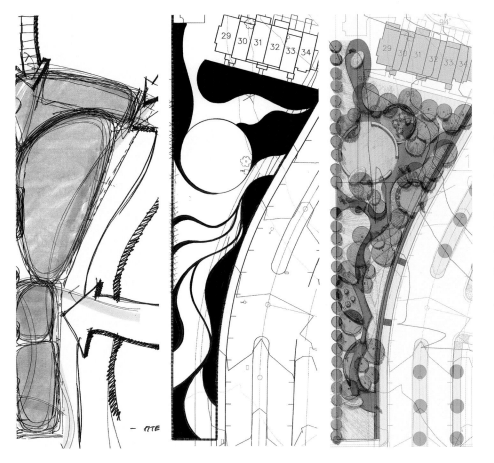

ROSLYN PARK

This angular, 1-acre space along the edge of a street serves as a connector between Crescent Park and the town center. The parcel begins at the south end as a narrow passage, growing to 120 feet wide on the north where it is edged by town homes. The park was conceived as an exhibition garden, with sinuously shaped walls and a colorful palette of drought-tolerant plants layered to create both open and intimate spaces.

The main challenges were the odd, narrow shape of the parcel and its immediate proximity to existing housing, which threatened to usurp the space as its own. The design converts the intimate-sized space into a public garden that stimulates the senses with sculptural changes in level and form and immerses people in a quiet space of fragrance and color.

Walls and plantings along the east edge shield the park from the street. A round expanse of grass at the widest point serves as a "sun room," a gathering spot that trails away to the south in a series of individually crafted gardens along a gravel pathway. The design buffers the north end from the adjoining town homes with a cluster of trees and partially screens housing on the west with an allée of trees that leaves a gap to give residents access.

The designers created numerous circulation studies of this small parcel to configure a tranquil gathering area for a space that serves primarily as a pass-through between Crescent Park and the town center.

By skewing the access corridor, the design
makes room for intimate gathering places
and creates a pleasant pedestrian link, sheltered by trees and infused with color.

POWERHOUSE PLAZA

This plaza, which lies between two newly constructed office buildings north of a roundabout and south of a residential district, was originally planned to be a 25-foot-wide, concrete emergency fire lane. The designers took advantage of its strategic location to make it into a gathering place for both office workers and residents and a high-visibility pedestrian walkway that links the area to Lowry's town center.

The main challenge was to produce an inviting social space within a 50-foot-wide sliver of land. The design-ers persuaded the local fire authority to reduce the width of the fire lane by 5 feet, then skewed the angle of this access lane to create "eddies" at opposite ends, giving pedestrians two points of respite. One is furnished with benches and tabletops for individual seating, the other with umbrella tables for group gatherings. A striped motif of colored concrete is echoed in strips of plantings of various colors. Custom light bollards along the sides are detailed with the neighborhood's star insignia, evoking the site's military history.

(above) What would have been simply a util-itarian corridor was transformed to become a place to gather and a unique passageway between residential neighborhoods and the town center. The plaza features both indi-vidual seating and tables and umbrellas for break areas (right). Custom light bollards stand along the length of the plaza, marked with the five-pointed star icon that evokes the site's military past.

THE READING GARDEN

As the design team began to create a system of parks and public spaces for the 180-acre northwest quadrant of the Lowry community, they discovered a small parcel between road elbows that transitioned from a residential area to office buildings. They asked to include it and proposed making the area into a hinge that would help draw people to the town center and encourage them to circulate throughout the community.

Because the community already featured several active outdoor spaces, the designers focused on how to create an intriguing passive use for this parcel. They learned that the board of the Lowry Foundation was seeking a way to honor a former member who had died unexpectedly, hoping to do something that would reflect his love of both reading and gardens. The designers suggested transforming this space into a small memorial park, and together they brainstormed ideas that would also give visitors a platform for creating their own meaning within the space.

The design produced a park and plaza with a wealth of sculptural forms, a host of literary quotes and several sculptures from the board member's own gardens. This intimate space is cut by a formal walkway running east-west and a more natural path that crosses north-south. Landforms, plant materials and hardscape differentiate a story-time area, a cluster of individual reading nooks and a tiny amphitheater arranged around a central gathering plaza whose seating walls are embossed with book-like shapes on which residents can have the names of their favorite novels etched. The walls, lawn and walkways are graced with quotations.

Because of utility easements that prohibit the planting of trees on the western half of the site, the plaza is shaded by large metal canopies. These are stenciled with the word READING, allowing sunlight to silhouette the word on the plaza floor, while the word GARDEN emerges from the ground in three-dimensional stone letters in a substantial bench that is also an impromptu stage. The grassy hillside to the north, which slopes down on three sides of the plaza, creates an audience space for this stage.

(top left) This pocket of parkland lies between two elbows of roadway, connecting them in both formal and informal ways. It offers both the public space of an open plaza, with a stage-like word sculpture (bottom left), and several different intimate spaces under the trees.

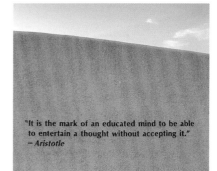

"It is the mark of an educated mind to be able to entertain a thought without accepting it."
— *Aristotle*

(this page) Spines of books are carved into the low walls around the central canopied plaza. The park space is enriched with sculpture and a variety of quotations in several settings and media.

When the Gates Rubber Factory closed in 1991, it left

a complicated, contaminated industrial site that cut off

surrounding neighborhoods from each other. A new

vision orchestrates the site's transit assets to support

creation of a lively, dense urban sector.

PROJECT DISCUSSION:
CHEROKEE REDEVELOPMENT

Denver, Colorado

An abandoned site transcends its history to become a vibrant district

The Gates Rubber Company was founded in Denver in 1911, where it served the nearby Ford Motor Company's Model T factory by producing replaceable rubber rims that extended the life of metal automobile tires. In the course of eight decades, Gates became a major employer in the Denver area, with 10,000 workers manufacturing a large variety of automobile belts and hoses and other rubber-based products. The Gates corporate campus, a self-contained, full-service community with 24-hour activity, spanned industrial space, offices and warehouses, cafeterias, a company store, a state-of-the-art medical facility and outdoor gathering spaces, including rooftop gardens. In the late 1950s, Interstate 25 was routed past the site, but over time, Gates shifted its major functions abroad and ceased all manufacturing activities on the site in

1991, leaving a large, deserted industrial swath in the south-central area of the city.

As city officials began to plan light-rail transit in the 1990s, the Gates area became a focus. Its central location offered a place where light-rail lines could converge, giving people access to large portions of the city. The local transportation district decided to link two light-rail lines at the site, funding a $1.2 billion light-rail expansion that opened for service in 2006. This new use lends the site a certain irony: A place that had thrived on the proliferation of the automobile is evolving to become a major transit site.

Cherokee Investment Partners, a manager of private equity funds specializing in the remediation and reuse of environmentally impaired properties, took an interest in the 50-acre parcel in 2001 and worked with the designers to

determine its economic viability. The unsightly and contaminated site is isolated from surrounding neighborhoods by arterial highways, a rail corridor and the city's extensive industrial swath along the South Platte River. Because it was centrally located and graced with a major transit hub, the planners saw the chance to create a sizable transit village there, with a mix of uses and pedestrian links to build on assets of transportation, historical buildings and views of downtown and the mountains. Such a place could also heal physical barriers between neighborhoods and reweave this outlying urban fabric.

The firm's urban plan called for creating a walkable community with a thoughtful mix of residential, office, retail, hotel and entertainment spaces. This new vision reclaims the site from its industrial past by reconnecting it to surrounding neighborhoods, developing at a scale that is sensitive to them, maximizing transit use, conserving water and energy, decreasing automobile use and celebrating the public realm with lively civic spaces and ground-floor uses.

The team worked to devise a collaborative process and a public-private partnership and to create a forum that welcomed community input. The planners guided Cherokee in undertaking a community involvement process

unprecedented for a private developer in the city of Denver. This included direct mail to 33,000 homes in the surrounding neighborhoods, dozens of meetings with key stakeholders, two rounds of public work sessions and formation of a neighborhood advisory group representing a dozen registered neighborhood organizations, with meetings on a monthly basis for over four years.

City officials invested in the project by forming planning and transportation work groups that included representatives of the Regional Transportation District and the Colorado Department of Transportation. They also supported the project by enacting an innovative zoning category, Transit Mixed-Use (T-MU-30), that allows a mix of uses and urban densities, including floor-area ratios of up to five-to-one and parking requirements that can be reduced by 50 percent for areas close to a light-rail station.

The final plan redevelops the former manufacturing site into a large-scale, mixed-use transit village that will serve as a central hub for people from all over the city and connect neighborhoods that had been disrupted by highways and industry. Four districts make up the planned site: regional retail and office uses on the northwest where visibility from Interstate 25 is high, residential devel-

(above) The Gates Rubber Factory, shown toward the bottom of this 1925 aerial photograph, was built on the edge of Denver, whose downtown can be seen at upper right. (opposite) Now the site lies in the middle of the metropolitan area, with immediate interstate highway and transit access as well as a view of the city center.

the master plan envisions a dense urban district on the former industrial site

(1)

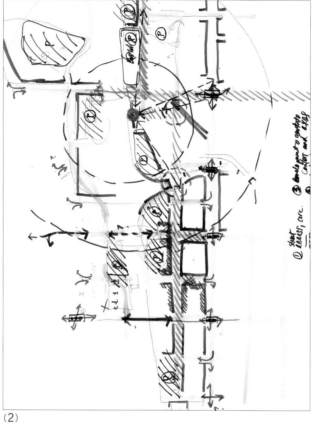

(2)

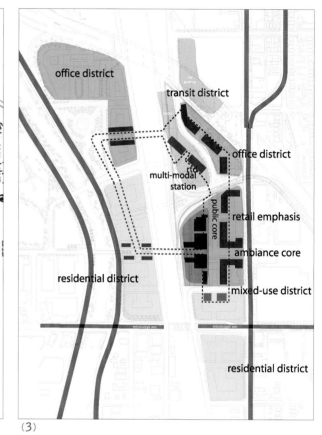

(3)

STUDIES

(1) Red and yellow outline the redevelopment site. The white circles are drawn at quarter-mile intervals to measure walkability from the transit station.

(2) This blocking diagram shows build-to lines and building frontages that support pedestrian links to transit.

(3) The proposed urban village comprises four separate districts, each with its own core and each linked to the others and to surrounding neighborhoods.

(4) Streets, streetscapes, open space and pedestrian ways are designed to integrate the project into the surrounding community.

(5) The organization of the intermodal transit system helped define and activate the redevelopment areas within the site.

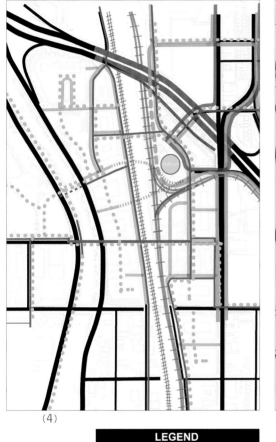

(4)

(5)

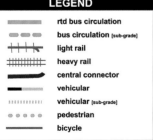

LEGEND	
	rtd bus circulation
	bus circulation [sub-grade]
	light rail
	heavy rail
	central connector
	vehicular
	vehicular [sub-grade]
	pedestrian
	bicycle

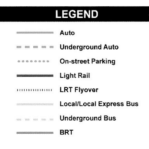

LEGEND	
	Auto
	Underground Auto
	On-street Parking
	Light Rail
	LRT Flyover
	Local/Local Express Bus
	Underground Bus
	BRT

opment to the south as an appropriate transition to surrounding neighborhoods, a retail-office-residential core potentially reusing portions of historical buildings and the transit hub to the north. The plan connects these districts with a series of dynamic public spaces, including links to the city's open-space trail system as well as pedestrian bridges over the rail corridor that bisects the site. At full buildout in 10 to 20 years, the redevelopment is expected to comprise 7 million square feet in four- to 12-story buildings, including up to 4,000 residential units and as much as 2 million square feet of office, retail, entertainment, hotel and civic uses.

Among the project's sustainability features are a reduction of water use by a factor of 70 compared with traditional, single-family, detached housing; reduction of pollution through mass-transit use; an increase and rejuvenation of park spaces; and encouragement of LEED-certified building practices.

PROJECT CREDITS

URBAN PLANNING/ENTITLEMENTS/
COMMUNITY OUTREACH:
Design Workshop, Inc.
  PIC: Rebecca Zimmermann
  Urban Planners: Kurt Culbertson, Todd Johnson, Todd Wenskoski, Geoff Gerring, Michael Hoffman, Dan Ford, Jeremy Alden, Paula Espinosa

CLIENT: Cherokee Investment Partners, LLC

Public Affairs: CRL Associates

Engineers: Nolte Associates

Land-Use Attorney: Brownstein Farber Hyatt

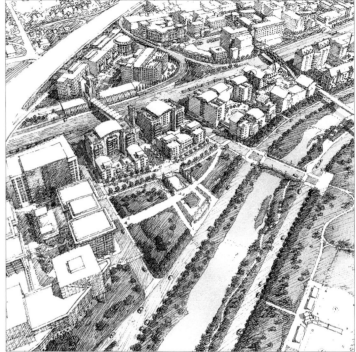

An artist's renderings demonstrate the project's relationship to both Denver's urban core and the regional Platte River trail system. The redevelopment is planned to be high-density, with a network of plazas, courtyards and other public spaces. Pedestrian bridges over the rail corridor bisecting the site will connect its eastern and western halves.

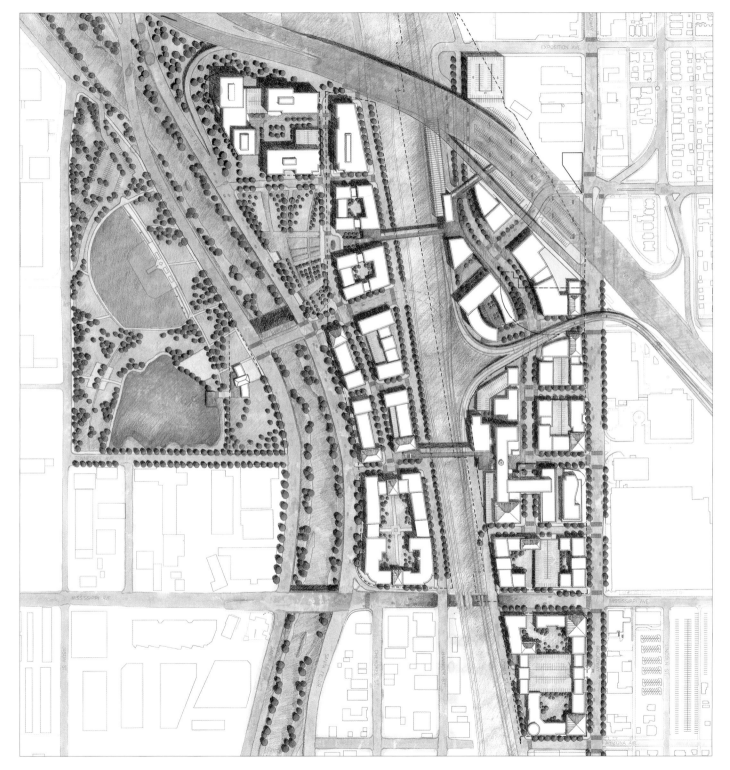

The final master plan links the two halves of the project to each other and connects the new urban district to the river and its trail system, to residential neighborhoods on the east and, by transit, to much of the rest of the city.

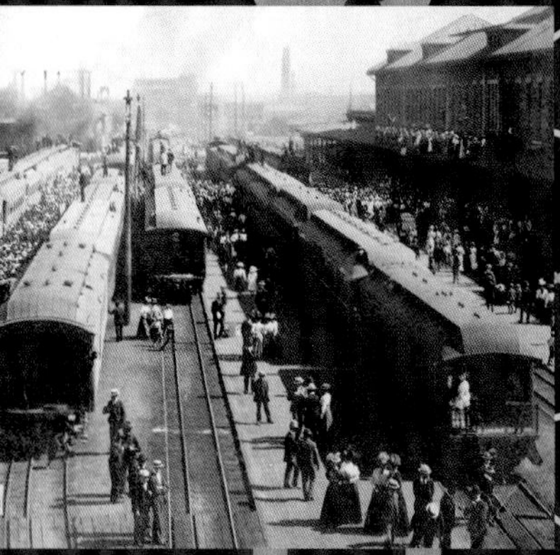

DILEMMA: When Union Pacific closed down all but two main lines through Denver, the former rail yard was just a big, unused space at the western end of downtown. Many ideas were proposed for this empty brownfield over several years, but none that engendered enough enthusiasm to be viable.

LEGACY GOALS:

Community
Create a new multi-use district that uses strong new links to downtown and surrounding neighborhoods to draw on the energy of those areas; fashion new gathering spots to attract visitors; connect the new district with the city's system of walking trails.

Environment
Remediate the site to accommodate residences, office uses, parklands and trails; concentrate development in urban-scale buildings to boost density, minimize the footprint and increase open space; introduce light rail to give easy access to the district.

Economics
Secure city support for infrastructure investment; plan and design the district so that it attracts support for mixed uses from surrounding areas and capitalizes on such amenities as close proximity to the Platte River and views to the Rocky Mountains.

Art
Use a distinctive, large-scale icon near high-traffic areas to mark this urban destination for visitors; connect open space with a network of plazas to create an urban adventure; grace the district with beautiful objects to make outdoor rooms inviting.

THESIS: Connection to the rest of the city will revitalize and activate this new district if the plan and design effectively link it with light-rail transit, the downtown grid, historical neighborhoods and the adjacent mixed-use warehouse district of Lower Downtown.

CASE STUDY

RIVERFRONT PARK

Denver, Colorado

New district is a phoenix rising from the ashes of a rail yard

Overview

Planning for Riverfront Park began in the early 1990s, on the heels of several failed plans for the remediated site. As demographics began to shift and the city's sprawl and traffic congestion worsened, city fathers decided to make a major reinvestment in the urban core, including a commitment to mass transit. This helped support a vision for a plan that is translating a 65-acre former rail yard into a 21-block mixed-use urban village centered on a multi-modal transit center — a new district that will build on the assets of the surrounding urban core and link to the city's dynamism. Already, the project has stimulated a return of private investment in the area.

History/Context

With the discovery of gold in 1858, the city of Denver was founded at the confluence of the Platte River and Cherry Creek, an area that had been sacred to the Ute and Arapaho peoples. Colorado's mining boom would eventually fuel a parallel boom in railroading, bringing the first rails to Denver in 1870 and running them along the river to supply the steam trains with water. To make a huge rail yard that would accommodate as many as 80 trains a day, the railroad bought up the neighborhoods that had grown up around the confluence of Denver's rivers.

By the middle of the 20th century, the city's business district began to shift from the train station toward the neoclassical civic center a mile away and the railroad district fell into disuse. At the same time, city fathers embraced the rhetoric of urban renewal and began to demolish parts of downtown, many of which would stand

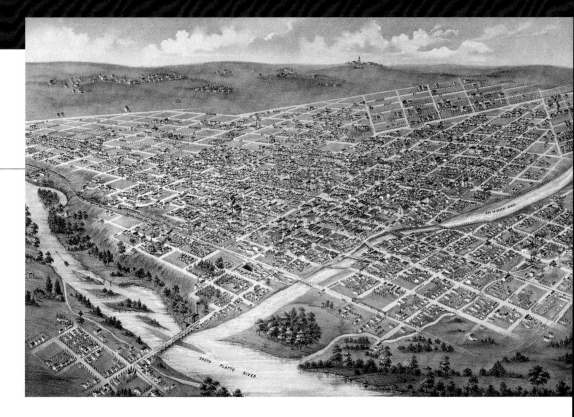

A bird's-eye rendering of early Denver at the confluence of Cherry Creek and the South Platte River shows the city before the arrival of the railroad, which wiped out many early neighborhoods.

CASE STUDY

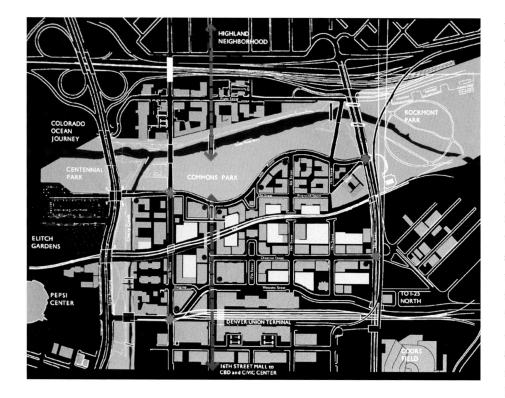

The extension of the 16th Street pedestrian mall through the site and across the river with footbridges became crucial to maintaining the new district's connection with the city's assets.

vacant or be turned into parking lots. The district near the train station became increasingly isolated, disreputable and dangerous. But in 1965, developer Dana Crawford took a stand against the demolition of a single block of Larimer Street, Denver's Skid Row, and was able to quickly renovate the buildings and turn them into a thriving urban marketplace known as Larimer Square. Crawford's next move was to preserve the 25-block warehouse district around the old train station, turning it into a vibrant mixed-used district of housing, offices, restaurants and entertainment. Building on this dynamism, the City constructed dams to make the nearby floodplain safe and threw its support behind several new large-scale attractions in the Central Platte Valley, including major venues for football, baseball and basketball. In the middle of this burgeoning area lay the vast, mostly unused rail yards. When Union Pacific consolidated its rail lines in the early 1990s, private interests finally moved to develop the area, seeking and securing city help to do so.

Aging viaducts that once stretched above this land were demolished, along with railroad storage facilities. This left behind land that needed environmental remediation and an area that was devoid of infrastructure — no sewer, no utilities, no streets. But the bigger problem was

how something new could insure that the area didn't become an isolated pocket. A series of plans, including a stadium, a convention center and an office park, were proposed over the course of several years, but none could find backing. In 1995, Design Workshop finally created a viable master plan for the site, leading a team of consultants that included businessmen, finance experts, real-estate economists, transportation planners, engineers and lawyers.

Process

The design began with a contextual understanding of the site's position in relation to the rest of the city, including its links to transportation and the possibilities for open space. Bounded by an interstate highway, a viaduct, an arterial and historic Union Station, the site had excellent potential for connection. The design team focused on how the area connected to the rest of the city — historically, physically and symbolically — and found that the same things that nourished the city into being around the rail yards were still ranged around the site: a street grid, the river and the renovated warehouse district that was now a vibrant sector. Linking the site to the surrounding neighborhoods became the key to creating a new district that would thrive. Through scores of public

The rail yard and the city's industrial swath separated downtown and other parts of the city from the Platte River, shown winding from the top center of this aerial photograph, down the right side to bottom center.

CASE STUDY

A hand rendering delineates the transportation connections to this new urban district. The 16th Street Mall is noted with red asterisks at either end, with the Millennium Bridge and Commons Park above it. Circles denote major transportation connections (red) in the surrounding area and the project arterials (gray) that feed into that system.

The top right drawing shows the existing site conditions and the disrupted link between the seat of power and the original site of the city; the bottom right drawing shows the reconnection. The site is outlined in red and the confluence of the two waterways is marked with a red dot.

meetings with concerned citizens, neighborhood groups, city staff and downtown businesses, the team established a set of design principles to guide the planning of this new district.

Using these principles, the design team built on the assets of the urban core and fashioned a flow of energy into and out of the new district that would allow it to participate in, benefit from and contribute to the city's vibrancy. This design responds to the greater growth pattern of Denver by reconnecting the former rail yard to the city grid and to northwest neighborhoods across the river. Symbolically, the project reconnects what was once a gathering ground for Native Americans to the civic center built by white settlers.

The primary method for linking the city and the rail yard was to extend the spine of downtown — the 16th Street pedestrian mall — into the newly created district, running it up and over the remaining main line with a bridge that would serve as a landmark for the district. Past the bridge, the design creates a major gathering point, new housing and a 25-acre park and riverside green space that are tied into the city's trail system. A network of streets and public spaces fans out through the 21-block district to give people easy access to its attractions and to surrounding city neighborhoods. The team also persuaded transportation officials to bring a new light-rail spur into the district to connect it to the rest of the metropolitan area and to create a multi-modal hub that links to local and regional bus lines, the mall shuttle, bicycle parking facilities and an anticipated airport train and commuter rail line.

Plan

Input from city staff, local architects and engineers helped the team create studies of massing, view-planes and vertical and horizontal uses, leading to a Planned Unit Development (PUD) submission, which was approved by the city in 1997. The focus of the firm's Urban Design Standards and Guidelines was the importance of creating a pedestrian-oriented and pedestrian-scaled, economically viable neighborhood that is also visually cohesive and aesthetically stimulating.

The plan, its zoning entitlements and ongoing implementation encompass:

- 4,000,000 square feet of commercial and office space
- 500,000 square feet of retail
- 1,500 hotel rooms
- 2,500 to 3,500 residential units, with 10 percent affordably priced
- a school
- a post office

Design

The master plan and architectural guidelines bring beauty to the district, for instance with the welcoming curve of Little Raven Street where Riverfront Plaza embraces Commons Park; the

style of the new loft-living residential units, which resonates with the nearby historic warehouse district, and gathering places for special events, such as concerts and festivals. The guidelines foster the engagement of people with each other by carefully positioning public spaces, ground-floor retail and building entrances. The district's iconic bridge was also required to serve both as a backdrop against the city skyline and as a place where people could linger and enjoy the urban setting.

The firm's design of Riverfront's plazas and streetscapes also imbues the district with exquisite details, such as the plaza floor, which juxtaposes formal strips of black granite with patchwork configurations of rose granite; obsidian-sand concrete, which alternates in a subtle rhythm with traditional sidewalks; graceful wooden-slat benches along the 16th Street pedestrian extension; large, amorphously shaped black planters draped with cascades of hanging flowers; and angular, elegant stone benches in the public plaza.

Outcome

The new streets of the district now bear names from a hundred years ago: Chestnut, Wewatta, Little Raven. The Millennium Bridge, which identifies the district, opened in 2002 and has become a city landmark. In the space of a decade, the value of the land increased by a factor of 200, from 1993's official asking price of 75 cents per square foot to $150 per square foot. The marketplace affirmed the plan with brisk sales of the first housing units, and the project has stimulated a return of investment in the city core, as well as inspiring mixed-use, new construction in other parts of Denver. The project is also believed to have encouraged other developments on the western side of the Platte River, which are connected to Riverfront by pedestrian bridges.

PROJECT CREDITS

URBAN DESIGN/MASTER PLAN:
Design Workshop, Inc.
  PIC: Todd Johnson
  Entitlements: Gregory Ochis, Sue Oberliesen
  Landscape Architect: Kim Swanson

STREETSCAPE DESIGN: Design Workshop, Inc.
  PIC: Todd Johnson
  Landscape architects: Todd Wenskoski, Jamie Fogle, Chuck Ware, Chad Klever, Heath Mizer, Jeff McMenimen, Jeremy Alden, Yu-Ju Liu, Kirby Hoyt, Paula Espinosa, Robert Matsuda

CLIENTS: Trillium Development, East West Partners

Architecture: Urban Design Group

Bridge design: Architecture Denver

Park design: Civitas

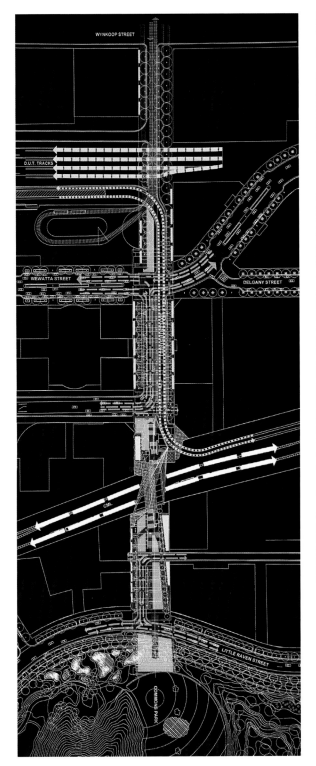

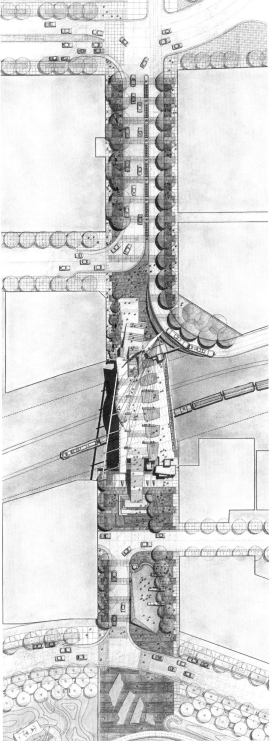

(left) A transit diagram of the 16th Street corridor shows the main-line tracks in white (passenger rail at top, freight lines toward the bottom), roadways in blue, pedestrian access in red, the free mall shuttle in orange and major public spaces in yellow-orange.

(near left) The hand rendering delineates the streetscape and plaza design that fleshes out pedestrian walkways and gathering spaces, both intimate and expansive. The bridge is at center, crossing over the mainline tracks, with Commons Park at the bottom.

(above) Bringing light rail into the new Riverfront Park district was key to its success. The first residential buildings are seen behind a light-rail train on its way to nearby Union Station. Part of the Millennium Bridge stands at right, with stairs up and over the remaining rail lines.

(this page) The district positions its highest density and greatest massing nearest downtown and across from Union Station, transitioning to lower urban density along the edge of the park. The district is helping galvanize existing redevelopment, including the vibrant

Lower Downtown district east of Union Station and attractions like Coors Field, at upper left, and the Pepsi Center, at middle right. The edge of the existing downtown is seen at the back.

(opposite) The master plan extends the city's grid into the district, configuring buildings around a series of public spaces and plazas. Its southern and northern boundaries are major arterials that lead into downtown.

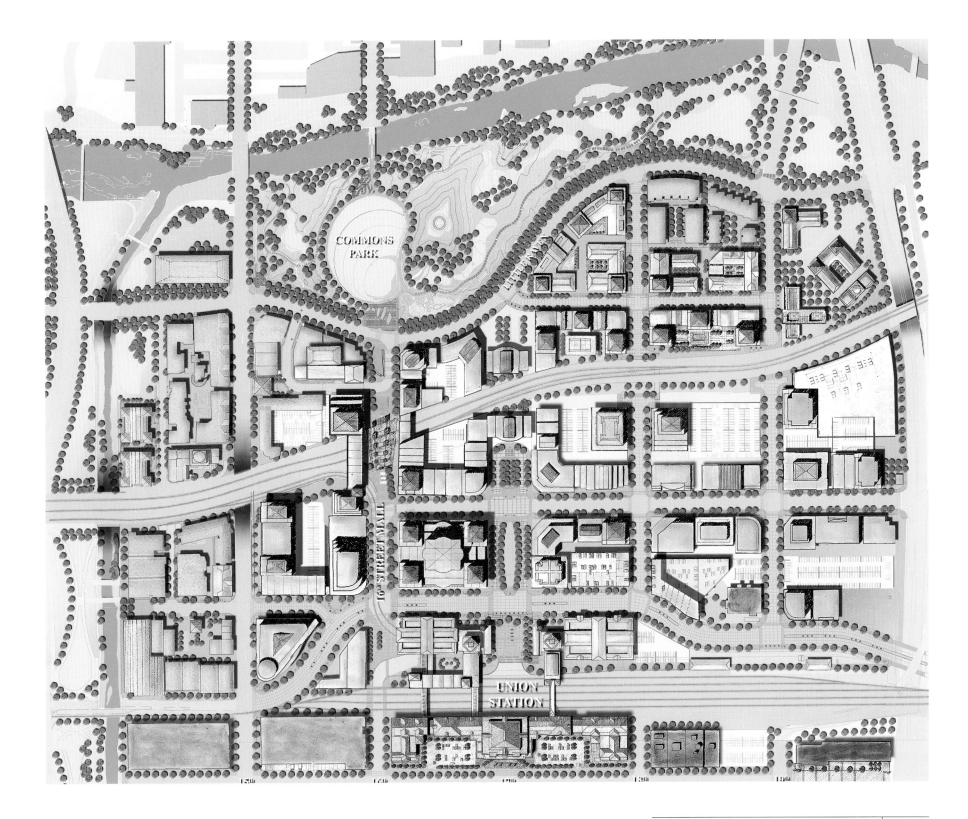

CASE STUDY

(this page) From the beginning, Riverfront was envisioned as an intensively urban district invigorated by a mix of residential, office and retail uses. The drawing at right is an aerial view looking up the 16th Street corridor, across the Millennium Bridge, toward the park and the river.

(opposite) Riverfront Plaza is the heart of the project, supported by the assets of the iconic bridge, the park and stimulating architecture with ground-floor retail. It has become a popular venue for festivals and special events of all kinds and also serves bicyclists and walkers through its connection to the Platte River trail system.

CASE STUDY

The plaza has become a favored gathering space for both informal and formal occasions. It is used regularly for special events and is also a stop-off for bicyclists using the nearby trail system that runs along the edge of the South Plate River.

LEGACY

5

Leading Change

ESSAY

Partners Kurt Culbertson, Richard Shaw, Rebecca Zimmermann and Greg Ochis collaborate here in the culmination of the book to consider projects that have involved significant public process. Through the narration of several projects, this chapter ventures into the challenging sphere of finding consensus in often crisis situations — a discipline that requires extensive and continually expanding skills, drawing deeply on the personal resources of those who engage in it.

PROJECT DISCUSSIONS

Flathead County Master Plan: In the face of runaway growth, residents near Glacier National Park curb their antagonism toward planning.

North Lake Tahoe: Strategies help boost the economies of unincorporated towns and give them more clout.

Canyon Forest Village: Groups of all stripes join to help plan and design a gateway village for the Grand Canyon.

Chalalan Ecolodge: Villagers win the support of outsiders to create an ecotourist camp in the Madidi region of Bolivia.

IN-DEPTH ACCOUNT

Park Avenue Redevelopment: Comprehensive, long-term public process solves environmental and economic problems in South Lake Tahoe.

Bringing people together to create a vision for the future is the only way a community can successfully navigate change.

AN ESSAY BY DESIGN WORKSHOP

Change is one of the greatest challenges any community will ever face. It can also be one of the most rewarding. Change is a great opportunity but it can also be daunting, even change that is positive, clear and tailored to the expressed desires of the people who live in a community. How change is managed will determine how a community evolves and what it will be in the future. The most successful and satisfying change emerges from the collective will of a community once it has addressed its long-term social, economic, environmental and aesthetic implications.

Change may come with an influx of newcomers, an economic decline or a threat to the environment. It may be needed to help a community adapt as it switches its economic base from agriculture or mining to tourism. Or it may be prompted by rapidly increasing real estate values that are pricing the middle class out of a community. Sometimes it's a crisis, sometimes a slow burn. It is not simple or quick and it is often unwelcome.

Creating change that helps a community flourish requires a thoughtful and thorough engagement of the people who live there — rarely an easy task. Helping communities manage change is less about change in the landscape and more about bringing people together to create a future, because the process of change begins in the hearts and minds of human beings.

The Importance of Vision

When a community undertakes change, everyone will be touched by it, but touched in different ways — some positively, some negatively, some drastically, some only a little. Change may occur or be needed in more than one system at a time and put civic objectives into conflict, for instance, if a community's environmental goals are not compatible with those supporting the economy or social conditions. Responses to change will vary: Government entities may contradict each other; residents may disagree about what constitutes success; and there will almost certainly be competing business interests.

To get a community back on its feet so that it can proactively manage change, it is necessary to build trust. That requires untangling a giant web of relationships. The vested, entrenched interests that guard the

(above) Master city planner Robert Moses stands on an I-beam over the East River on Roosevelt Island June 4, 1959, in New York City. Moses became a symbol for the sweeping changes that urban renewal brought, often without community input.

(opposite) American writer Jane Jacobs (third from right) and architect Philip Johnson (far right) stand with picketing crowds outside New York City's Penn Station in 1963 to protest the building's demolition. Jacobs successfully opposed Moses on some projects.

[Change] is a great and yeasty time, filled with opportunity.

— *John Naisbitt,* Megatrends

At times the journey feels awkward or perilous: you're asking questions that everyone wishes would go away; you don't know how to put into words what you're searching for; you're wondering just how big an idiot you really are for leaving what felt sure and safe and comfortable. And at times, the freshness and exhilaration of setting out for new territory are pure pleasure.

— *Paul Ray and Sherry Ruth Anderson,* The Cultural Creatives

Without effective community input, growth can consume land in a way that has a far-ranging impact. At left, a new housing development is sited along a mountain ridge near Castro Valley, California.

current state of the place and the reason it exists — these forces must be reckoned with before a new vision has any hope of being established. All stakeholders must be heard and understood. Their mindsets, their fears and even elements that have nothing to do with the change process will all emerge in the process of sorting out issues. And all of this must be dealt with.

The most effective and important tool for reconciling a community's diverse reactions to change is forming a vision for the future. In a time of great uncertainty, a vision serves as a guiding force. A successful vision is one that touches on all aspects of a community — not just making a better place but also creating a true image of how a place will evolve, grow and mature to become something it isn't today. This vision governs how the economic system creates the opportunity for tomorrow, how the community will benefit and respond and how the transformation will influence outsiders' perceptions of the possibility of change. The broadest view is the most helpful. The narrower the vision, the more likely there will be unforeseen and undesired consequences. Starting from scratch can be an act of liberation. It allows people to think comprehensively, to imagine on the grandest scale what this place, this society, this economic system could be.

The hard work is the process of engaging and consolidating and getting everybody to agree, weaving together the strands of a community like a twisting DNA helix. This is the major accomplishment of change: not what ends up on the ground as redevelopment, but what changes inside people and forges new bonds among them. Investors must engage with people, be willing to look beyond short-term economic return to support the community and work for the public good. Government has to recognize the risk for those who will be acting as the agents of change — private investors — and work toward minimizing it, whether by providing infrastructure with bond initiatives, using the bully pulpit or reconfiguring regulations to give broader support.

Vision, Plan and Pitfalls

Plans for the future hinge on the viability of the vision behind it. But even high buy-in to vision cannot guarantee a plan's success. A plan must result in specific, understandable action that people will take because they know what it means and how it will affect them. It's necessary to come up with implementation strategies that fit the stakeholders and it's necessary for those strategies and the plan itself to be adopted by the governing entities. If not, the plan may languish. If it is adopted, it will function at the very least as a set of guiding principles and recommendations for all future plans.

Part of the reason why such projects are so difficult and prone to failure and why it's so humbling to work on them is that they are easy to derail. A single person in a group can thwart an entire redevelopment project. It's critical for planners and designers to maintain the vision and find stakeholders who are willing to do the same, despite the profound tactical and technical challenges and significant impediments and nuisances they will encounter in the process of effecting proactive change. The process often moves ahead by simply solving one problem at a time and keeping the sticking points from becoming spoilers.

Story is a critical element of success. Even the most sincere and needed efforts can be overthrown by opposition forces if the process has no compelling story. Here the perception or character of the change agent becomes paramount and charisma and narrative play important roles. When a strong leader, like Mayor Federico Peña of Denver or Guilherme Frering of Minerações Brasileiras Reunidas (MBR), can frame the debate within the larger community, that chances for change are greatly improved. Such people and actions bring to the task what Harvard's educational innovator Howard Gardner (*Changing Minds*) terms "resonance" and author Malcolm Gladwell (*The Tipping Point*) terms "stickiness." Leaders of this kind can call for public sacrifice and continually tell the story of a great future. Designers support this by helping to craft and tell the story through presentations, visualizations and writing. These stories must be sufficiently complex to be compelling but straightforward enough to gain a hearing.

The success of change hinges on leadership. Change leadership means being able to articulate, illustrate and write to alternative futures without

And say, finally, whether peace is best preserved by giving energy to the government or information to the people. This last is the most certain, and the most legitimate engine of government. Educate and inform the whole mass of people. Enable them to see that it is their interest to preserve peace and order, and they will preserve them ... They are the only sure reliance for the preservation of liberty.

— *Thomas Jefferson*, letter to James Madison, 1787

Ultimately, leaders cannot be effective — and cannot call for sacrifice — unless their stories and their persons strike a resonant chord with their audiences.

— *Howard Gardner*, Changing Minds

... one must be willing to look ahead and consider uncertainties ... Rather than asking such questions, too many people react to uncertainty with denial. They take an unconsciously deterministic view of events.

— *Peter Schwartz*, The Art of the Long View

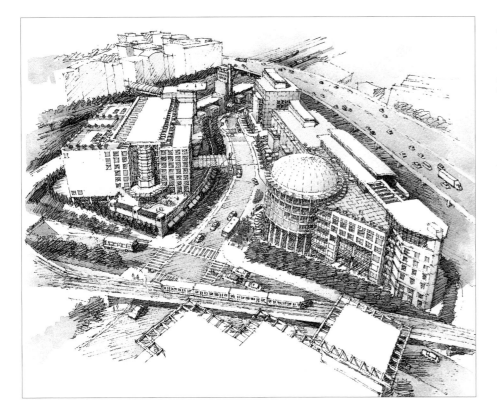

The Cherokee redevelopment, discussed in the chapter on connection, required the city to embrace an entirely new zoning category in order to convert a former industrial swath to an urban, mixed-use district.

relying upon dogma. It requires the humility to set aside the arrogance of the "expert" and to recognize the wisdom of crowds and of Thomas Jefferson's yeoman farmer. Change leadership requires the ability to align risks and resources, to redeploy resources and, in some cases, to capitalize on world events. Most importantly, change requires the perseverance and patience to work through the resistance that is inevitably encountered.

If a community becomes proactive in dealing with change, it is possible to reinvent the economic community and social future of a place. But it takes time and persistent, long-term efforts — some would say, the devotion of a mother and the patience of a saint. Forces of opposition can be enormous and resistance of all kinds is to be expected. Perhaps the greatest force is time itself, simply because such projects are often extremely complex and can take a very long time to bring to completion.

Resources, Skills and Challenges

In recent years, the process of helping people manage change has been articulated in detail by insightful people such as Gardner, Gladwell and public-opinion scholar Daniel Yankelovich (*Coming to Public Judgment*). Such work can give people a basis for dealing with change, but its main gifts may lie in reminding us that change takes time, is almost always met with resistance and begins within us.

It is impossible to lead others through change if one is not open to it oneself. Those who simply apply early learning over and over again without questioning basic assumptions and beliefs will not succeed in this work. If one is not personally striving for innovation and new ideas, why expect the pursuit of excellence from others? Special qualities are needed to lead change, including both conviction and openness. A change agent needs to be confident and secure in his or her position, yet at the same time sensitive to criticism, open and courageous — not an easy balance to maintain. Success comes from constantly seeking to dig deeper into the professional and personal issues and challenges of life.

Those who tackle change management must be able to work within a setting of confusion and ambiguity and to process information at multiple levels to allow social, economic, design and environmental components to cohere. They must be able to face — and help others face — the fact that the outcome is uncertain. There is no such thing as perfect information, and the change may not be what was the hoped for. Study and analysis mitigate the danger; the more information there is, the more certainty there is. But the early work is a leap of faith with no guarantee.

We have found some of the most intensive laboratories of change near scenic destinations, places threatened with the loss of scenic beauty, degradation of the environment or economic decline. Communities near such destinations have often experienced conflicts over natural resources, people and economic interests, often to the point that communities no longer function well and problems seem intractable. These places frequently have little inherent support and present complex challenges. At some major vacation destinations, tourism pressures inflict hardship on local populations, whose services and infrastructure suffer by comparison. At others, economic decline has compounded threats to the quality of life or the environment. There are also vested economic interests in such places that may see profound threats in change and may do everything they can to frustrate efforts to manage change. In the United States, nearly all land-use decisions are based on local politics, and even when a major national asset is involved, local political considerations govern any proposed use of private property. Local politics can easily override innovative design, national publicity and the best of intentions.

Change is the Future

Change is unavoidable. We grapple with it at all scales of our lives. To do so effectively, it is critical that the vocabulary and tools of the process become familiar to us. We must also acknowledge that change is difficult. In 35 years of leading change, we have seen startling successes and piecemeal adoption of measures, as well as projects that simply could not survive the process. Our guideposts have always been taking a holistic approach and cultivating a comprehensive grasp of all issues — the tools formalized in the Legacy philosophy. Our decision to follow Legacy is a commitment to move from a simple way of thinking about landscape architecture and urban design to a more complex concept that ultimately

embraces the mythic and the spiritual. This allows us to seek meaning in our lives and work as we grapple with changes in the world, in our firm and in ourselves — and to support others in seeking meaning as they face the inevitable changes of life.

We shall not cease from exploration
And the end of all our exploring
Will be to arrive where we started
And to know the place for the first time.

— *T. S. Eliot,* Four Quartets

The central irony of the runaway growth near Glacier National Park is that people who live there have a strong aversion to planning. But the population explosion eventually prompted residents to band together and try to solve the resulting challenges.

PROJECT DISCUSSION:
FLATHEAD COUNTY MASTER PLAN

Flathead County, Montana

A scenic community tackles the agendas spawned by growth

Flathead County is a 3.8-million-acre expanse just south of the Canadian border, containing half of both Glacier National Park and Flathead Lake, the largest freshwater lake west of the Mississippi. Once a loggers' outpost and a haven for fishermen, in the 1980s the area began to attract urban refugees, retirees and significant numbers of wilderness tourists. Between 1970 and 2000, the population of this Rhode Island-sized county grew by almost 90 percent to 65,000. The area was playing host to more than 2 million visitors a year, and the second-home market, which was dividing ranches into 20-acre "ranchettes," was booming.

This skyrocketing growth made Flathead County the hottest real estate market in the country in 1993, and also outstripped the county government's resources and made its 15-year-old master plan obsolete. By the end of the decade, roads were clogged and schools were packed and development threatened the scenic assets that had originally drawn people to the Flathead area. Land once used for agriculture or open space was converted to housing: In a single year, subdivision lots increased 15 percent; in two years, new construction requests almost doubled. Between 1973 and 1992, 135,000 acres were subdivided, 94 percent without public review. Projects that did come up for public review often failed because of pressure from one or another stakeholder. This tended to preserve the scenery but stymie attempts to deal with growth. Financial crises kept government institutions from acting quickly, but the real obstacle to management of this sudden growth was Montana residents' property rights orientation and the failure of

A satellite image of the mountainous Flathead County shows Flathead Lake. The area's spectacular scenery has fueled significant growth in recent decades, a trend that overwhelmed local infrastructure and services.

(top) Scattered retail and service corridors resulted from the growth and tourism pressures building in the scenic areas around Flathead County.

(bottom) Population growth and a lack of planning allowed former agricultural lands to be consumed by sprawling development, as newcomers and longtime residents vied for prime locations on the lakefront or other waterways.

top-down planning in community after community in the area.

No countywide zoning existed in any county in Montana when the master plan process was undertaken. Flathead County's population is quite varied socioeconomically, including the very liberal and the very conservative, the extremely wealthy and the working poor, staunch environmentalists and equally passionate supporters of the timber industry, real cowboys and "cappuccino cowboys." The one thing they have in common is a notorious dislike for public planning. With residents' fervent independence and their hostility to government intervention, the county's widely divergent population could not agree on how to proceed. Flathead needed to invent its own decision-making process and its own kind of plan — one that would embrace broad citizen involvement.

When development pressures reached a pitch in 1992, a consortium of traditional opponents – timber, agricultural, environmental, development, political and real estate interests – joined forces in a grassroots organization called the Cooperative Planning Coalition (CPC). Its goal was to develop a master plan to guide growth in a sustainable way. Community support was immediate and strong and brought $350,000 in

private donations to fund the initiative, making it the largest-known privately funded public planning process as well as one of the largest master-planning efforts ever undertaken in the United States. But by the end of 1993, the process had overwhelmed the capacity of the CPC, which sought planning assistance from Design Workshop.

A new comprehensive planning process began by seeking the participation of people of all stripes, from natural scientists to small-business owners. The goals were to streamline local land-use approval processes, to protect natural resources and the valley's rural character and to plan public facilities and services in a cost-efficient and proactive way. Once a month for a year, the team descended on the Flathead Valley in exhaustive week-long efforts as strategists, facilitators and coordinators, helping residents craft the larger vision while managing specific concerns of separate areas and constituencies. The team met with 165 service organizations and hosted 80 public meetings as well as a television show and radio call-ins. The process began with having residents define their neighborhoods and visualize each area's future, in order to configure a framework of public facilities to serve as a platform for residential, commercial and industrial development and

Somers/Lower Valley - Public Services Proximity

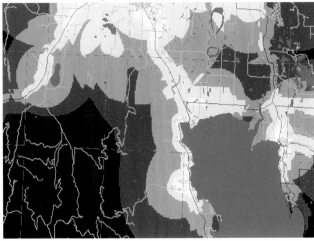

Creston Area Resource - Land Use Fit

Kalispell - Preliminary Land Use

Final Land Use Plan

	RURAL LANDS	SHORELINE AREAS	FOREST LANDS	AGRICULTURAL LANDS	URBAN LANDS	STATUTORY LANDS
less development sensitivity						
↓						
more development sensitivity						

(left) The team analyzed both physical features and population and market trends across the county, working with substantial community involvement to grasp the impact of growth and to craft a plan for managing it — one that would be acceptable to the county's widely diverse population.

(above) The final plan left much of the county untouched and negotiated a delicate balance of public and private rights.

to determine what population levels the land could comfortably support. Volunteers took on major obligations: The effort included 26 working groups of 300 people who drafted sections of the final plan. It was estimated that one in five Flathead residents ultimately participated in some way.

Eighty percent of the county is public lands. Its economy is so dependent on activities on these lands that it became critical to deal with how public and private lands fit together and how those uses needed to be managed in order to sustain the area's overall ecosystem. With a survey of 33,000 residents, the firm used Geographic Information Systems (GIS), then in its early stages, to create inventory maps showing where development would have the greatest impacts on resources like agriculture, timber, floodplains and wetlands. With the help of the National Park Service, the U.S. Forest Service and several local agencies, the team produced more than 100 maps documenting both natural and manmade conditions, from vegetation, wetlands and wildlife to transpor-

tation, utilities and cultural and historic sites, creating the foundation for a plan that would reconcile diverse agendas.

The centerpiece of the final plan is a performance-standard review system that allows residents to do what they want with their land so long as it doesn't negatively impact their neighbors and neighborhoods. It also offers economic incentives to develop in areas with low ecological sensitivity, protects forests and agricultural lands with a real-estate transfer tax and an increased use of land trusts, and modifies existing rules and regulations to better suit community interests.

But property rights sentiments ran deep and sometimes dark. Weeks before the project began, the passing of the Brady gun-control amendment led to the massing of a militia on the Flathead County fairgrounds in protest of all government controls, including the new county plan that was then being formulated. During the project, bomb threats forced the CPC board to meet in a room over the sheriff's office in Kalispell. And although the plan was

unanimously approved by the Flathead County Board of Commissioners, it was overturned in a contentious referendum in 1996. Individual agencies and communities adopted numerous aspects of the plan, but the plan itself was never implemented. In 2005, the county undertook a new master-planning effort, as officials agreed that the same development pressures are at work in the county today and the need and support for a comprehensive master plan are greater than ever.

PROJECT CREDITS

MASTER PLAN: Design Workshop, Inc.
  PIC: Kurt Culbertson
  Project Manager: Deanna Weber
  GIS Specialist: Steve Mullen
  Project Planners: Bill Kane, Marty Zeller, Tomas Gal

CLIENT: Cooperative Planning Coalition

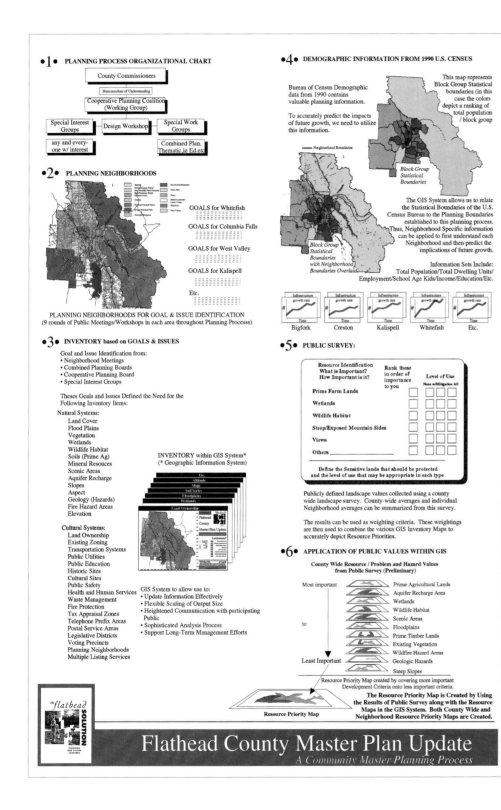

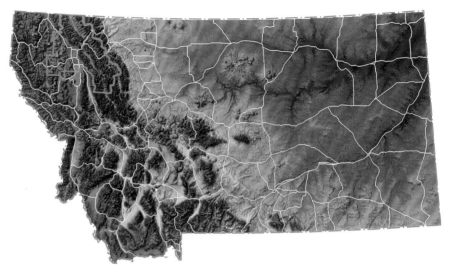

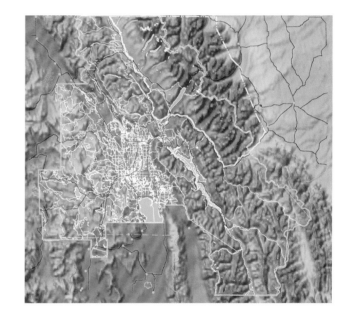

(left) An early diagram helped people understand how land analysis would be reconciled with the public values expressed in the planning process.

(above) This regional planning effort covered a piece of land the size of Rhode Island, addressing an extremely broad spectrum of stakeholders.

The unincorporated towns along the north shore of Lake Tahoe were economically stagnant, losing their tourism market position and didn't have the political or tax support they needed to change course. A series of strategic plans brought the area's stakeholders together, giving them the clout to attract substantial reinvestment.

PROJECT DISCUSSION:
NORTH LAKE TAHOE

Lake Tahoe, California

Consolidating scattered interests gives a tourist economy a new future

By the mid-1990s, the infrastructure and built environment of North Lake Tahoe's resort communities were in a steady decline and skier visits were down. Major resorts such as Squaw Valley had been established after World War II, but surrounding communities' development had never kept pace. These towns remained unincorporated, their growth neither guided by formal planning nor directly supported by tax revenue.

The region was hampered by stringent environmental regulations enacted in the late 1960s that made new development and redevelopment difficult. The commercial core areas and lodging facilities that had once looked fun and funky had become old and tired and people stayed in them less and less frequently. Tahoe became a haven for day-trippers, which increased traffic congestion and air pollution and

reduced income from the area's bed tax. Communities couldn't fund basic infrastructure like sidewalks, which frustrated pedestrians and negatively affected hundreds of local businesses, 80 percent of which depended on tourism. These interests had no unified voice, no clout at the county level and no means for solving problems of infrastructure and transportation. Individual towns conducted dozens of studies on transportation, marketing, recreation, redevelopment and marketing. But often their recommendations were in conflict with each other, or, because of the region's staunch resistance to governmental entities of any kind, they failed to find funding or means of implementation.

In 1995, Placer County hired Design Workshop to create a tourism development master plan. Ultimately, the firm would complete three such

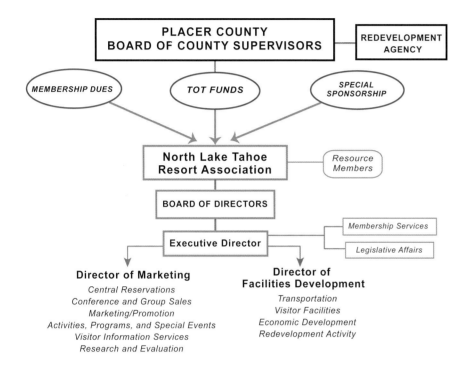

PLACER COUNTY
BOARD OF COUNTY SUPERVISORS

REDEVELOPMENT
AGENCY

MEMBERSHIP DUES

TOT FUNDS

SPECIAL
SPONSORSHIP

**North Lake Tahoe
Resort Association**

*Resource
Members*

BOARD OF DIRECTORS

Executive Director

Membership Services

Legislative Affairs

Director of Marketing

*Central Reservations
Conference and Group Sales
Marketing/Promotion
Activities, Programs, and Special Events
Visitor Information Services
Research and Evaluation*

**Director of
Facilities Development**

*Transportation
Visitor Facilities
Economic Development
Redevelopment Activity*

(above left) An organizational chart reflects two years of negotiation that brought stakeholders together to create a resort association that could channel tax revenue and handle tourist-related issues.

(above right) Recreational enthusiasts, who dominate the economy of the unincorporated towns along the north shore of Lake Tahoe, take a toll on infrastructure and impact communities, sometimes in unforeseen ways.

plans over eight years to solve increasingly complex issues. These were essentially business plans for a tourism-based economy, helping to guide much-needed upgrades and leverage public funds to attract private investment. For each, the planners formed a citizens' advisory committee, held public meetings, assessed the area's strengths and weaknesses and its standing in national competition, produced working papers, suggested priorities and made recommendations.

In the first master plan, the planners wove together previous studies to give officials a coherent approach to local issues. Their analysis showed that North Lake Tahoe had the lowest amount of public investment, the smallest marketing budget and the least public transit in operation of all mountain resort communities studied. The designers focused on finding a way to give the area's seven communities political muscle and leverage public funds so that they would serve as a catalyst for private investment. By merging the 500 businesses of the local Chamber of Commerce and the Visitor & Convention Bureau, the plan created a resort association with a board of directors representing small and large

lodging facilities, ski areas, retail interests and restaurants. This group had the power to implement changes locally in place of county agencies. The plan also increased the transient occupancy tax (TOT) to fund tourism infrastructure and created a mechanism for the county to disburse its revenues, an increase approved by public vote in 1997. The plan also focused on seasonal traffic congestion and the need to find funding for an efficient, environmentally friendly public transit system, an issue that is still one of North Lake Tahoe's most significant ongoing challenges.

Three years after the first plan, the resort association asked Design Workshop to help it set priorities for investing TOT monies in order to encourage longer and more frequent tourist visits. But by then the resort association had fallen victim to its own success: Locals were pressuring it to deal with things outside its purpose and capability, including daycare and workforce housing. The association used the new TOT tourism plan internally but did not release it to the public, finally turning its attention to issues of community investment in 2004, when it undertook a new plan

that would also clarify its role. In that document, it pledged to bring its power to bear on local issues that have tourism impacts, for instance by supporting construction of a much-desired recreation center that could also enhance the visitor experience, and by agreeing to sit on the board of the housing authority to advocate for workforce housing. The plan also focused on the land, linking the area's economic vitality to the health of its ecosystems, since the area depends so heavily on its scenic qualities, emphasizing the need for environmental care in all infrastructure changes. But the 2004 plan also restated in a public forum that the resort association is not a government entity and doesn't have the expertise, training or funding to solve community problems.

The three consecutive tourism master plans for North Lake Tahoe resulted in far-reaching positive impacts. At the largest scale, once the resort association was in place and the TOT was increased, investors undertook new multimillion-dollar developments at both Squaw Valley and Northstar. Effects at the local level were significant as well. TOT revenues funded modest

redevelopment of the commercial cores of several communities, which encouraged private improvements. When Tahoe City installed sidewalks and drainage systems to create a pedestrian ambience, adjacent landowners began improving their properties almost immediately. A year after the 2004 master plan was instituted, local officials praised it for having made significant strides in aligning agencies and removing competition for grant funds, while bringing a $2.1 million investment in new infrastructure, trails, parks and transportation improvements to communities along the north shore.

PROJECT CREDITS

MASTER PLAN: Design Workshop, Inc.
  PICs: Richard Shaw (Phases 1 and 2)
  Rebecca Zimmermann (Phase 3)
  Project manager: Rebecca Zimmermann
  (Phases 1 and 2)
  Planners: Sarah Chase, Amy Capron,
  Kristen White

CLIENTS: Placer County, California, North Lake
Tahoe Resort Association

Tourism Data: BBC Research (Phase 1)

Transportation Consulting: LSC Transportation
Consultants, Inc. (Phases 1 and 3)

Survey Data: RRC Associates (Phases 1 and 3)

Rising visitor numbers threatened to degrade the scenic qualities at the edge of one of the world's premier places. An array of interests came together to plan and design a gateway village that would give people access to the canyon while allowing them to enjoy their visits more fully.

PROJECT DISCUSSION:
CANYON FOREST VILLAGE

Grand Canyon, Arizona

Gateway village aims to mitigate pressures at the Grand Canyon's rim

Like many national parks, the South Rim of the Grand Canyon offers access to its spectacular landscape but must also protect it. Five million people visit the Grand Canyon annually, which challenges its fragile ecosystem, and funding cuts have compounded problems such as overtaxed infrastructure at the rim's existing village. In 20 years of debate, officials had come to believe that the most helpful ways with which they could preserve the canyon would be to exclude private cars from the South Rim by bringing in public transit and to move besieged services out of the park to a gateway community.

In 1989, the designers helped a developer plan and design just such a gateway community, proposing to create a mixed-use development in the town of Tusayan, 7 miles south of the rim, with upgraded worker housing,

needed social services and a light-rail connection to the canyon. This planned community would use income from hotels and shops to subsidize permanent housing and the community services that were missing from Tusayan, including fire, emergency, medical, banking, churches and a school. To maintain long-term tourist revenues, the development would have to be consistent with park ideals, address environmental concerns and meet the economic and social needs of the South Rim communities. The developer made an exchange of 2,100 acres of inholdings in South Kaibab National Forest for 270 acres of developable land adjacent to Tusayan. Because of the high profile of the park, the designers felt that the project needed to be an international educational model for cutting-edge sustainable design, and they assembled a team that included law,

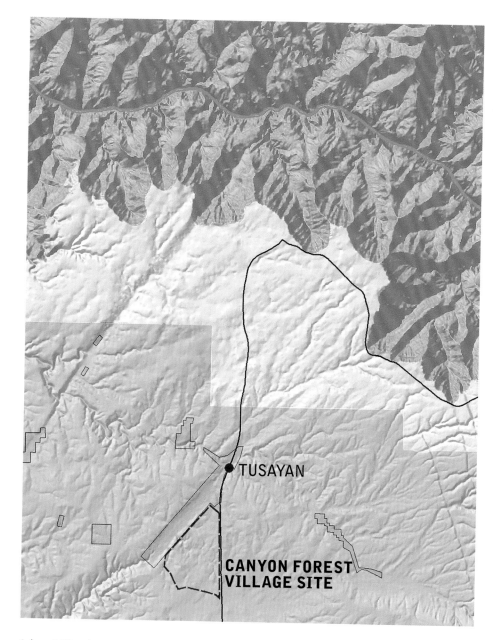

(above) The site was due south of the main tourist stop along the South Rim of the Grand Canyon, far enough from the canyon to divert uses away from its edge. The Tusayan airfield is located along the northwest edge of the site. At top, the Colorado River, which is at the bottom of the canyon, is shown in blue.

(opposite) Development at the existing town of Tusayan had grown without any guiding policies that could have created a sense of gateway for the Grand Canyon. The town offers scattered services and accommodations for tourists as well as rudimentary housing for canyon staff.

planning and "green" architecture experts.

The project was subject to rigorous scrutiny by an array of stakeholders, including environmental groups, Native American tribes, workers and even visitors. The design included housing for park employees and Tusayan workers, hotels for visitors, a market featuring Native American craftspeople, a research facility, churches and other community institutions and a satellite facility of the Museum of Northern Arizona to add a cultural and educational layer over the tourism base. Retail and hotel offerings were reduced and phased so as not to overwhelm local competitors. Architectural guidelines required buildings to follow historical styles, and codes were drafted requiring straightforward "green" building practices.

Sustainability was the single most persuasive aspect of the project, bringing people together no matter whether their prime concern was the environment, economics or community issues. The entire village was designed to be LEED-certified, with a review board to ensure it met measurable "green" building objectives, including such widespread use of photovoltaic cells and passive solar design that it would be the largest solar installation in the United States. Environmental scientists coun-

seled against the use of groundwater wells, which could deplete the aquifers beneath the rim. Local Native American tribes joined them, citing the impact the project could have on canyon springs, which they consider sacred. By designing such features as rainwater harvesting, low-flow fixtures, reuse of graywater and a solar-aquatic sewage treatment facility, the team was able to gain support for a legally binding commitment to use no groundwater.

The plan was endorsed by federal, state and county officials; the Hopi, Navajo and Havasupai tribes; environmentalists; and cultural organizations, including the Grand Canyon Trust. Other groups, like the Sierra Club, opposed the plan in favor of creating a quota on canyon visitation. Local landowners and merchants in Tusayan vehemently opposed the plan, seeking to extend the monopoly they had held on the tourist trade since homesteading days. The nearby communities of Flagstaff and Williams were split between those who saw benefit in improving the canyon visitation experience and those who saw only the threat of a potential competitor.

Ultimately, the plan was approved by a seven-to-one vote of the county planning commission and a unanimous vote of the local board of supervisors.

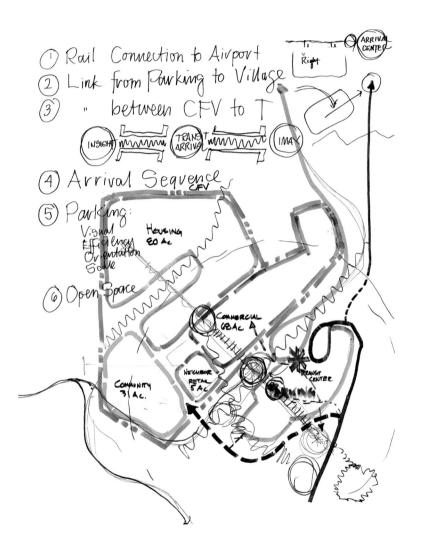

1. Rail Connection to Airport
2. Link from Parking to Village
3. " between CFV to T

INSIGHT TRANSIT ARRIVAL IMAX
ARRIVAL CENTER
Right

4. Arrival Sequence CFV
5. Parking:
   Visual
   Efficiency
   Orientation
   Scale
   HOUSING 80 Ac.
6. Open Space

COMMERCIAL 60 Ac. A
NEIGHBOR RETAIL 5 AC.
COMMUNITY 31 AC.
PARKING
TRANSIT CENTER

However, using the Arizona law that permits any rezoning decision to be taken to local referendum, the opposing business interests allied themselves with the anti-development faction of the environmental community and circulated petitions to have the decision put on a county-wide election ballot. After a divisive and expensive campaign, Coconino County voters rejected the Canyon Forest Village proposal. Just days after the project was defeated in November 2000, local merchants began construction of a strip mall in Tusayan.

The town still has no schools and very poor worker housing and offers no social services. Housing for Park Service employees still consists of largely run-down homes, including mobile homes, within the park itself. The only access Tusayan residents have to medical, fire, banking and other community facilities is through services that are paid for by the federal government and available in Grand Canyon Village. Tusayan still has only limited standards for development.

PROJECT CREDITS

MASTER PLAN: Design Workshop, Inc.
PIC: Kurt Culbertson
Project Managers: Deanna Weber,
Sarah Chase Shaw

CLIENT: Grand Canyon Exchange
Limited Partnership
General Partner: Tom DePaolo

Architecture: Bob Berkebile, BNIM Architects

Governance: Wayne Hyatt, Hyatt and Stubblefield

(above) The team linked the assets of the new village with transportation from the canyon to both preserve the South Rim and offer pedestrian access.

(opposite) The master plan created a gateway community for the canyon. Renderings, top to bottom, show the plan's proposed walking trails and open spaces, central public gathering places, employee housing and a solar sewage treatment facility.

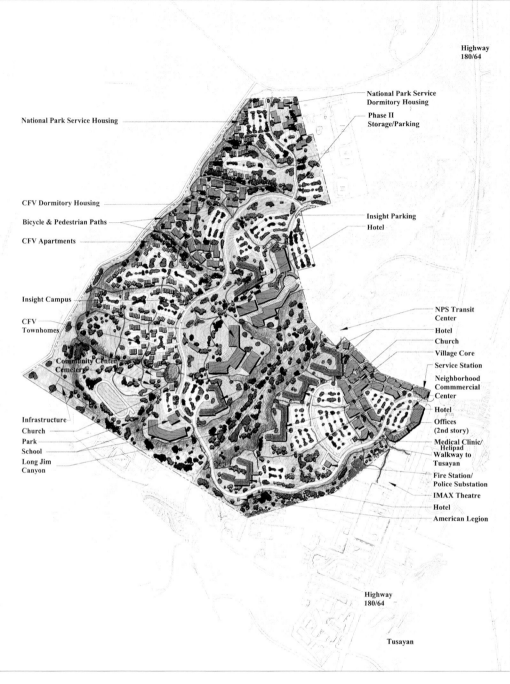

Highway
180/64

National Park Service Housing

National Park Service
Dormitory Housing

Phase II
Storage/Parking

CFV Dormitory Housing

Bicycle & Pedestrian Paths

Insight Parking

Hotel

CFV Apartments

Insight Campus

NPS Transit
Center

CFV
Townhomes

Hotel

Church

Village Core

Community Center

Service Station

Cemetery

Neighborhood
Commmercial
Center

Infrastructure

Hotel

Church

Offices
(2nd story)

Park

Medical Clinic/
Helipad

School

Walkway to
Tusayan

Long Jim
Canyon

Fire Station/
Police Substation

IMAX Theatre

Hotel

American Legion

Highway
180/64

Tusayan

Locals have been trying to make an ecotourist camp in the Madidi region of Bolivia for years. It took a convergence of forces inside and outside of the country to finally make it happen. In order to ensure that the camp would thrive, its planning and design focused on making it economically, socially and environmentally viable.

PROJECT DISCUSSION: CHALALÀN ECOLODGE

Madidi National Forest, Bolivia

Sustainability of many kinds achieved with ecotourism outpost

The idea of creating an ecolodge on Lake Chalalàn in northwestern Bolivia got its start in 1976 when a travel agency in La Paz set up a rudimentary sleeping platform there and hired hunting guides from among the people of San José de Uchupiamonas, a nearby village of Tacana-Quechua Indians. Because of the area's abundant monkey, peccary and jaguar, the agency hoped to bring in wildlife tourists, but the site had little success and was eventually abandoned. Several years later, it was popularized as a backpacking destination after the publication of the book *Back from Tuichi*, later republished as *Heart of the Amazon*, by Israeli adventurer Yossi Ghinsberg.

The book recounts the author's harrowing adventure when he became lost in the Bolivian rainforest for three weeks in 1982 and nearly died. After he was rescued by a friend, a hunter and a guide from San José, Ghinsberg offered to help the people of the village in any way he could. Villagers had earned their livelihoods from logging the area's abundant mahogany, guiding hunters and helping with oil exploration. In 1991, when a group of residents decided to build a tourist lodge at Chalalàn, Ghinsberg introduced locals to Conservation International (CI), which has a major initiative to preserve tropical environments. This second tourism venture also failed, but CI, which had long debated an initiative to create ecotourism destinations as a means of protecting rainforest locales, took an interest in the area and did an assessment of the region's biodiversity. This played a major role in helping the Bolivian government create the 7,000-square-mile Madidi National Park in 1995, in which both Chalalàn and San José lie.

Leaders of the project engaged villagers and the team in intensive discussion of the possibilities for creating an ecotourist lodge on Lake Chalalàn.

Scientists characterized Madidi as the most biologically diverse wilderness reserve on Earth. CI chose to launch its first ecotourist project, thereby creating an entirely new facility in this remote location, which is reached by small commuter planes from La Paz to Rurrenabaque, followed by a five-hour motorized canoe trip up the Beni and Tuichi rivers. Though the people of San Jose wanted to build the ecolodge for economic reasons, CI wanted to help prevent or minimize illegal logging and oil drilling by putting "eyes" on the new national park. The planning process recognized that these goals could only be reconciled by giving project ownership to area residents. If the ecolodge succeeded, the new economy would make locals' livelihood dependent on preservation of the park, which would in turn encourage residents to act as the guardians of that fragile landscape.

Design Workshop did pro bono planning and design of the new ecotourist resort, including economic, community and environmental assessments and design of its facilities. Ghinsberg lent support by helping villagers win a $1.25 million grant from the Inter-American Development Bank, $200,000 of which went to building the Chalalàn Ecolodge.

The team began by crafting a financial pro forma, assessing market demand in order to establish the project's feasibility. Design and planning were done on site, which presented significant challenges. Locals constructed a rudimentary shelter for the team to live and work in and built a table for them to work on, but there were no utilities within 50 miles and no available mapping of any kind, in part because of constraints imposed by the U.S. Department of Defense's war on drugs. The team finally crafted crude base maps by combining global-positioning system data and handheld altimeters.

Working with CI and Cornell University ecologists, the designers surveyed local wildlife, soils and other conditions and explored regional building forms and site locations that would protect guests from animals, insects and significant rainfall. They worked with 25 residents of San José in on-site charrettes to do site design, planning and design, all of which depended on local technologies and extensive fieldwork. Local residents became so engaged in the process that the designers had to wait to work until they had gone to bed. The designers served as ad hoc architects and construction supervisors, gaining knowledge of local construction materials and methods for building in hot humid conditions, averting rapid decomposition and managing climate

The team worked with villagers to enhance local building techniques using sustainably harvested materials from the nearby forest.

(left) Local craftsmen use split chonta palms for the walls of one of the cabins, with jatata leaves for the roofing.

(right) Villagers split fibrous materials to use as binding.

(above) The table on which they created the plans and designs was constructed by villagers from San José, along with a shelter for them to sleep in.

(opposite) The designers created both the master plan and a series of designs for individual buildings.

control. Design of individual facilities relied entirely on building materials that could be harvested sustainably from local forests, including chonta palms, which were used for the walls of lodges, and jatata leaves, used to make the roofs.

To meet the challenges of a fragile site that had only a small, untrained labor pool and to centralize guest services and reduce the overall impact of the project, the design clustered a series of small buildings near the lake. This made it possible to construct the project with relative ease and phase it in response to market demand and funding. The team also trained villagers in marketing, management, housekeeping, food preparation and tour-guiding.

The Chalalàn Ecolodge, which has been operated for several seasons by the people of San José, opened in May 1998 and now has 24 beds. Lodge buildings run on solar power; a shallow well suggested in planning documents provides the site with abundant potable water. A network of trails allows visitors to explore the surrounding rainforest, both with and without guides. The facility is recognized in the industry as having achieved a good balance between what it offers tourists and what it does for locals. In February 2001, the community received full ownership of the lodge. Today, 74 families receive regular

direct economic benefits from employment and management of the ecolodge.

Tours to the ecolodge are booked by several specialty tour companies in North America and the lodge has been featured in such publications as *Outside* magazine and the *Washington Post*. Chalalàn's setting, a misty jungle lake ringed by low hills, has been rhapsodized by travel writers for its network of trails and "spooky beauty," while its cabins and lodges have a reputation as stylish and comfortable. It is considered upmarket, as opposed to rugged tented camps at other sites on the Tuichi River, which are known to cause environmental degradation by operating in a non-sustainable manner.

PROJECT CREDITS

PROJECT COORDINATOR: Joe Vieira, Conservation International

MASTER PLAN: Design Workshop, Inc.
  PIC: Kurt Culbertson
  Landscape Architect: John Suarez
  Project Architect: Rich Carr

CLIENT: Conservation International

Collaborators: Guido Mamani, Zenon Limaco and Alejandro Limaco, villagers and tourism entrepreneurs who took lead roles in the planning workshops

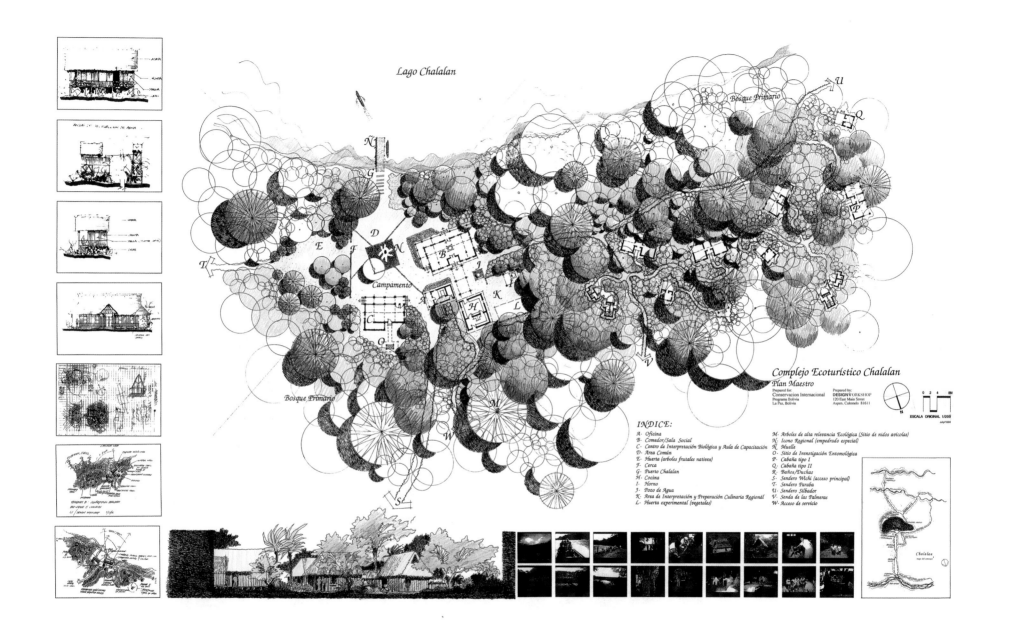

Lago Chalalan

Bosque Primario

Bosque Primario

Campamento

Bosque Primario

Complejo Ecoturístico Chalalan
Plan Maestro

Prepared for: Prepared by:
Conservacion Internacional   DESIGN WORKSHOP
Programa Bolivia   120 East Main Street
La Paz, Bolivia   Aspen, Colorado 81611

ESCALA ORIGINAL 1/200

INDICE:

A- Oficina
B- Comedor/Sala Social
C- Centro de Interpretación Biológica y Aula de Capacitación
D- Area Común
E- Huerta (arboles frutales nativos)
F- Cerca
G- Puerto Chalalan
H- Cocina
I- Horno
J- Pozo de Agua
K- Area de Interpretación y Preparación Culinaria Regional
L- Huerta experimental (vegetales)

M- Arboles de alta relevancia Ecológica (Sitio de nidos avícolas)
N- Icono Regional (empedrado especial)
Ñ- Muelle
O- Sitio de Investigación Entomológica
P- Cabaña tipo I
Q- Cabaña tipo II
R- Baños/Duchas
S- Sendero Wichi (acceso principal)
T- Sendero Puraba
U- Sendero Silbador
V- Senda de las Palmeras
W- Acceso de servicio

Chalalan

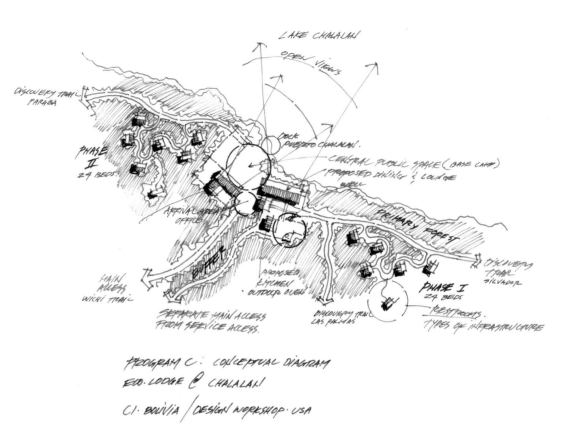

PROGRAM C: CONCEPTUAL DIAGRAM
ECO·LODGE @ CHALALAN

CI·BOLIVIA / DESIGN WORKSHOP·USA

(above left) Villagers now serve as guides taking visitors into the surrounding rain forest to view the abundant wildlife, insect population and botanical attractions.

(above right) The dining and lounge building is situated on the lake to maximize views, while individual cabins are clustered under the forest canopy with a buffer of trees between them and the lake.

Chalalàn's finished cabins are elevated, with all windows screened to keep out insects and guard against decomposition.

DILEMMA: The environment and economy of South Lake Tahoe deteriorated over several decades until, by the mid-1980s, problems looked intractable. Undisciplined development left the city with overwhelming environmental and economic problems.

LEGACY GOALS:

Community
Rescue the town from decline by creating a new public face, transforming strip development to make the street a place where people can connect with each other and establishing a central gathering place.

Environment
Improve the lake's water quality by filtering runoff and reducing the building footprint; foster a pedestrian-friendly village, networking with public transportation, which will reduce traffic volume and air pollution; preserve mature trees.

Economics
Re-establish South Lake Tahoe as a worthy destination by linking it with the ski area and redeveloping a portion of downtown; support the project with public funding and private investment, boosting property values and increasing tax revenue.

Art
Elevate the style of the built environment to match the area's spectacular surroundings; craft a series of spaces that encourage exploration and discovery and create scenic corridors with sequenced spaces to reveal views to the mountains and the lake.

THESIS: Residents, officials and developers working together can overcome differences to craft an environmentally sustainable and financially viable vision for Tahoe's future; this will bring people together and reinvent the area as an appealing destination.

PARK AVENUE REDEVELOPMENT

South Lake Tahoe, California

Economic revitalization rescues the environment of a national treasure

Overview

The community of South Lake Tahoe overcame serious environmental and economic problems to create a $260 million, mixed-use redevelopment project that includes a gondola to nearby Heavenly Ski Area and a consolidated transit center. The 11-year planning, approvals, entitlements and construction process required the forging of a public-private partnership and an intensive negotiation process among widely diverse stakeholders. This public process guided locals to find the legislative support, revision of regulations and careful deployment of development monies that have given the town a new future. The final plan, which clarified stringent environmental regulations that were choking off economic development in the area, won the support of both the Tahoe Regional Planning Agency and the League to Save Lake Tahoe, both well-known for their staunch environmental stands.

History/Context

Because of its recreational and gaming assets, the Lake Tahoe area became a popular vacation spot with Californians in the 1950s and 1960s. But the resulting unplanned development spelled disaster for the environment, degrading the scenic assets of the area and also despoiling the clarity and purity of the highest and clearest lake in the world. In response, the governors of California and Nevada created the Tahoe Regional Planning Agency (TRPA) in 1969, and environmental groups like the League to Save Lake Tahoe called for stringent environmental regulations, which were enacted. These were put in place to change future development, but the

funding that was allocated was inadequate to the task and new investment in the area had essentially ceased because of the daunting challenges of the new requirements. Conditions became dire: The lake's water quality had not improved; the TRPA had no money left for environmental work; the town's economy was in serious decline; and there was serious in-fighting among stakeholders in the basin.

In 1984, the City of South Lake Tahoe asked the California state legislature to declare the city a blighted area, something that required lawmakers to enlarge the definition to include environmental blight. This granted the town new powers, which allowed a newly formed redevelopment agency to condemn land and relocate tenants so the town could acquire areas ripe for redevelopment and create a financial mechanism to fund projects through tax-increment financing and municipal bonds.

The first project created under this aegis was the Embassy Suites hotel (1986-1988), which had good occupancy and boosted tax revenues. On the heels of this, Heavenly Ski Area officials introduced the idea of building a gondola that would connect South Lake Tahoe to the ski area. This was the key feature of what eventually would become the Park Avenue redevelopment. But at the

time, because of economic decline and uncertainty, neither Heavenly nor the redevelopment agency was willing to commit to building any part of it.

Process

The obstacles to redeveloping the proposed gondola site seemed insurmountable. Other planning consultants and developers had tried to redevelop portions of South Lake Tahoe and failed because of the environmental regulations, the absence of capital and the community's lack of a vision for the future. The members of the redevelopment agency (city officials, a representative of the Japanese-owned Heavenly Ski Area, property owners and developers) had little in common and no coherent plans for the site. But the agency proceeded, entering into development agreements with the city to create a mixed-use base area that would be linked to the Heavenly Ski Resort by gondola.

In 1992, Design Workshop began developing a master plan for the 34-acre site in the center of downtown and, over time, assembled and led a team of architects, civil engineers, transportation planners, market researchers and economists, soil scientists, hydrologists, native plant and tree preservation specialists, ski-area planners and gondola engineers. Many factors militated

Tahoe Aims for Change: From Seedy to Sleek

By Jim Carlton

South Lake Tahoe, Calif.

THIS CROWDED RESORT TOWN is trying to lose its seedy image by going green.

The bustling south shore of Lake Tahoe, unlike the more open and upscale north-shore area, is undergoing an estimated $500 million makeover to replace most of its 1950s and 1960s-era budget motels with sleeker, more environment-friendly buildings. Already in place are an Embassy Suites Resort and two Marriott vacation properties, plus a new $28 million gondola that conveniently whisks skiers from the town's center to the slopes of the nearby Heavenly Ski Resort.

PROPERTY REPORT

The facelift, being paid for with a combination of municipal bonds and California state funds, is winning accolades from environmentalists, among others, because it has been designed to take up as much as a fifth less land space than the earlier construction.

Not only will that bring an aesthetic improvement to the year-round mountain resort, but it is expected to significantly reduce the engine oil and other contaminants that flow with rain and snow runoff into Lake Tahoe on the border between California and Nevada. In recent decades, overdevelopment on Lake Tahoe's shores has turned its famed crystalline waters cloudier.

This miniature golf course has been torn down to make way for a more upscale South Lake Tahoe.

"We think the environmental benefits of this project are substantial," says Rochelle Nason, executive director of the League to Save Lake Tahoe, a local environmental group, which had bitterly resisted many other large-scale developments in the past.

The Lake Tahoe redevelopment scheme, following a type of development known as "land intensification," is one of the more ambitious involving this Western tourist attraction. Urban planners say such development, featuring fewer but taller buildings that use less land, could serve as a model to many sprawling urban areas, such as greater Los Angeles.

Blessed by stunning scenery, including Ponderosa pine forests and snow-capped mountains hemming a mirror-like lake, the resort has long been a draw for its hiking and water sports in summer, and skiing in winter. Tahoe's location bordering Nevada, once the only state in the U.S. that allowed casinos, had made it a gambling destination, too.

But the gambling business, some locals say, didn't spur the right kind of development. "A lot of the motels were designed for people to have a roof over their head and a bed so they could go gamble," recalls Lew Feldman, a local attorney who has represented the project's developers, including Marriott.

Outside the casino district, the lakefront began to fill in the 1970s and 1980s with new subdivisions catering to second-home owners. Prompted by a public outcry over the pell-mell growth, the Tahoe Regional Planning Agency was formed in 1970 to rein in development. Given final say on all projects around the lake's entire 72-mile shoreline, the agency succeeded in corralling the region's runaway growth. However, it also came under fire from some motel owners who said it prevented

Please Turn to Page B8, Column 1

Tahoe Aims to Change Seedy, Polluted Ways

Continued From Page B1

them from making modest upgrades to their aging establishments.

Agency officials deny they hampered motels from making improvements and regular maintenance. Planners say that economic problems—caused by a glut of motels—prevented the lodging owners from keeping their property in good repair.

Whatever the cause, South Lake Tahoe had gained such a bad reputation by the 1990s that local officials say their

community began to lose tourism business to other resorts. Then, the proliferation of casinos nationwide further siphoned off gamblers.

Meanwhile, during those decades, lake pollution continued. According to the League to Save Lake Tahoe, the lake's cleanliness has declined to the point that the water's clarity has sharply diminished. A white plate that could be seen at 102 feet in 1965 can now be seen at only about 70 feet. In 1997, the region's efforts gained national attention when President Clinton attended a federal government summit here to coordinate various state, county and federal environmental projects in the area, including erosion-control efforts.

"The city of South Lake Tahoe decided they had to change their direction, or they wouldn't have a future," says Richard Shaw, a principal of Design Workshop, an Aspen, Colo., design firm that has helped spearhead the local makeover.

In 1988, city officials declared much of their half-mile motel strip along U.S. Highway 50 (which runs from Maryland's coast to Sacramento, Calif.) a blighted zone and formed a redevelopment agency to clean it up. Using its power of eminent domain, the city demolished about a half-dozen motels and shops lining the edge of U.S. 50 nearest

the Nevada border after paying off the owners. Then, in 1990, in place of the tumbledown motels, a 400-room Embassy Suites Resort was built.

The following year, the redevelopment agency commissioned Design Workshop to develop a map for a much larger project on roughly 34 acres of land where nearly two dozen motels, mostly one-story wood-frame buildings with neon signs, and small businesses were situated. The project was endorsed by the local planning agency and environmentalists because it was designed to reduce the footprint of de-

New hotels and shops, set back from the street, have been designed to fit in with Tahoe's natural surroundings.

veloped land and add retention basins to catch and filter street runoff before it could wash into the lake.

Through the 1990s, however, the city encountered some obstacles in pursuing the plan. Some motel owners sued for, and won, more money after their properties were condemned. Owners of the now-razed Red Carpet Inn, for exam-

ple, said they managed to increase to $4.1 million from $3.2 million the total the city paid for their property.

More hurdles had to be overcome after the projects were issued construction permits in 1996. For example, the regional planning agency has a 28-foot, or three-story height limit, but the plan called for buildings as high as 76 feet, or six floors, so buildings would take up less land. Developers gained an exemption after showing that the buildings would be set back about 75 feet from the highway so their added height wouldn't obscure mountain views.

Other troubles popped up. For example, the project's principal developer, Maine-based American Skiing Co., then-owner of Heavenly Ski Resort announced in early 2000 it was in such financial straits it could no longer back two big vacation-ownership hotels it was planning to build. But Marriott stepped in to take the place of American, which has since sold the resort to Colorado's Vail Resorts. Vail officials said a major reason they decided to buy Heavenly was the redevelopment plan for South Lake Tahoe.

Since then, the redevelopment has proceeded fairly smoothly. In November, Marriott opened its 261-room Timber Lodge and 199-room Grand Residence Club. More attractions, including a new cinema complex and ice-skating rink, are set to open next winter. Across the street on the north side of U.S. 50, a hotel and convention center is planned on property owned mostly by Harrah's Entertainment Inc.

(above) The environmental significance of the new development was noted by the *Wall Street Journal* in May 2004 coverage.

(right) An early rendering shows the connection the gondola has made between the town of South Lake Tahoe and the Heavenly Ski Area, which has helped reduce air pollution by minimizing driving between the two.

CASE STUDY

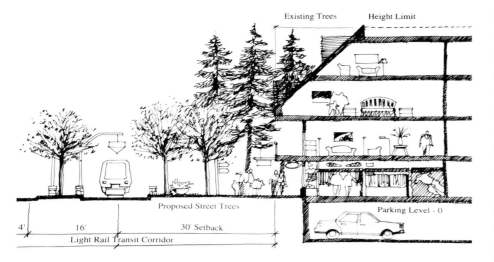

Vertical stacking of parking, retail and accommodations gave the site the density it needed to support construction of the gondola (located in the clock-tower building) and an adjacent intermodal transit center.

against success, including the area's weak economy and the town's emerging reputation as a rundown place of low-rent motels for skiers and gamblers. It was the town's newly granted redevelopment powers, the kind of powers previously reserved only for urban entities, that would eventually make it possible to effect change in South Lake Tahoe.

Site analysis, an assessment of the political environment, funding mechanisms and the redevelopment's legal status revealed that the area was one of the biggest contributors to the poor water quality of the lake and had no economic life left — no manmade or built part of the site could be salvaged. What was needed was a vision of the future that had been denied under the existing, unplanned development pattern, a vision that would bring a significant upside for the community.

The first step was to create a plan to align the economic and market interests of the redevelopment proponents, a process that took almost a year and made it clear to the development group that they couldn't proceed under the current regulations enforced by the TRPA. The team began a series of informal conversations with the agency with the goal of demonstrating the positive contribution the redevelopment could make.

One demonstration included a built model of the development program as it would exist under then-current regulations. The agency had imposed a height limit of 32 feet in order to protect views of the mountains and also required any new development to reduce its footprint on the land. But the height limit meant the development had to spread out across the site, so ground coverage couldn't be reduced. It also meant there was no space for the setbacks and wide sidewalks the TRPA wanted. The team illustrated how allowing taller buildings but moving them back from the highway would still preserve views of the mountains, even enhancing them by creating specific view corridors and framing the landscape more artfully. The model also illustrated how the TRPA's ban on below-grade construction (because it would touch groundwater) conflicted with its desire to conceal parking. The team demonstrated how such issues could be handled with environmental mitigation, such as detention ponds, lower groundwater and manmade wetlands to ensure higher water quality before drainage reaches the lake.

Capitalizing on the city's desire for a ski gondola to Heavenly, the team introduced the idea of a transit center adjacent to the gondola, which could reduce the number of car trips to the area and improve air quality —

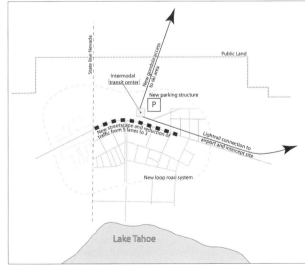

Early concepts included light rail and a loop road that would divert traffic from Highway 50 and give visitors easier access to the town's other assets. The model was created to demonstrate how changing height restrictions would not obscure views of the mountain.

CASE STUDY

The redevelopment enhanced the pedestrian experience of South Lake Tahoe by creating new public spaces and connections between spaces within the site.

something the State of California offered funding for. Rather than making this a one-time zoning exception, the design team argued that they were actually creating a new standard for development in the area, one that would achieve the TRPA's goals through the introduction of transit, mixed uses and intensive environmental measures. Gradually, agency officials realized that in some ways its regulations were at odds with the larger goals of scenic and environmental preservation, and they began to work with the team to rewrite regulations to accommodate development in new ways.

With regulatory issues out of the way and public support strong, the individual members of the redevelopment project began to compete for the most favorable positions on the site. The vision for the community helped guide a long series of redesigns, deepening the stakeholders' understanding of such issues as circulation patterns, the design of public spaces and transit use. The city issued $50 million in bonds to support the redevelopment but external events began to intrude. In 1996, supported by the success of its initial public offering, American Skiing Company bought Heavenly Ski Area and the hotel development rights in the belief that linkage of the commercial and hotel properties

to Heavenly was crucial to its success. The company had capital to invest in the mountain and agreed to build the gondola. By 1999, the $28 million gondola had been constructed but was the only element on the site. The skiing company, which suffered a series of setbacks, sold the hotel sites to Marriott Corporation, which began construction in 2000, and two years later, it sold Heavenly to Vail Resorts. The team moved ahead to resolve institutional governance issues, which allowed the project to open in November 2002.

Outcomes

The redevelopment took 11 years to be realized. Although it had public support from an early stage, people often despaired that it would ever be built because so many projects in South Lake Tahoe had failed in the past. No individual entity had the capability to manage so large-scale and complex a project and none could tackle the major regulatory obstacles on its own. At times, the only rational course of action was to move forward in whatever way possible, solve immediate problems and trust that the process would eventually bear fruit. Once the right economic purpose for the site had been found, people came together around that vision, with the design team serving as problem solvers,

(opposite) The gondola building, with a clock-tower steeple, is positioned between two new hotels that offer ground-floor retail.

(above) New private spaces, like this courtyard pool, complement the extensive new streetscape, which was made possible by the elimination of curb cuts along the main arterial.

negotiators and vision keepers, along with such dedicated locals as Lew Feldman, attorney for the project; Jaye Von Klug, director of the redevelopment agency, who engineered the public-private partnership; and Stan Hanson, vice president of Heavenly.

In all, 700 hotel rooms were incorporated into two large structures that operate either as time-share or interval ownership hotels in order to ensure a steady stream of income to the area. To enhance aesthetics, the design guidelines for the project specified an architectural style similar to that of Tahoe mountain lodges and setbacks that preserve scenic vistas. The project sets aside 20 percent of all units for affordable housing to meet pressing community needs and diversify the social fabric. It has spawned other redevelopment projects in the area, including a 19-acre site across the street. The plan remade an arterial roadway of scattered retail into an essentially auto-free destination, revitalizing it with retail and housing, inviting streetscapes, public spaces for people to gather and a way to connect to the ski mountain — as well as reducing the number of curb cuts on the highway from 27 to two.

Because of the plan's adherence to a much higher standard of environmental rigor than had ever been practiced in the Tahoe basin, the plan was fully endorsed by the TRPA, arguably as restrictive a planning agency as any that exists in the United States. Its main successes include creation of a consolidated transportation system that resulted in a 10 percent decrease in traffic volume, preservation of more than 100 existing mature conifer trees, replacement of billboards with street trees and public open space and filtration of approximately 1,000 pounds of contaminants annually through manmade wetlands.

PROJECT CREDITS

MASTER PLAN: Design Workshop, Inc.
  PIC: Richard Shaw
  Project managers: Deanna Weber, Steve Noll, Taber Sweet
  Landscape Architects: Gyles Thornely, Suzanne Richman, Corey Brooks, Rob Breeden, Rich Carr, Rich Sharp, Denise George

CLIENTS: City of South Lake Tahoe Redevelopment Agency, Marriott, Heavenly Ski Area, Trans Sierra Investments

Master Plan Architects: Cottle Graybeal Yaw, Jung Brannen

Architects: Jung Bramien Architects, Theodore Brown and Partners

Collaborator: Lew Feldman/Feldman, Shaw and DeVore, LLC

The gondola connects skiers to the redevelopment, which has created a series of public gathering spaces that bring people together.

LEGACY

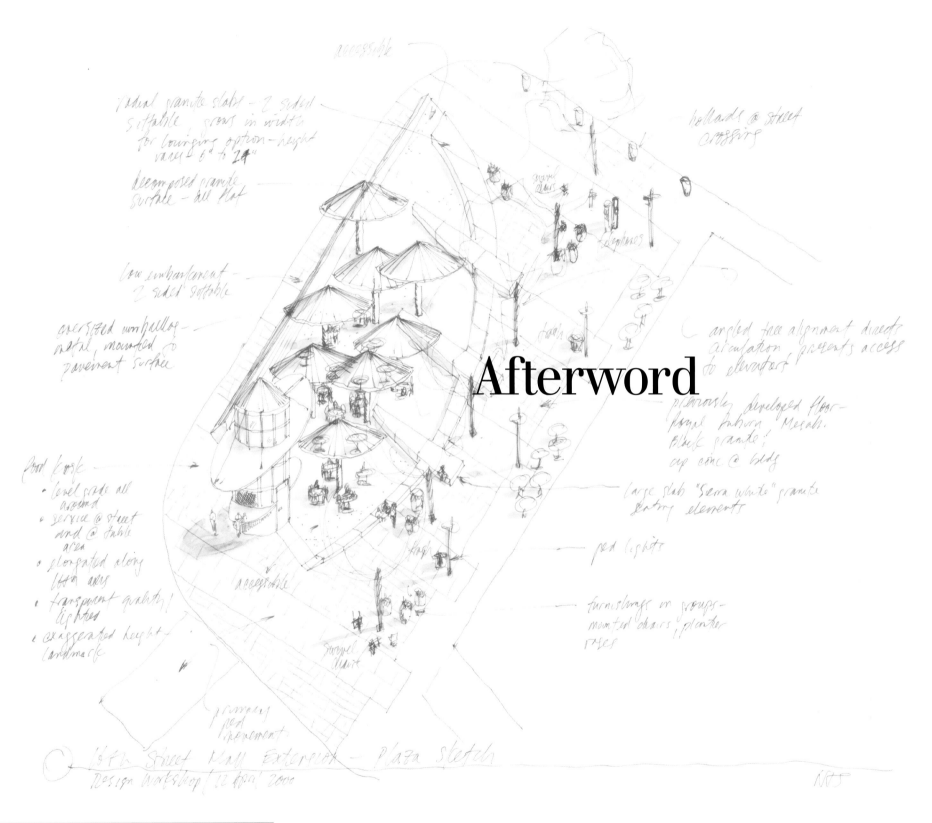

Afterword

In this book, we have tried to demonstrate the essence of Legacy Design through projects we have undertaken over the years, but this is also a book about people — people striving together to achieve an ideal. From the beginning, the partners have sought a higher purpose for their work, and the professionals that joined with them over the years, forming more than ten offices across the country and into South America, have shared that vision. The workshop environment brings people together, testing, questioning, pushing and supporting one another so that they can reach higher than they might on their own. We seek to do work of exceptional quality in landscape architecture, community planning and urban design. To do that we need great clients, great challenges and great colleagues. Legacy is a quality that can only be judged over time. Design Workshop has been organized from its inception to outlast its founders with the understanding that Legacy requires multiple generations to test its mettle. Legacy is neither a product nor a process, it is a way of thinking — a culture based on trust, transparency and holism. The people of Design Workshop are truly the engine that propels us further and higher, always seeking to do better as we journey toward Legacy.

The Partners

Joe Porter, FASLA, helped found Design Workshop in 1969. Porter earned his bachelor's degree in landscape architecture from Utah State University and his master's from the University of Illinois. He served as an assistant professor in both the Department of Landscape Architecture at Louisiana State University and in the School of Design at North Carolina State University. More recently, he has served as an adjunct professor in the Department of Architecture and Planning at the University of Colorado at Denver. Porter, who is a registered landscape architect in Montana and North Carolina, is a full member of the Urban Land Institute and received a fellowship from the American Society of Landscape Architects in 1988. He has served as a board member and past president of the Landscape Architecture Foundation and The Center for Design Innovation.

Don Ensign, FASLA, helped found Design Workshop in 1969. Ensign holds a bachelor's degree in landscape architecture from Utah State University and a master's from the University of Michigan. He was an assistant professor in the School of Design at North Carolina State University and an instructor in the Department of Landscape Architecture and Environmental Planning at Utah State University. He is a registered landscape architect in Michigan and North Carolina.

Kurt Culbertson, FASLA, is the chairman and chief executive officer of Design Workshop, and the president of Design Workshop/South America. A graduate of Louisiana State University, Culbertson holds a master's degree in business administration in real estate from Southern Methodist University. He is a full member of the Urban Land Institute, participating in the Recreation Development Council, and served as chapter chair of the Rocky Mountain chapter of the Young Presidents Organization. He has served as a fellow of Dumbarton Oaks, the American Society of Landscape Architects and the Institute of Urban Design and received a Fulbright Scholarship to the Wirtschaft Universitat in Vienna, Austria. He currently serves as co-chair of the Cultural Landscape Foundation. He is a registered landscape architect in Arizona,

Florida, Idaho, Louisiana, Nevada, New Mexico, South Carolina, Texas, Utah, Virginia and Wyoming.

Richard W. Shaw, FASLA, joined Design Workshop in 1976. He graduated with honors from Utah State University and earned his master's from the Graduate School of Design at Harvard University, where he was awarded the Jacob Weidenman Traveling Fellowship. Shaw is a full member of the Urban Land Institute and has held council memberships in the Retail Development Council and the Recreation Development Council. He has taught Resort Design through Harvard University's School of Design Professional Development Series and his work in both small-scale residential garden design and large-scale resort redevelopment, planning and design has garnered many awards and commendations. Richard is a fellow of the American Society of Landscape Architects and a board member of the Landscape Architecture Foundation. He is a registered landscape architect in Arizona, Nevada and Wyoming.

Greg Ochis is the president and chief operating officer for Design Workshop. Greg joined the firm in 1981 after receiving his bachelor's degree in landscape architecture from the University of Minnesota. He earned his master's in real estate and construction management from the University of Colorado at Denver in 1995. Greg is a full member of the Urban Land Institute, a board member of the University of Minnesota's College of Architecture and Landscape Architecture, of the Landscape Architecture Foundation and the CEO Roundtable of the American Society of Landscape Architects (ASLA), as well as a member of the Colorado Real Estate Council and ASLA. He is a registered landscape architect in Iowa.

Rebecca Zimmermann specializes in real estate advisory services, market and economic analysis, and tourism planning. She joined Design Workshop in 1985 after graduating from Trinity University. In 1992, she received a master's degree of business administration from the University of Colorado at Denver. She is a full member of the Urban Land Institute, chair of the Recreation Development Council and instructor of the ULI Real Estate School. She is also a member of the Travel and Tourism Research Association. Becky has received numerous awards for her work in tourism planning and resort redevelopment, including being named to the Denver Business Journal's 2004 Who's Who in Construction, Architecture and Engineering and its 1999 Top 40 Under 40 Business Leaders and one of the Top 100 Business Women in Arizona by Today's Arizona Woman in 2000.

Todd Johnson, FASLA, joined Design Workshop in 1996. A founding partner and principal with Civitas, Inc., in Denver, Johnson holds a bachelor of landscape architecture from Utah State University and a master's from the Graduate School of Design at Harvard University. Under a Harvard Jerusalem Fellowship, he produced an urban design master plan for the Damascus Gate area that won first prize for urban design in Progressive Architecture's annual awards programs. He is a member of the Urban Land Institute and the American Society of Landscape Architects and serves as an associate adjunct professor with the Department of Architecture and Planning at the University of Colorado at Denver.

Terrall Budge, the firm's newest shareholder, is the principal of Design Workshop's Salt Lake City office. He earned a bachelor's degree in landscape architecture from Utah State University and a master's with distinction from Harvard University's Graduate School of Design. At Harvard, he was awarded the Jacob Weidenman Prize for outstanding design talent. He is LEED-accredited, is a member of the Urban Land Institute and the American Society of Landscape Architects and is a registered landscape architect in Utah.

Staff over the Years

Aboulafia, Sari
Adams, Carol
Adams, Peter
Affenburg, Marquita
Al-Hatabeh, Hesham
Al-rubaiy, Amir
Albert, Mike
Alden, Jeremy
Aldrete, Laura
Alexander, Tiffany
Alexander, Valerie
Allen, Alisa
Allen, Joe
Allen, Tawny
Allis, Ashley
Alsup, Jim
Amalong, David
Ambron, Corinne
Ames, Lisa
Amore, Richard
Anderson, Eric
Anderson, Kelly
Andreasen, Joseph
Armani, Lorna
Atterbury, Chad
Austin, Norecia
Bader, Michael
Baker, Shannon
Balabani, Monica
Balcer, Christian
Balgooyen, Steve
Balzer, Jennifer
Barbour, John
Barré, Kirsten
Basso, Cristian
Barrett-Osborne, Hillary
Bathgate, Judy
Battleson, Jay
Bayens, Cari
Beals, Jeramy
Bear, Jennifer
Bedell, Mark
Bell, Dave

Bellville, Linda
Bennish, Christopher
Benton, Emily
Berg, Robb
Bergeron, Kate
Bernard, Eric
Bernotas, Christopher
Beyer, Marc
Bhuthimethee, Tara
Blau, Ryan
Blue, Amie
Boesch, Amara
Bogaski, Kathy
Boggs, Zachary
Boldu, Mariana
Borkovetz, Rick
Borthwick, Bradley
Bousquet, Marla
Boyd, Phyllis
Bradley, Kobi
Braun, Peter
Braun, Rebecca
Breeden, Robert
Brenes, Juan Garcia
Britton, Pamela
Brockwell, Geraldine
Brooks, Corey
Brown, David
Brozo, Steven
Brunet, Thomas
Bruno, Vincent
Budge, Michael
Budge, Terrall
Burkhardt, Roger
Burns, Mimi
Busch, Carmen
Byers, Casey
Byron, Shawn
Byun, HyunJung
Cagnina, Maria
Cahir, Kathryn
Campbell, Craig
Campbell, Jill

Campbell, Sara
Campos, Pedro
Canfield, Jessica
Capron, Amy
Carlson, David
Carr, Rich
Carroll, Pat
Carrizo, Valeria
Case, Diedra
Castillo, Fernando
Cerqueira, Andrea Callonere
Cenzano, Christina
Chanslor, Mary Alison
Charles, Joseph
Chau, Eddie
Chen, Ting-chieh
Cheri, Robin
Cheung, Kenneth
Chidgey, Dominic
Chiesa, Alejandra
Chipman, Robert
Chomiak, Scott
Choules, Julie
Christensen, E.
Churchill, Beth
Clark, Erin
Cohon, Cindy
Cole, Walter
Colgan, Breena
Condon, Anne
Consiglio, Dina
Cook, Brian
Cook, Troy
Corbett, Brian
Costner, Jerod
Cress, K.C.
Culbertson, Kurt
Cullimore, Blake
Curtis, Jim
Czerny, Craig
Dake, Glen
Dallmann, Gustavo
Dapolito, Dana

Davidson, Tracy
Davis, David
Davis, Heather
Delcambre, Carla
Desjardins, Anne
Dewing, Mary
Dillon, Eric
Dimmig, Janna
Dorward, Sherry
Doskocil, Megan
Dowgiallo, Emily
Du, Fenglin
Du, Shaobo
Ellis, Dave
Emilie Gravel, Anne
Ensign, Donald
Erle, Claudia
Escorcia, Kelly
Espinosa, Paula
Essex, Katherine
Estes, Michelle
Evans, Amy
Evans, Mathew
Faber, Natalie Shea
Faber, Stephen
Fay, Jennifer
Feldmann, Mark
Fernandez de Boggs, Isabel
Fish, Benjamin
Fogle, Jamie
Fontaine, Sara
Foote, Vince
Ford, Daniel
Forry, Shannon
Foss, Marilyn
Fowler, Drake
Fox, Mary
Frailey, Brian
Francis, Kenneth
Fredd, Felicia
Frk, Bret
Fry, Katherine
Fuller, Christopher

Gagne, Anna
Gailey, Izzi
Galante, Cherrie
Garcia, Celine
Gardiner, Devin
Garibotti, Laura
Gavalas, George
Gelman, Ariel
George, Denise
Gerring, Geoffrey
Gerstenberger, Hillary
Gildner, Geoff
Giner, Florencia
Glazier, Christine
Goodner, William
Granade, Pam
Grant, Andrea
Gray, Alan
Gregory, David
Greig, Bruce
Grigsby, Stephanie
Grillo, Natalie
Gustafson, Bradley
Haas, Jennifer
Hamlin, Caprice
Hamula, Justin
Hanson, Scott
Harding, Bryan
Hare, Charles
Harrington, Teresa
Harris, Luke
Harwood, Trevor
Haswell, Jim
Haughey, Megan
Hauri, Sharen
Hawkes, Jennifer
Hay, Justin
Haynes, John
Hazzard, Bruce
Hegvik, Emily
Hellund, Paul
Henry, Heather
Herd, Chad

Herman, Brenda
Hershberger, Bonny
Hershberger, Mark
Hicks, Jay
Himick, Jason
Hochrein, Joe
Hoden, Ash
Hoetmer, Larry
Hoffman, Michael
Hogan, Matt
Homuth, Sarah
Horchner, Dale
Horn, Claudia Meyer
Hottel, Elyse
Houghton, Amy
Hoyt, Eliot
Hoyt, Kirby
Huang, Wen
Huerta, Christina
Huey, Larry
Hughes, Gayle
Hulton-Larson, Lindy
Hunsinger, Patricia
Ingram, Todd
Isaacson, Elias
Jacobs, Shira
Jaszczak, Ela
Jaszczak, Joanna
Jeffreys, Philip
Jennings, Jill
Jennings, John
Johns, Gregory
Johnson, Dorinda
Johnson, Jerrod
Johnson, Kristofer
Johnson, Natalie
Johnson, Rebecca
Johnson, Scott
Johnson, Todd
Johnston, John
Johnston, Sophie
Jones-Wilson, Shafee
Jordan, Scott

Junge, Erik
Kalback, Lindsay
Kambic, Kathleen
Kane, Bill
Kearns, Monica
Keefe, Susie Best
Kelley, Sarah
Kelly, Lara
Kennen, Kate
Kenyon, David
Kessel, Laura
Kest, Jarrett
Kiersztyn, Nicole
Kiley, Christopher
Kim, Seung
Kim, Yun Soo
Kirby, Kevin
Kirby, Lisa
Kirk, Catherine
Kirschner, Lisa
Klein, Thomas
Klever, Chad
Kmetzsch, Justin Carl
Kneisel, Connie
Knightley, Angela
Koh, Moon-Gi
Kolberg, Judy
Koto, Karl
Kring, Rebecca
Kronenwetter, Angie
Kruse, Alexis
Kvarfordt, Kristofor
Lagarrigue, Juan
Lamprell, Susan
Landis, Matthew
Langdon, Micah
Langhart, Karen F.
Lares, Dee
Larson, Bill
Larson, Michael
Lasek, Matt
Laser, Ginger
Lassiter, Allison

Layton, Dinah
Lee, Linda
Leib, Karrie
Lendon, David
Leonard, Gregory
Leonard, Rebecca
Liechty, David
Lilyblade, Sara
Lindars, Scott
Liu, Yu-ju
Liu, Yuwen
Locke, Nancy
Lopez, Juliana Maria
Lopez, Mark
Lusi, Mike
MacRae, James
Madden, Matthew
Madden, Nicole
Majcher, Todd
Malby, Sean
Mannelly, Brian
Mansfield, Jacqueline
Mardones, Cristian
Marquis, Matthew
Martignoni, Maria Jimena
Martin, Sophie
Massey, Kurt
Mathe, Carol
Mathis, Joseph
Mathis, Sam
Matsuda, Tetsu
Mattil, Marcy
McCubbin, Mary Beth
Mcginnis, Cathy
McGrew, Julie
McGuire, Lisa
McKeown, Keith
McMenimen, Jeff
McMurray, Erik
Meacci, Grant
Meeker, Andy
Mendenhall, Allyson
Meriwether, Melanie

Merkl, Stacey
Michael, Jesse
Miles, Leigh Ann
Miles, Matthew
Miller, Laura
Miller, Suzanne
Mills, Jennifer
Milnes, Daniel
Misheau, Anne
Mitchell, Shannon
Mitton, James
Mizer, Heath
Molins, Maria
Molska, Kasia
Mondragon, Anna
Monteith, Nancy
Moore, Ethan
Moran, Jennifer
Morgan, Devon
Morgan, Heather
Moses, Val
Moss, Layne
Mouzo, Sebastian
Moyse, Shari
Muir Owen, Sara
Mulholland, Alison
Mullen, Steve
Mullins, Ann
Murphy, Chad
Murray, Cecilia
Murray, Jocelyn
Nakano, Deb
Naknakorn, Ekpanith
Navarro, Judith
Neale, Steven
Negretti, Glenn
Nelson, Aaron
Nevins, Bob
Newman, Gweneth
Nicholas, David
Nichols, Lynn
Noble, Josh
Noll, Steve

North, Peter
Norwood, Carrie
Oberliesen, Susan
Ochis, Gregory
Ochis, Heidi
Oden, Hunter
Okuma, Faith
Olson, Katherine
Oost, Dennis
Ortiz, Marcos
Ortiz, Sebastian
Owen, Cameron
Owen, Travis
Oz-Golden, Liza
Page, Jan
Palmberg, Britt
Parker, Douglas
Parker, Jordan
Paul, Marie
Peralta, Carla
Perkins, William
Pero, Nino
Peters, Scott
Petersen, Kirsi
Pierce, Benjamin
Pinto Eid, Cristhian
Pitenko, Olga
Pitts, James
Porter, Joe
Porter, Margaret
Price, Rose Marie
Pruett, Theresa
Putra, Angga
Raber, Cynthia
Rachmawati, Kartika
Raol, Susan
Rashbaum, Lisa
Redcay, Brittain
Reich, Bill
Rhoades, Conrad
Rice, Jennie
Richman, Suzanne
Riera, Ana

Rilzeff, Kathy
Robertson, Jonathan
Rodgers, Robyn
Roggenburk, Betsy
Roman, Michael
Roverud, Eric
Ruggeri, Deni
Ruhland, Kelly
Russig, Cornelia
Ryan, Marc
Sachs, Sarah
Sager, Marsha
Sanderson, Wayne
Sandridge, Jim
Sands, Alesha
Santana, Luiz Sergio
Santana, Peggy
Sanzone, Sheri
Sauve, Sophie
Saw, Olivia
Saydek, John
Schenk, Patty
Schoeder, Todd
Schroder, Max
Schuler, Dee
Schwellenbach, Susan
Scott, Jill
Seely, Becky
Segura, Carolina
Serna, Suzanne
Serquis, Solange
Sevy, Sara
Sharp, Rich
Shaw, Karen
Shaw, Richard
Shaw, Sarah
Shawaker, Matt
Shoplick, Jane
Simon, Keith
Simpson, Kelly
Sippy, Jacob
Siroky, Jared
Slifer, Seth

Smiley, Stephanie
Smith, Karla
Smith, Kelan
Smith, Reshelle
Smith, Scott
Smith, Terri
Snyder, Deanna
Snyder, Thomas
Soares, Tattana Maria
Socha, Roger
Soden, Mark
Somerfeldt, Cheryl
Son, Glenda
Souza, Aaron
Spears, Steven
Sperat, Carol
Squadrito, Paul
Stach, Glenn
Stacishin-Moura, Elizabeth
Stander, Marilee
Starcher, Amanda
Steinberg, Marcy
Stenquist, Tina
Stepp, Paula
Stevens, Michael
Stevens, Patti
Stevens, Tom
Stewart, Greg
Stokes, Jacqueline
Storheim, Steven
Strachan, Kim
Stutzman-Solitario, Leslie
Suarez, John
Supawongse, Chon
Sutherland, Annie
Sutherland, Jennifer
Sutterfield, Chris
Swanson, Kim
Sweet, Taber
Sylvester, Dana
Szabo, Trimbi
Szot, Amanda
Takeuchi, Lin

Tanner, James
Tanniehill, Ramona
Tarbet, Jennifer
Tautges, Alan
Taylor, Scott
Tennian, Sarah
Teo, Lai-teck
Thiltgen, Anne
Thomas, Briana
Thomas, Henry
Thompson, Linda
Thornely, Gyles
Thurlow, Alexis
Tidbeck, Elin
Timmer, Julie
Timmons, Sean
Tolderlund, Leila
Toliver, Merrilee
Toneatto, Andres
Tremblay, Emilienne
Trivedi, Dipti
Troukens, Philippe
Truesdale, Kristy
Trujillo, Bruce
Turner, Kristin
Turner, Rebecca
Vaca, Alfredo
Valinotto, Maria Cecilia
Van Der Wal, Benny
Van Gilder, Jennifer
Van Woerkom, Jessica
Variava, Binaifer
Vehige, Donald
Velasquez, Alvaro
Vincent, Sulin
Viola, Sylvie
Vogele, Ad
Vora-Akhom, Kotchakorn
Wallstrom, Pete
Walsh, Chris
Walsh, Kristen
Walters, Glenn
Wang, Fan

Ware, Charles
Washburn, Lori
Watada, Stuart
Waters, Missy
Watters, Emie
Way, Gregg
Weber, Deanna
Wells, Andrew
Wells, Joe
Wenskoski, Todd
Wescoat, Chappell
Westermann, Marcelo
White, Kristen
Wilkinson, Dick
Williams, Kimberly
Wilson, Pamela
Winters, Alexis
Witherspoon, Gregory
Wittman, Matt
Wolf, Anna
Wolfgang, Greg
Wood, Carlie
Wood, Jerome
Woodruff, Julie
Worthley, Gary
Wright, Kristi
Wyda, Stephen
Wyszynski, Brandon
Yamada, Sergio
Yela, Allison
Yoshimura, Daisuke
Zimmermann, Jeffrey
Zimmermann, Rebecca
Zinn, Rebecca
Zodrow, Michelle

BIBLIOGRAPHY

Adler, Mortimer. *The Time of Our Lives,* New York : Holt, Rinehart and Winston, 1970.

Aguilar, Orson. *Why I Am Not an Environmentalist,* http://www.alternet.org/envirohealth/22002/ May 17, 2005.

Anderson, Ray. *Mid-Course Correction,* White River Junction: Chelsea Green Publishing, 1998.

Bacon, Edmund N. *Design of Cities,* New York: Viking Press, 1967.

Baudrillard, Jean. *Simulacra and Simulation,* Ann Arbor: University of Michigan Press, 1994.

Carter, Stephen L. *Civility: Manners, Morals, and the Etiquette of Democracy,* New York: Basic Books, 1998.

Christensen, Clayton M., Anthony, Scott D., and Roth, Erik A. *Seeing What's Next,* Boston: Harvard Business School Press, 2004.

Cronon, William. *Uncommon Ground: Rethinking the Human Place in Nature,* New York: W.W. Norton & Company, Inc., 1996.

Daly, Herman E. *Beyond Growth: The Economics of Sustainable Development,* Boston: Beacon Press, 1996.

DeBord, Guy. *The Society of the Spectacle,* New York: Zone Books, 1994.

Diamond, Jared. *Guns Germs and Steel,* New York: W.W. Norton & Company, Inc., 1996.

Doppelt, Bob, *Leading Change Toward Sustainability,* Sheffield: Greenleaf Publishing, 2003.

Doxiadis, Constantine. *Anthropolis: City for Human Development,* New York: Norton, 1974.

_____. *Ecology and Ekistics,* Boulder, Colorado: Westview Press, 1977.

_____. *Ekistics: An Introduction to the Science of Human Settlements,* London: Hutchinson, 1968.

Gardner, Howard. *Changing Minds: The Art and Science of Changing Our Own and Other People's Minds,* Boston: Harvard Business School Press, 2004.

Gladwell, Malcolm. *Blink: The Power of Thinking Without Thinking,* New York: Little, Brown and Company, 2005.

_____. *Tipping Point,* Boston: Little, Brown and Company, 2000.

Grove, Andrew S. *Only the Paranoid Survive: How to Exploit the Crisis Points that Challenge Every Company,* New York: Currency Doubleday, 1999.

Hegemann, Werner, and Elbert Peets. *The American Vitruvius: An Architects' Handbook of Civic Art,* New York: Princeton Architectural Press, 1988 reprint.

Jacobs, Jane. *The Death and Life of Great American Cities,* New York: Random House, 1961.

_____. *Systems of Survival: A Dialog on the Moral Foundations of Commerce and Politics,* New York: Random House, 1992.

_____. *The Nature of Economies,* New York: Modern Library, 2000.

Kemmis, Daniel. *Community and the Politics of Place,* Norman, Okla.: University of Oklahoma Press, 1990.

Klaus, Susan L. *A Modern Arcadia: Frederick Law Olmsted Jr. and the Plan for Forest Hills Gardens,* Amherst: University of Massachusetts Press, 2002.

Kuhn, Thomas, *The Structure of Scientific Revolutions,* Chicago: University of Chicago Press, 1970.

Kunstler, James Howard. *The Geography of Nowhere,* NewYork: Simon & Schuster, 1993.

McHarg, Ian. *Design with Nature,* Garden City, N.Y.: Natural History Press, 1969.

May, Rollo. *The Courage to Create,* New York: W.W. Norton & Company, Inc., 1975.

Naisbitt, John. *Megatrends,* New York: Warner Books, 1982.

Olsen, Joshua. *Better Places, Better Lives: A Biography of Jim Rouse,* Washington, D.C.: Urban Land Institute, 2003.

Porter, Joe. "Collaborative Community-Building," *Practicing Planner,* Vol. 2, No. 4, Winter 2004. http://www.planning.org/practicingplanner/member/04winter/case1.htm

Putnam, Robert D. *Bowling Alone: The Collapse and Revival of American Community,* New York: Simon & Schuster, 2000.

Ray, Paul and Sherry Anderson. *The Cultural Creatives,* New York: Harmony Books, 2000.

Root-Bernstein, Robert and Michele. *Sparks of Genius,* Boston: Mariner Books, 2001.

Schama, Simon. *Landscape and Memory,* New York: Vintage Books, 1994.

Schon, Daniel. *The Reflective Practitioner: How Professionals Think in Action,* New York: Basic Books, 1983.

Schwartz, Peter. *The Art of the Long View: Planning for the Future in an Uncertain World,* New York, Doubleday, 1991.

Senge, Peter, Otto C. Schwarmer, Joseph Jaworski and Betty Sue Flowers. *Presence, Human Purpose and the Field of the Future,* Cambridge: The Society for Organizational Learning, 2004.

Shaw, George Bernard. *Man and Superman: A Comedy and A Philosophy,* Baltimore, Maryland: Penguin Books, 1931. First published 1903.

Shaw, Sarah Chase. *New Gardens of the American West,* New York: Watson Guptill, 2004.

Sorkin, Michael. *Some Assembly Required,* Minneapolis: University of Minnesota, 2001.

Surowiecki, James. *The Wisdom of Crowds: Why The Many Are Smarter Than the Few and How Collective Wisdom Shapes Business, Economies, Societies, and Nations,* New York: Doubleday, 2004.

Thoreau, Henry D. *The Natural History Essays,* Salt Lake City: Peregrine Smith Books (reprint), 1980.

Treib, Marc. "Must Landscapes Mean? Approaches to Significance in Recent Landscape Architecture," *Landscape Journal,* Vol. 14: No. 1, 1995.

Unwin, Raymond. *Town Planning in Practice: An introduction to the art of designing cities in suburbs,* New York: Princeton Architectural Classic Reprint, 1994 (originally published in 1909).

Yankelovich, Daniel. *Coming to Public Judgment: Making Democracy Work in a Complex World,* Syracuse, N.Y.: Syracuse University Press, 1991.

_____. *The Magic of Dialogue,* New York: Simon and Schuster, 1999.

ACKNOWLEDGMENTS

We would like to acknowledge the efforts of many staff members, including Todd Johnson, principal-in-charge of this project; Joe Porter, who invested a great deal of time in it; Kurt Culbertson, whose impulse it first was, and Greg Ochis, Don Ensign, Richard Shaw and Becky Zimmermann, who reviewed the book. The firm's head of training, Pam Britton, was instrumental in re-focusing our efforts midway in the process. Todd Wenskoski served as an advisor on the project from an early stage and helped shape the book's framework. Former employee Marc Ryan completed our first graphic design. Several staff members helped with, provided or participated in research (including Jim MacRae, Sue Schwellenbach, Anna Mondragon-Metzger, John Suarez, Greg Witherspoon, Faith Okuma, Matt Shawaker, Judy Kolberg, Kristin Turner, Carol Sperat, Bret Frk, Linda Thompson, Don Ensign, Dori Johnson, Pao Cagnina, Kirby Hoyt, Tom Snyder, Jennifer Van Gilder, Zac Boggs and Leila Tolderlund) and many made or adapted drawings for the book (including Kartika Rachmawati, Suzanne Serna, Nino Pero, David Liechty, Keith McKeown, Fenglin Du, Jesse Michael, Ying Zhang, Moon-Gi Koh, Carolina Segura, Nancy Monteith and Robert Matsuda). Our internal reviewers included Nino Pero, Kelly Ruhland, Kelan Smith and Natalie Grillo. Outside reviewers were also enormously helpful, including our former partners, Dick Wilkinson and Vince Foote; Carl Steinitz of Harvard's Graduate School of Design; Fritz Steiner of the University of Texas at Austin; developer Jim Chaffin of Chaffin/Light; attorney Wayne Hyatt of Hyatt & Stubblefield, P.C.; architect Rebel Roberts of VOA Associates; Charles Birnbaum of the National Park Service; Jim Wescoat of the University of Illinois at Urbana-Champaign; landscape architect Bill Johnson; economist Michael Hoffman, and author Joy Hakim. Many people outside the firm were instrumental in helping us enrich the project descriptions and make them accurate, and others went above and beyond the call of duty in providing us with images, including:

Arbolera de Vida: Dory Wegrzyn, Sawmill Community Land Trust

Blackcomb: photographer Greg Griffith

Canyon Forest Village: Grady Gammage and Wayne Hyatt

Chalalan Ecolodge: Stephen Edwards, Vlasova Urrea and Joe Vieira of Conservation International and photographer Sergio Ballivian

Cherokee redevelopment: Coi Drummond-Gehrig at the Denver Public Library, Western History Photography Collection

Clark County Wetlands Park: Elizabeth Bickmore of the Las Vegas Wash Coordination Committee, Pat Glancy of the U.S. Geological Survey, and Bruce Sillitoe and Jeff Harris of Clark County Parks and Community Services

Connection essay: Mandi Johnson at the Georgia Historical Society in Savannah, Georgia

Flathead County Master Plan: Tom Jentz, former deputy director of the Flathead Regional Planning Office, Marty Zeller of Conservation Partners, Michael Collins, former president of Winter Sports, Inc. and Steve Mullen of Community Viz

Inn on Biltmore Estate: Kathleen Mosher of Biltmore Estate

Interstate 25 Conservation Corridor: Nate Forst of Great Outdoors Colorado and photographer John Fielder

Little Nell: John Cottle of Cottle Carr Yaw Architects of Basalt, Colorado

Nature essay: Gayle Lucas of Kings County Library, Hanford, California

Pittsburgh World War II Memorial: Cheryl Hyatt of The Charitable Resources Group, the Honorable John G. Brosky, Stanley J. Roman and sculptor Larry Kirkland

RidgeGate: Coventry Development's Lone Tree, Colorado, office

Riverfront Park: Rebecca Lintz at the Colorado Historical Society

Walnut Creek Wildlife Refuge: Dave Schaeffer and Mark Marxen of the U.S. Fish & Wildlife Service

We are indebted to all of you for your generous contributions and guidance.

INDEX

affordable housing
    Arbolera de Vida, 144-149
    Rancho Viejo, 159, 161, 167
    Riverfront Park, 219
Aguas Claras, 036-041
Arbolera de Vida, 144-149
Blackcomb, 092-099
brownfields
    Aguas Claras, 036-041
    Clark County Wetlands Park, 066-075
    Cherokee redevelopment of the former Gates
        rubber factory, 206-213
    Riverfront Park, 214-227
Canyon Forest Village, 246-251
Chalalàn Ecolodge, 252-259
change management, 228-235
Cherokee redevelopment of the former Gates rubber
    factory, 206-213
Clark County Wetlands Park, 066-075
community planning, 130-137
    Aguas Claras, 036-041
    Arbolera de Vida, 144-149
    High Desert, 138-143
    Rancho Viejo, 158-173
    RidgeGate, 150-157
conservation easements
    Interstate-25 Conservation Corridor, 050-057
Flathead County Master Plan, 236-241
garden design
    Gardens on El Paseo, 106-113
    Rio Grande Botanical Garden, 086-091
Gardens on El Paseo, 106-113
Glacier Club, 058-065
golf course design
    Glacier Club, 058-065
High Desert, 138-143
infrastructure as amenity
    High Desert, 139-140, 142
    RidgeGate, 156-157

Rancho Viejo, 167-170
Inn on Biltmore Estate, 100-105
Interstate-25 Conservation Corridor, 050-057
Kierland Commons, 182-187
La Posada, 114-119
landscape design
    Inn on Biltmore Estate, 100-105
    Gardens on El Paseo, 106-113
    Glacier Club, 058-065
    La Posada, 114-119
    Rio Grande Botanical Garden, 086-091
Legacy theory, 010-015
Little Nell, 188-195
Lowry Parks, 196-205
master planning
    Aguas Claras, 036-041
    Blackcomb, 092-099
    Cherokee redevelopment of the former Gates
        rubber factory, 206-213
    Clark County Wetlands Park, 066-075
    Flathead County Master Plan, 236-241
    Inn on Biltmore Estate, 100-105
    Park Avenue redevelopment, 260-271
    Riverfront Park, 214-227
mixed uses
    Canyon Forest Village, 246-251
    Cherokee redevelopment of the former Gates
        rubber factory, 206-213
    Kierland Commons, 182-187
    Park Avenue redevelopment, 260-271
    Riverfront Park, 214-227
new communities (see community planning)
North Lake Tahoe Resort Association, 242-245
open space
    Canyon Forest Village, 246-251
    High Desert, 138-143
    Interstate-25 Conservation Corridor, 050-057
    Rancho Viejo, 158-173
    RidgeGate, 150-157

Walnut Creek Wildlife Refuge, 042-049
Park Avenue redevelopment, 260-271
parks
    Clark County Wetlands Park, 066-075
    Hills Park at Summerlin, 020-021
    Lowry parks, 196-205
    RidgeGate, 150-157
    Rio Grande Botanical Garden, 086-091
Pittsburgh World War II Memorial, 120-129
place-making, 076-085
plazas
    Arbolera de Vida, 149
    Gardens on El Paseo, 109, 113
    Inn on Biltmore Estate, 104-105
    Kierland Commons, 183, 187
    La Posada, 115
    Little Nell, 189
    Lowry Parks, 199, 200, 202-205
    Park Avenue redevelopment, 267, 270-271
    Pittsburgh World War II Memorial, 120-129
    Riverfront Park, 220, 224-227
preservation, 030-035
    Clark County Wetlands Park, 066-075
    Interstate-25 Conservation Corridor, 050-057
public process, 230-235
    Arbolera de Vida, 144-149
    Canyon Forest Village, 246-251
    Chalalàn Eco-Lodge, 254-256
    Cherokee redevelopment of the former Gates
        rubber factory, 208
    Clark County Wetlands Park, 068-071
    Flathead County Master Plan, 237-240
    North Lake Tahoe Resort Association, 242-245
    Park Avenue redevelopment, 260-271
    Rancho Viejo, 158-173
    Riverfront Park, 214-227
Rancho Viejo, 158-173
redevelopment, 230-235
    Aguas Claras, 036-041

Chalalàn Ecolodge, 252-259
Cherokee redevelopment of the former Gates
    rubber factory, 206-213
Clark County Wetlands Park, 066-075
La Posada, 114-119
Little Nell, 188-195
Park Avenue redevelopment, 260-271
Rio Grande Botanical Garden, 086-091
Riverfront Park, 214-227
regional planning
    Flathead County Master Plan, 236-241
    Interstate-25 Conservation Corridor, 050-057
    North Lake Tahoe Resort Association, 242-245
    Rancho Viejo, 158-173
resorts and tourist destinations
    Blackcomb, 092-099
    Canyon Forest Village, 246-251
    Chalalàn Ecolodge, 252-259
    Flathead County Master Plan, 236-241
    Inn on Biltmore Estate, 100-105
    La Posada, 114-119
    North Lake Tahoe Resort Association, 242-245
    Park Avenue redevelopment, 260-271
retail
    Gardens on El Paseo, 106-113
    Kierland Commons, 182-187
RidgeGate, 150-157
Rio Grande Botanical Garden, 086-091
Riverfront Park, 214-227
sustainable design
    Arbolera de Vida, 144-149
    as a Legacy goal, 009-015, 130-137
    Canyon Forest Village, 246-251
    Chalalàn Ecolodge, 252-259
    Gardens on El Paseo, 106-113
    Glacier Club, 058-065
    High Desert, 138-143
    Interstate-25 Conservation Corridor, 050-057

Park Avenue redevelopment, 260-271
RidgeGate, 150-157
Rancho Viejo, 158-173
transit-oriented development
    Canyon Forest Village, 246-251
    Cherokee redevelopment of the former Gates
        rubber factory, 206-213
    Park Avenue redevelopment, 260-271
    RidgeGate, 150-157
    Riverfront Park, 214-227
urban design
    Cherokee redevelopment of the former Gates
        rubber factory, 206-213
    Kierland Commons, 182-187
    Little Nell, 188-195
    Lowry Parks, 196-205
    Riverfront Park, 214-227
Walnut Creek Wildlife Refuge, 042-049

AWARDS

Design Workshop, Inc. is recognized by the professional design community as a creative and innovative planning and design firm. The following is a list of the awards the firm has received.

The Village at Ribbon Creek, Kananaskis County, Alberta, Canada, Merit Award, Colorado Chapter – American Society of Landscape Architects, 1982

North Village at Mt. Crested Butte, Colorado, Honor Award, Colorado Chapter – American Society of Landscape Architects, 1984

Castle Rock Master Plan, Castle Rock, Colorado, Merit Award, Colorado Chapter – American Society of Landscape Architects, 1985

Village at Blue Mountain, Collingwood, Colorado, Honor Award Colorado Chapter – American Society of Landscape Architects, 1985

The Meadows, Castle Rock, Colorado, Merit Award, Colorado Chapter – American Society of Landscape Architects, 1986

Wolf Creek Valley, Mineral County, Colorado, Honor Award Colorado Chapter – American Society of Landscape Architects, 1986

Canyon Village Lodging Redevelopment, Yellowstone National Park, Honor Award, Colorado Chapter – American Society of Landscape Architects, 1987

Seventh Street Esplanade, Glenwood Springs, Colorado, Merit Award, Colorado Chapter – American Society of Landscape Architects, 1987

Berger Residence, Aspen, Colorado, Merit Award, Colorado Chapter – American Society of Landscape Architects, 1988

Cherry Creek Redevelopment, Denver, Colorado, Merit Award, Colorado Chapter – American Society of Landscape Architects, 1988

Red Mesa Communication, Denver, Colorado, Merit Award, Colorado Chapter – American Society of Landscape Architects, 1988

Estrella New Community, Goodyear, Arizona, Merit Award, Colorado Chapter – American Society of Landscape Architects, 1989

Kananaskis Village, Alberta, Canada, Merit Award, Colorado Chapter – American Society of Landscape Architects, 1989

Kananaskis Village, Alberta, Canada, National Regional Merit Award, Canadian Society of Landscape Architects, 1989

Getz Residence, Aspen, Colorado, Honor Award, Colorado Chapter – American Society of Landscape Architects, 1990

Little Nell Hotel, Aspen, Colorado, Honor Award, Colorado Chapter – American Society of Landscape Architects, 1990

The Hills Park Las Vegas, Nevada, Merit Award, Colorado Chapter – American Society of Landscape Architects, 1991

Bow Canmore Visual Impact Assesment, Alberta, Canada, Merit Award, American Society of Landscape Architects – National, 1991

Banff Downtown Enhancement Conceptual Plan, Alberta, Canada, 1st Place, International Design Competition, 1992

Banff Downtown enhancement Conceptual Plan, Alberta, Canada, National Citation Award, Regional Merit Award, Canadian Society of Landscape Architects, 1992

Bow Canmore Visual Impact Assesment, National Merit Award, Regional Honor Award, Canadian Society of Landscape Architects, 1992

Aguas Claras Minas, Gerais, Brazil, Honor Award, Colorado Chapter – American Society of Landscape Architects, 1992

Banff Downtown Enhancement Conceptual Plan, Alberta, Canada, Honor Award, Colorado Chapter – American Society of Landscape Architects, 1992

Rosa Vista Resort Community, Urban Design Citation, Progressive Architecture, 1993

Summerlin New Community, Nevada, Gold Nugget Merit Award for Best Community Site Plan, Pacific Coast Builders, 1993

The Hills at Summerlin, Las Vegas, Nevada, Merit Award, Arizona Chapter – American Society of Landscape Architects, 1993

Special Events Piece, New Year's Card, Gold Award, Society for Marketing Professional Services, 1994

Special Market Brochure, Gold Award, Society for Marketing Professional Services, 1994

Snowmass Ski Area, Colorado, Ski Area Award, Colorado Chapter – American Society of Landscape Architects, 1994

Starr Pass,Tucson, Arizona, Merit Award, Arizona Chapter – American Society of Landscape Architects, 1994

Verde River Greenway, Cottonwood, Arizona, Honor Award, Arizona Chapter – American Society of Landscape Architects, 1994

Loveland: In the Nature of Things report, Colorado, Merit Award, Colorado Chapter – American Society of Landscape Architects, 1995

Special Events Piece, New Year's Card, Gold Award, Society for Marketing Professional Services, 1995

Special Market Brochure, Silver Award, Society for Marketing Professional Services, 1995

Flathead County Master Plan, Montana, Honor Award, Colorado Chapter – American Society of Landscape Architects, 1995

High Desert Community, Albuquerque, New Mexico, Honor Award, Colorado Chapter – American Society of Landscape Architects, 1995

Maricopa Association of Governments Desert Spaces Plan, Arizona, Merit Award, Arizona Chapter – American Society of Landscape Architects, 1995

Mill Creek, Illinois, Honor Award, Illinois Chapter – American Society of Landscape Architects, 1995

The Life and Times of George Edward Kessler, Research & Communication Merit Award, Colorado Chapter – American Society of Landscape Architects, 1995

Town of Vail Comprehensive Open Lands Plan, Colorado, Merit Award, Colorado Chapter – American Society of Landscape Architects, 1995

Snake River Basin Plan, Colorado, Outstanding Efforts in Smart Growth and Development, Colorado Governor's Award, 1995

Little Nell Base Redevelopment, Aspen, Colorado, Award of Excellence, Urban Land Institute, 1995

Flathead County Regional Master Plan, Montana, Merit Award, American Society of Landscape Architects – National, 1995

North Lake Tahoe Tourism Development Master Plan, California, Merit Award, American Society of Landscape Architects – National, 1995

Town of Vail Comprehensive Open Lands Plan, Colorado, Merit Award, American Society of Landscape Architects – National, 1995

Town of Vail Comprehensive Open Lands Plan, Colorado, Honor Award, Colorado Chapter – American Planning Association, 1995

Direct Mail Piece, Corporate Announcements, Silver Award, Society for Marketing Professional Services, 1996

Donnell Residence, Jacobs Residence, New Mexico, Western Garden Design Award of Excellence, Sunset magazine, 1996

Special Events Piece, New Year's Card, Gold Award, Society for Marketing Professional Services, 1996

Clark County Wetlands Park, Nevada, Excellence in Communications, Landscape Architecture Magazine, 1996

Clark County Wetlands Park, Nevada, President's Award of Excellence, Colorado Chapter – American Society of Landscape Architects, 1996

I-25 Conservation Corridor Plan, Colorado, Merit Award, Colorado Chapter – American Society of Landscape Architects, 1996

Los Padillas Elementary School, New Mexico, Honor Award, Colorado Chapter – American Society of Landscape Architects, 1996

Santa Fe County Visual Inventory and Analysis, New Mexico, Honor Award, Colorado Chapter – American Society of Landscape Architects, 1996

McDowell Mountain Ranch, Scottsdale, Arizona, Merit Award, Pacific Coast Builders Gold Nugget Awards, 1996

Design Workshop, Inc., Company of the Year, Service category, Colorado Association of Commerce and Industry, Colorado Business magazine, Coopers & Lybrand L.L.P., 1996

San Luis Valley Trails and Recreation Master Plan, Colorado, Smart Growth Award, Colorado Governor's Office, 1996

Santa Fe County Visual Inventory and Analysis, New Mexico, Smart Growth Award, Colorado Governor's Office, 1996

McDowell Mountain Ranch Community Center & Trails, Scottsdale, Arizona, Environmental Excellence Award of Merit, Valley Forward Association, 1996

Las Campanas Golf Clubhouse, Grand Award, National Association of Home Builders, 1996

Barr Lake Conservation Vision, Colorado, Land Stewardship Award, Colorado Chapter – American Society of Landscape Architects, 1997

Rio Grande Botanic Garden, Award of Excellence, New Mexico chapter – American Society of Landscape Architects, 1997

Los Angeles River Corridor, California, Honor Award for Communication, American Society of Landscape Architects, 1997

Rocky Mountain Arsenal National Wildlife Refuge, Commerce City, Colorado, Honor Award, Colorado Chapter – American Society of Landscape Architects, 1997

San Luis Valley Trails and Recreation Master Plan, Colorado, Honor Award, Colorado Chapter – American Society of Landscape Architects, 1997

I-25 Conservation Corridor, Colorado, Smart Growth Award, Colorado Governor's Office, 1997

Clark County Wetlands Park, Nevada, Merit Award, American Society of Landscape Architects, 1997

Maricopa Association of Governments Desert Spaces Plan, Arizona, Environmental Excellence Award of Merit, Valley Forward Association, 1997

South "Y" Transit Transfer Station, South Lake Tahoe, California, Helen Putnam Award - Public Works & Transportation Excellence, League of California Cities, 1997

W.A. Hover Building (Denver office of Design Workshop), Community Preservation Award, Historic Denver Inc., 1997

Barelas Streetscape, Albuquerque, New Mexico, Community Award of Excellence City of Albuquerque Environmental Planning Commission, 1997

High Desert Community, Albuquerque, New Mexico, Community Award of Excellence, City of Albuquerque Environmental Planning Commission, 1997

High Desert Sustainable Community, Award of Honor, New Mexico Chapter – American Society of Landscape Architects, 1997

Ski Tip Town Homes, Award of Merit for Best Condo/ Attached Home, PCBC/ Western Building Show and Builder Magazine, 1997

Tesuque Residence, Award of Excellence, New Mexico Chapter – American Society of Landscape Architects, 1997

Arbolera de Vida Master Development Plan (Sawmill Neighborhood), President's Award of Excellence for Planning and Urban Design, Colorado Chapter – American Society of Landscape Architects, 1998

Chalalan Ecolodge, Merit Award for Design, Colorado Chapter – American Society of Landscape Architects, 1998

Commons Neighborhood, Honor Award for Planning and Urban Design, Colorado Chapter – American Society of Landscape Architects, 1998

"Landschaft und Gardenkunst: The Contribution of German-Americans to the Development of American Landscape Architecture" research project, Research & Communication Merit Award, Colorado Chapter – American Society of Landscape Architects, 1998

Platte Canyon Outdoor Resource Master Plan, Smart Growth and Development Award, Colorado Governor's Office, 1998

Canyon Forest Village Master Plan, Merit Award, American Society of Landscape Architects – National, 2000

Pikes Peak Resource Plan Management, Merit Award, American Society of Landscape Architects – National, 2000

Arbolera de Vida, Community Building by Design Award, American Institute of Architects / HUD, 2001

La Posada Resort and Spa, Honor Award, New Mexico chapter - American Society of Landscape Architects, 2001

The Colony at White Pines, President's Award of Excellence, Colorado Chapter - American Society of Landscape Architects, 2002

Redstone Parkside, 2002 Award of Merit for Design/Planning, The Envision Utah – Governor's Quality Growth Award, 2002

Superstition Area Land Trust and Superstition Area Land Plan, Award of Merit, Valley Forward Association, 2002

Lake Tahoe Sand Harbor Restoration and Facilities Upgrade, Merit Award, Washoe County Design Awards Program, 2002

Summerlin, Merit Award, Awards for Excellence: New Community, Urban Land Institute, 2002

Mesdag Residence, Honor Award, Colorado Chapter - American Society of Landscape Architects, 2002

Light Residence, Merit Award, Colorado Chapter - American Society of Landscape Architects, 2002

Wexner Residence, Honor Award, Colorado Chapter - American Society of Landscape Architects, 2002

Wise Residence, Honor Award, Colorado Chapter - American Society of Landscape Architects, 2002

Stock Farm, Merit Award and Land Stewardship Award, Colorado Chapter - American Society of Landscape Architects, 2002

Fitzsimmons Army Base Redevelopment, Award for Technology-led Economic Development, U.S. Department of Commerce, 2003

The Commons/ Riverfront Park, Charter Award, Congress for the New Urbanism, 2003

Rocks at Reatta Pass, Best Community Site Plan, Gold Nugget Award, Pacific Coast Builders, 2003

Grand Junction Veterans Cemetery, Exceptional Design Services, Division of Veteran Affairs, 2003

Santa Fe Community College District Plan and The Villages of Rancho Viejo, Innovation in Private Zoning, New Mexico chapter – American Planning Association, 2003

Goldwater Boulevard Tributary Wall, Honor Award, Arizona ASLA, 2003

16th Street Mall Extension, Honor Award for Urban Design, Colorado Chapter - American Society of Landscape Architects, 2003

Fitzsimmons Army Base Redevelopment, Merit Award for Planning, Colorado Chapter - American Society of Landscape Architects, 2003

Rancho Viejo Water Management Manual, Honor Award and Land Stewardship for Planning, Colorado Chapter - American Society of Landscape Architects, 2003

Crown Residence, Merit Award, Colorado Chapter - American Society of Landscape Architects, 2003

Pole Residence, Merit Award, Colorado Chapter - American Society of Landscape Architects, 2003

Teton Club, Merit Award, Colorado Chapter - American Society of Landscape Architects, 2003

Tessler Residence, Merit Award, Colorado Chapter - American Society of Landscape Architects, 2003

Dorros Residence, Merit Award, Colorado Chapter - American Society of Landscape Architects, 2003

Marriott Grand Residence Club, California Construction, Best of 2003

Rocks at Pinnacle Peak Multi-Family Residential, Crescordia Environmental Excellence Award, Valley Forward Association, 2003

Kierland Commons, Site Development and Landscape Design - Commercial Plazas, Crescordia Environmental Excellence Award, Valley Forward Association, 2003

Rocks at Pinnacle Peak, Best Community Site Plan (0 to 15 Years), Award of Merit Excellence and Value, Gold Nugget Awards Program, Pacific Coast Builders, 2003

Lair of the Golden Bear Family Camp, University of California, Berkeley, Merit Award, Northern California Chapter - American Society of Landscape Architects, 2004

Dorros Residence, Award of Excellence (Regional Awards), Sunset Western Gardens Design Award, 2004

Aspen Sundeck, Merit Award for Planning, Gold Nugget Award, Pacific Coast Builders, 2004

The Inn on Biltmore Estate, Award of Excellence (Large-Scale Projects), North Carolina Chapter - American Society of Landscape Architects, 2004

Kierland Commons, Honor Award, Arizona Chapter - American Society of Landscape Architects, 2004

Rocks at Pinnacle Peak, Merit Award, Arizona Chapter - American Society of Landscape Architects, 2004

Santa Fe Community College District Master Plan, Merit Award, Colorado Chapter - American Society of Landscape Architects, 2005

Gardens on El Paseo, Merit Award, Colorado Chapter - American Society of Landscape Architects, 2005

Union Park Design Guidelines, Honor Award, Colorado Chapter - American Society of Landscape Architects, 2005

Private residence, Aspen, Colorado, Honor Award, Colorado Chapter - American Society of Landscape Architects, 2005

Book/monograph, Marketing Excellence Award, Colorado Chapter - Society for Marketing Professional Services, 2005

Nevada Department of Transportation, Project of the Year, Nevada Chapter - American Society of Landscape Architects, 2005

Mesa Arts Center, Tempe, Arizona, Award of Excellence, Urban Land Institute, 2006

Private residence, Denver, Colorado, Dream Garden Award, Sunset magazine, 2006

PHOTOGRAPHY CREDITS

All photographs are © D.A. Horchner/ Design Workshop unless specified below and all illustrations are by Design Workshop unless noted below.

Location notes as follows: (a) above, (b) below, (l) left, (c) center, (r) right

Table of Contents
005 (l) © Sergio Ballivian

Introduction
013 Design Workshop
018 (l) Design Workshop
021 Tom Craig/Opulence Studios, Inc.

Chapter 1 Nature
030 (l) NASA photo
031 © Sime/eStock Photo
032 © Wendy Shattil/Bob Rozinski
033 Photograph in permanent collection of the Kings County Library, Hanford, CA. Also part of the San Joaquin Valley and Sierra Foothills Photo Heritage Project.
036 Design Workshop
039 (l) Design Workshop
041 (b) Design Workshop
043 Design Workshop
051 © Willard Clay
057 Photograph by John Fielder
069 Courtesy of U.S. Geological Survey
071 Courtesy of U.S. Geological Survey

Chapter 2 Places
078 (l) © Julia Timmer
079 © Sergio Ballivian
080 © Michael S. Yamashita/CORBIS
083 © Royalty Free/Corbis
088 Design Workshop

089 Courtesy of City of Albuquerque
093 © Greg Griffith/ Mountain Moments Photography
094 Design Workshop
095 (r) © Greg Griffith/ Mountain Moments Photography
098 © Greg Griffith/ Mountain Moments Photography
099 (l) © Greg Griffith/ Mountain Moments Photography
100 Used with permission, Biltmore Estate, Asheville, NC.
121 (a) Photo Courtesy of The Charitable Resources Group, Sewickley, PA.; (bl) Photo Courtesy of Judge John G. Brosky; (br) Photo Courtesy of Stanley J. Roman
122 (a) Design Workshop (b) Map from Greater Pittsburgh Convention and Visitors Bureau (www.visitpitts- burgh.com)
123 Design Workshop
125 Design Workshop
127 Design Workshop
128 Design Workshop

Chapter 3 Community
132 (l) © Margaret Bourke-White/ Time Life Pictures/Getty Images
133 Design Workshop
134 © John Loengard/Time Life Pictures/Getty Images
140 (a) © Lee B. Morgan— EaglesEyePhoto.com
146 Design Workshop
150 © Jay Simon
151 Illustration by Carl Dalio/carldalio.com
162 (a, b) Design Workshop
167 Illustration by William Rotsaert for

Rancho Viejo de Santa Fe, Inc.
168 Design Workshop

Chapter 4 Connection
177 (a) Courtesy of the Georgia Historical Society, Savannah; (b) © Dia Max/ Getty Images
178 (a) Photo courtesy of DigitalGlobe; (b) "Illustration" by Elliot Arthur Pavlos, from DESIGN OF CITIES by Edmund Bacon, copyright © 1967, 1974 by Edmund N. Bacon. Used by permission of Penguin, a division of Penguin Group (USA) Inc.
179 © Bob Krist/CORBIS
180 © Lester Boswell/ Getty Images
191 (bl) Courtesy of Cottle Carr Yaw Architects; (al, ar, br) Design Workshop
192 Design Workshop
193 (b) Design Workshop
194 (l) Design Workshop
206 Denver Public Library, Western History Collection, X-24537
208 Denver Public Library, Western History Collection, X-24514
212 Illustrations by Sneary Architectural Illustration
214 Image, Courtesy of Colorado Historical Society (F26,913), All Rights Reserved
215 Image, Courtesy Colorado Historical Society (Map G4314D4A5, 1874, G5a), All Rights Reserved
217 Landiscor, Inc.
222 © Dann Coffey/danncoffey.com
224 Illustrations by Sneary Architectural Illustration

Chapter 5 Leading Change
229 (l) Design Workshop ; (c) Drawing by Jeffery Joyce
230 © WalterDaran/HultonArchive/ Getty Images
231 © 1959 Arnold Newman
232 © Phil Schermeister/CORBIS
234 Illustration by Sneary Architectural Illustration
236 Design Workshop
237 © CORBIS
238 (a) Design Workshop ; (b) © Kevin R. Morris/CORBIS
243 © Court Leve/Gravity Hook
248 Base map courtesy of Coconino County US Geological Survey
249 Design Workshop
251 (l) Drawings by Jeffery Joyce
252 © Sergio Ballivian
253 © Sergio Ballivian
254 © Joe Vieira
255 © Joe Vieira
256 Design Workshop
258 (l) © Sergio Ballivian
259 © Sergio Ballivian
262 (a, c) © Tahoe Daily Tribune; (b) Design Workshop
263 (l) Reprinted by permission of The Wall Street Journal, Copyright © 2003, Dow Jones & Company, Inc. All Rights Reserved Worldwide. Lic#1377740437120
265 (br) Design Workshop